Children and Youth
in Sickness and in Health

Children and Youth in Sickness and in Health

A Historical Handbook and Guide

Janet Golden, Richard A. Meckel, and Heather Munro Prescott

Children and Youth: History and Culture
Miriam Forman-Brunell, Series Editor

GREENWOOD PRESS
Westport, Connecticut • London

Library of Congress Cataloging-in-Publication Data

Golden, Janet.
    Children and youth in sickness and in health : a historical handbook and guide /
Janet Golden, Richard A. Meckel, and Heather Munro Prescott.
      p. cm. — (Children and youth: history and culture, ISSN 1546–6752)
    ISBN 0–313–33041–7 (alk. paper)
    1. Children—Health and hygiene—United States—History. 2. Children—Diseases—
United States—History. 3. Youth—Health and hygiene—United States—History.
4. Youth—Diseases—United States—History. 5. Child health services—United States—
History. 6. Youth—Medical care—United States—History. I. Meckel, Richard A., 1948–
II. Prescott, Heather Munro. III. Title. IV. Children and youth (Westport, Conn.)
  RJ102.G65   2004
  613′.0432′0973—dc22   2003064259

British Library Cataloguing in Publication Data is available.

Library of Congress Catalog Card Number: 2003064259
ISBN: 0–313–33041–7
ISSN: 1546–6752

First published in 2004

Greenwood Press, 88 Post Road West, Westport, CT 06881
An imprint of Greenwood Publishing Group, Inc.
www.greenwood.com

Printed in the United States of America

The paper used in this book complies with the
Permanent Paper Standard issued by the National
Information Standards Organization (Z39.48–1984).

10 9 8 7 6 5 4 3 2 1

Contents

Series Foreword

Pocahontas, a legendary figure in American history, was just a pre-adolescent when she challenged two cultures at odds to cooperate instead of to compete. While Pocahontas forged peace, many more now forgotten Native American, Anglo-American, African American, and other children contributed to their families' survival, communities' development, and America's history in just as legitimate, though perhaps less legendary ways. Contracts and correspondence from colonial Chesapeake reveal that even seventeenth-century toddlers labored. But the historical agency of the vast majority of children and adolescents has been undervalued and overlooked in dominant historical narratives. Instead, generations of Americans have credited fathers and other hoary leaders for their actions and achievements, all the while disregarding pivotal boyhood experiences that shaped skills and ideals. Reflecting these androcentric, Eurocentric, and age-based biases that have framed the nation's history, American history texts have reinforced the historical invisibility of girls and boys for centuries. For students searching libraries for scholarly sources and primary documents about children and adolescents in various historical contexts, this near absence of information in master narratives has vexed their research.

The absence of children in standard history books has not only obscured children's history but also the work of scholars who have been investigating youth's histories and interrogating their cultures since the turn of the last century. A new curiosity about children in times past was generated by the progressive era agenda which sought to educate, acculturate, and elevate American children through child study and child welfare. In *Child Life in Colonial Days* (1899), "amateur historian" Alice Morse Earl drew upon archival sources and material culture in order to examine the social history of Puritan girls and boys. Children were also included in Arthur W. Calhoun's

A Social History of the American Family (1917) and in Edmund S. Morgan's *The Puritan Family: Religion and Domestic Relations in Seventeenth Century New England* (1944), but few other professional historians within the male-dominated profession considered children worthy of study. Those children who made appearances in historical accounts were typically the privileged daughters and sons of white men of means and might.

In the 1960s, larger social, cultural, and political transformations refocused scholarly attention. The influence of sixties' youth culture and second wave feminism and renewed interest in the agency of "ordinary people," youth in particular, laid the foundation for a "new" social history. The confluence of a renewed interest in youth and the development of new methodological approaches led French demographer and social historian Philippe Ariès to study a nation's youngest population. Challenging a dominant assumption that childhood was transhistorical in *Centuries of Childhood: A Social History of Family Life* (1962), Ariès argued that over time, changing cultures and societies redefined notions of childhood and transformed children's experiences. Ariès work on European children was soon followed by Bernard Wishy's *The Child and the Republic: The Dawn of American Child Nurture* (1968), which explored the changing nature of child rearing advice in the United States.

Despite important inroads made by these and other scholars (e.g., Robert Bremner), the history of childhood became embedded within historical sub fields during the 1970s. The history of childhood was briefly associated with psychohistory due to the controversial work of Lloyd deMause who founded *The History of Childhood Quarterly*. It was largely historians of the family (e.g., John Demos, Philip Greven Jr.) and those in the history of education (who refocused attention away from the school and onto the student) who broke new ground. Essays appeared in scholarly journals in the 1970s but were not reprinted until the following decade when *Growing Up in America: Children in Historical Perspective* (1985) brought new visibility to the "vitality and scope of this emerging field" (preface). That important collection edited by historians Joseph M. Hawes and N. Ray Hiner, along with their *American Childhood: A Research Guide and Historical Handbook* (1985), served to promote research among an up-and-coming generation of historians whose work would be included in another path breaking anthology. By placing children at the center of historical inquiry, privileging gender as a critical factor in childhood socialization, and expanding social history to include cultural history, historians in *Small Worlds: Children and Adolescents in America, 1850–1950* (1992) demonstrated that the relationships between childhood and adulthood and kids and culture were historically significant. By privileging previously overlooked and disregarded historical sources, "reading" material culture artifacts as historical texts, and applying gender, race, and class analyses to an age-based one, these historians continued to the mapping of childhood's terrain. Creatively and methodically, they traced childhood ideals and children's experiences within cultures and over centuries.

In the early to mid 1990s, those in the fields of psychology and education initiated a scholarly debate about the dangers that popular culture posed to the healthy development of female adolescents in contemporary America. Those scholars influenced by a different scholarly trajectory—cultural studies and feminist theory—saw agency instead, illuminating the many ways in which girls and female adolescents (as other youth) resist, contest, subvert, and reappropriate dominant cultural forms. Moreover, scholars such as Kimberly Roberts brought to light the discursive nature of the contemporary "girl crisis" debate just as others have uncovered numerous other discourses that create, reflect, and reinforce the cultural norms of girlhood, boyhood, female and male adolescence. Trained in fields other than history (e.g., American Studies, communications studies, English, Rhetoric and Composition), the latest generation of scholars has blurred the boundaries and forged new fields. Informed by the work of cultural studies scholar Angela McRobbie, "girl's culture" aimed to balance the boy-centered biases of the older "youth studies." Nevertheless, such late twentieth-century anthologies as *The Children's Culture Reader* (1998), *Delinquents & Debutantes: Twentieth-Century American Girls' Cultures* (1998) and *Generations of Youth: Youth Cultures and History in Twentieth-Century America* (1998) reflect a new multi- and inter-disciplinarity in the study of children and youth which utilizes textual and representational analyses (as opposed to social history) to study the subcultures that children and youth have constructed within larger historical contexts. By developing new methods of inquiry and widening subjects of study, scholars have been able to examine "lived experiences" and "subjectivities," though most of the recent work focuses on teenagers in the twentieth century.

Today, there is an abundance of scholarly works (e.g., monographs, anthologies, and encyclopedias), book series on children (e.g., The Girls' History & Culture Series), national, regional, and local conferences, major academic journals, and in 2000, The Society for the History of Children and Youth, was finally founded by two of the field's pioneers, Joseph M. Hawes and N. Ray Hiner. That professional organization draws together the many college and university professors who teach courses on the history of children and youth, girlhood and female adolescence regularly offered in schools of education, departments of history, psychology, political science, sociology, and in programs on Women's Studies, Media/Communications Studies, and American Studies. But the history of children and adolescents has an even broader audience as media attention on bad boys and mean girls (e.g., "Queenbees") generates new questions and a search for answers in historical antecedents.

To meet the research needs of students of all ages, this accessibly written work—as the others in the series—surveys and synthesizes a century of scholarship on children and adolescents of different classes, races, genders, regions, religions, sexualities, and abilities. Some topics in the series have a gendered, racial, or regional focus while others (e.g., sickness and health, work and play, etc.) utilize a larger multicultural perspective. Whichever their focus, each and every book is organized into three equal parts to provide researchers with immediate access to historical overviews, primary source documents, and scholarly sources. Part I consists of synthetic essays written by experts in the field whose surveys are chronological and contextual. Part II provides access to hard-to-find primary source documents, in part or whole. Explanatory head notes illuminate themes, generate further understanding, and expedite inquiry. Part III is an extensive up-to-date bibliography of cited sources as well as those critical for further research.

The goal of the Children and Youth: History and Culture reference book series is not simply a utilitarian one but also to ultimately situate girls and boys of all ages more centrally in dominant historical narratives.

Miriam Forman-Brunell, Series Editor
University of Missouri, Kansas City

Acknowledgments

For research and transcription assistance we would like to thank Katherine Chavez, Bonnie Doyle, David Gartner, Mary Paula Hunter, and Cynthia Riccio. For indexing, we would like to thank Cynthia Monroe. For financial support we would like to thank the Brown University Departmental Research Fund for the Arts, Humanities, and Social Sciences; the Connecticut State University American Association of University Professors; the Rutgers Center for Children and Childhood Studies; and the Graduate Program in History of Rutgers University, Camden.

This book is dedicated to our families.

Introduction

This book provides an historical overview of the major issues in infant, child, and adolescent health in the United States from the colonial period through the twenty-first century. It is the first book to provide a comprehensive historical account of the ways in which professionals and the state have addressed child health problems. The book examines how family and community caretakers intervened in the lives of sick children and also how they became advocates for local child health initiatives. Most critically, this volume looks at how children and youth reacted to being sick and how these experiences affected their lives, the development of health care, and the creation of pediatric medicine.

The book is composed of three parts. The initial section consists of six original essays. The first, written by Richard A. Meckel, gives a broad demographic overview and explanation of the major trends and variables in infant, child, and youth death and disease since the seventeenth century. The second chapter, by Heather Munro Prescott, discusses representations of child sickness and health in memoirs, art, literature, and film. This is followed by an essay by Kathleen Jones exploring mental hygiene and children's experiences of mental illness. Jones argues that definitions of mental health and mental illness are functions of what society considers to be age-appropriate feelings and behaviors. The fourth chapter, by Janet Golden, looks at health care providers and institutions for children and youth. Golden argues that children's health care has been marked by both change and continuity. Chapter five, by Elizabeth Toon, examines advice literature and public school curriculum materials aimed at children and youth about health, illness, and personal hygiene. Bringing together a variety of historical scholarship in the history of medicine, education, and childhood, Toon argues that health education has frequently been viewed as a panacea for a variety of social ills affecting children. The sixth and final essay, by Kriste Lindenmeyer, looks at child health and the state, with an emphasis on the rise of state and federally funded programs designed to improve child health and welfare. A central question of this chapter is how maintenance of good health became one of the major rights to which children are entitled.

The six original essays in this volume reflect the growing scholarly interest in the history of childhood and youth, particularly in issues affecting child health and welfare. They show how changing patterns of health and disease have responded to and helped to shape notions of childhood and adolescence as life stages. The authors also describe numerous changes in the experiences of children and caregivers over time. Through the early twentieth century, for example, life-threatening illnesses were a constant threat to children of all social classes. Today, many diseases and threats to child health have been eliminated or alleviated, although critical problems remain and new ones, such as AIDS and violence, have begun to take a steady toll. Child health, therefore, continues to be an active concern for families, communities, and the nation. A second example of change and continuity can be drawn from the development of health care institutions and the rise of social welfare policies aimed at improving the health of children. Both have grown enormously over the course of American history, but the home remains, as it was in the colonial period, the most critical site of care, and parents the most critical actors in the preservation of child health.

The second section of this volume provides a selection of primary sources grouped into six categories: recounting health and illness, advice on child health, images of child health, institutions for child health, mental hygiene, and child health and the state. The third and final section of this book consists of an extensive bibliography of secondary sources.

This book is meant to be a starting point for students and scholars interested in exploring the history of child health and illness. Many important questions remain to be answered, and many critical sources have yet to be explored. In the future, as studies of children become even more important to the historical enterprise, knowledge about illness and health, caregivers and sites of care, mental health, experiences of illness, health education, and the role of the state in providing care will expand and grow.

Janet Golden
Richard A. Meckel
Heather Munro Prescott

I Essays

1 Levels and Trends of Death and Disease in Childhood, 1620 to the Present

Richard A. Meckel

Of all the changes that have transformed American childhood since the colonial era, perhaps none has been more significant than the dramatic reduction that has taken place in the likelihood of death, disease, or physical incapacitation during the early years of life. Today, the death rate of the nation's young is only a tiny fraction of what it was through most of the eighteenth and nineteenth centuries, when somewhere around 25 percent of all children born in the United States failed to survive the first five years of life and close to a third failed to make it to age ten. Similarly, in real terms, the incidence of serious disease and physical handicap has declined immensely. The so-called childhood diseases are infrequently contracted and almost never fatal, and, unlike in past centuries, it is no longer common to meet children who are blind or deaf from infection or accident, whose frames are stunted or twisted from rickets, scoliosis, or tuberculosis, who are disfigured or partially paralyzed by accidents, or who are condemned to lives as invalids by hearts damaged in bouts with diphtheria or scarlet fever. Most of this great improvement in children's health and survival took place in the twentieth century and was part of a larger mortality and epidemiological transition that saw life expectancy improve at all ages and infectious disease retreat from being the great killer of Americans. Driven initially by improving nutrition, living, and educational standards and by state-sponsored environmental sanitation, improvements in children's health and survival have increasingly been the consequence of developments in scientific medicine.

THE COLONIAL ERA

Although the lack of accurate birth, death, and population records for the colonies continues to obscure the rates and trends of infant and child mortality in the colonial period, historians in recent decades have made considerable progress in developing a far more complete and sophisticated understanding of what those rates and trends probably were (Alter 1997). For much of the twentieth century, historians—drawing upon such literary sources as diaries, sermons, travelogues, and histories written by colonists or those who traveled in the colonies—characterized the colonial period and especially the seventeenth century as extraordinarily inhospitable to infant and child life. In the Chesapeake infants and children were said to be the most favored victims of the agues, fevers, and various diarrheal fluxes that were reported by colonists as ever present. In New England, bitter winters and respiratory catarrhs were believed to have carried off the young in droves. Everywhere poor diet, primitive conditions, and the deadly epidemics that seemed continually to sweep through village and town were believed to put survival of the young always in doubt. Indeed, estimates of the proportion of those born in the colonies who failed to reach age ten often ranged as high as 50 and 60 percent (Vinovskis 1972; Earle 1899).

Lending both support and illustration to the estimates that over half of all colonial children perished before adolescence were the experiences of a number of prominent colonists. Cotton Mather saw nine of his fifteen children die before they reached the age of five. Samuel Sewell watched seven of his fourteen offspring perish within the first two years of life. The poet Edward Taylor suffered the loss of five of the eight children he had with his first wife. Moreover, the silent testimony of many colonial-era graveyards suggests that the experiences of these men were not unusual. Dotting such graveyards are markers like that of the Daggart family of New Haven. On it are listed the names of six Daggart offspring, the oldest of whom perished at the age of seventy-two days (Slater 1977).

In the 1970s, however, American colonial historians began challenging the traditional description of early America as uniformly deadly to infants and children and started to construct a much more nuanced description of mortality among the colonial young. Focusing on single villages, parishes, or towns and more systematically exploiting existing records by using quantitative techniques pioneered by English and European historical demographers, these historians produced a number of studies collectively suggesting that the most salient characteristic of colonial infant and child mortality was not that it was extraordinarily high but that it varied tremendously in level and cause over time, region, proximity to the coast, population density, and race. Although still too few in number and too focused on New England and the Chesapeake to support a definitive assessment of infant and child mortality in the colonies, these studies nevertheless allow us to arrive at a few tentative conclusions (Demos 1970; Greven 1970; Norton 1971; Smith 1978).

The first of these conclusions is that Arthur Calhoun was less than entirely correct when he wrote in his classic *A Social History of the American Family* that "it was difficult at first to raise children in the new country. In the bareness and cold of Massachusetts, mortality of infants was frightful" (Calhoun 1917). Based on the mortality rates of adults, studies of Plymouth and Dedham, Massachusetts, hypothesized that mortality among infants and children in seventeenth-century New England villages was anything but frightful and was probably lower than it was in rural England at the time. These hypotheses found significant support in a study done of the village of Andover by Philip Greven. Using family-reconstitution techniques developed by the French historical demographer Louis Henry, Greven examined the demographic characteristics of successive generations of colonial Andover residents and concluded that mortality among all ages, but especially among infants and children, had been astonishingly low in the seventeenth century before rising somewhat during the eighteenth. Indeed, for the generation born in Andover between 1640 and 1669, Greven calculated that 89 percent survived to the age of ten, a survival rate that would suggest that only 6 to 7 percent of Andover children failed to make it out of infancy. Today we would consider such a percentage tragically high, but for the seventeenth century it was extraordinarily low—and indeed would not be achieved in modern Andover until well into the twentieth century (Greven 1970).

Comparing the seventeenth-century Andover infant and child mortality rates to those that English historical demographers had computed for similar English villages, Greven challenged the often-stated judgment of historians that the early migrants to New England had paid for their venture with higher death rates for themselves and their children. Additionally, by calculating that infant and child mortality was significantly higher among the generations born between 1700 and 1729 and 1730 and 1759, he concluded that contrary to previous belief, the eighteenth century, with its improved living conditions and comforts, brought worse rather than better health to the infants and children who lived in villages like Andover. Indeed, according to Greven, only 52 percent of those born in the latter generation managed to survive to age ten (Greven 1970).

Subsequent demographic studies of colonial New England confirmed Greven's general findings while questioning whether seventeenth-century infant and child mortality was quite as low as he suggested. Noting that the failure to report deaths in early infancy was not uncommon in colonial America, they adjusted reported infant and child deaths or used model life tables to propose that a more realistic infant death rate for seventeenth-century rural Massachusetts would be somewhere between 10 and 15 percent. Subsequent research also demonstrated that colonial New England children born in commercial seaports had significantly lower chances of survival than did their rural village counterparts. Studies based on parish and town records of Salem and Boston suggest that between 20 and 30 percent of all infants born in colonial seaports may have died before their first birthdays, a rate that was lower than that obtaining at the time in Paris and London but considerably higher than that in villages away from the seacoast. Moreover, there is now considerable evidence indicating that the survival rate of such infants and children, unlike that of their rural counterparts, improved rather than deteriorated as the eighteenth century progressed, though it remained higher than it was inland (Vinovskis 1972; Archer 1990; Alter 1997).

Proximity to the coast and location in a seaport also seems to have made surviving more difficult for infants and children in the mid-Atlantic and southern colonies. Infant and child death rates in colonial New York and Philadelphia were as high as they were in Boston. In colonial Charleston, they were considerably higher. Indeed, infants and children throughout the South faced a significantly higher risk of dying than did their counterparts in the North and even England. This was especially true of those who had the misfortune to reside in coastal and tidewater settlements in the Chesapeake. Beginning with Jamestown, the early settlement of the Chesapeake was a demographic disaster. Death rates were so high and birthrates so low among the Anglo settlers that it took a constant flow of immigrants just to sustain the population. In such an environment, the few children who were born often did not make it out of infancy and childhood. Moreover, unlike in New England coastal areas, the coming of the eighteenth century did not bring significant relief. Although mortality rates for all ages were considerably lower in the new settlements being established in the Piedmont and other inland areas, in the Chesapeake they remained rather high. One estimate suggests that during the first third of the eighteenth century close to 20 percent of Chesapeake-born Anglo infants failed to survive the first year and that another 15 percent did not make it to puberty (Smith 1978).

As high as mortality was among the infants and children of the Anglo settlers in the coastal and tidewater regions of the southern colonies, it was significantly higher among another group of children with whom they lived in close proximity—the offspring of the expanding African slave population. Although mortality among slave children, like that among their white counterparts, varied considerably by region and environment, mid-eighteenth-century records from a few large coastal plantations suggest that fully 50 percent of slave children died before age ten, with at least 25 percent never making it to age one. Why this was so has not been established, but a number of historians suggest it was the result of poor nourishment combined with how difficult slavery made it for mothers to breast-feed and give their young the attention and care they required (Kulikoff 1986).

Even higher than the mortality experienced by African slave children was that suffered by the children of the aboriginal peoples who had occupied the eastern seaboard before European migration. Although no records exist from which even suggestive Indian birth and death rates can be calculated, historians have in recent decades established fairly concretely that the aboriginal population throughout the Americas declined catastrophically from the initial European contact onward. Probably four hundred thousand people lived east of the Appalachian Mountains when the first English and Dutch colonists arrived on the continent. By the time of the Revolution, there were only a few thousand left. Wars and migration were partly responsible for this drastic depopulation, but by far the major cause was exposure to the viral and bacterial infectious diseases that the Europeans brought with them. Having no previous contact and thus no biological defenses, the aboriginal population proved incredibly vulnerable. In the early seventeenth century, for instance, pneumonic or bubonic plague ravaged the Algonquin in northern New England, killing some 90 percent of the tribe. A decade or two later, smallpox swept through the Huron and Iroquois, leaving half of them dead (Duffy 1997).

Although children seem to weather certain viral infections such as smallpox, mumps, and measles better than do adults, it seems certain that the aboriginal young were in no way spared the slaughter that European and African diseases visited on the continent's native peoples. For such children, the coming of Europeans and the importation of African slaves drastically and catastrophically altered the disease environment with which they had to interact and in so doing exponentially decreased their chances of survival. Confronted with an environment newly filled with disease agents against which they had neither acquired nor inherited armament, they were decidedly disadvantaged in both resisting infection or surviving diseases once infected (Cook 1997).

If interaction with the disease environment explains why so many aboriginal children died, so too does it explain the variations in death rates among other colonial infants and children across time, place, and race. Unlike today, when infants and children who die do so primarily from congenital problems, degenerative disease, accidents, or violence, the vast majority of the colonial young who perished were the victims of infectious and parasitic diseases. Those who lived either avoided exposure, resisted being infected, or were able to survive disease. The ability to resist and survive is dependent on acquired immunities and general healthiness, while avoidance is dependent on how prevalent diseases are in the environment. In seventeenth-century rural New England, infants and children enjoyed relatively low death rates, because they were generally well fed and healthy and were protected from continued exposure to infectious human disease by the isolation of their villages. Their seaport counterparts, on the other hand, not only faced the constant exposure that is characteristic of places with a continued commerce of people but also were always in danger of being infected with insect-transmitted parasitic diseases like malaria, which was endemic to the colonial coastline all the way up to Salem. With the coming of the eighteenth century, malaria retreated from New England, and the isolation of inland towns and villages disappeared with the improvement of roads. The result was a drop in mortality along the coast and a rise inland, especially during the second quarter of the eighteenth century, when deadly epidemics of measles, diphtheria, and smallpox swept through a rural New England population that had avoided exposure and therefore lacked immunities (Duffy 1953; Kunitz 1984).

In the colonial South, malaria continued to threaten children, especially along the coast and inland waterways, throughout the colonial era. Although newborns may have enjoyed immunity for a few months, older infants and toddlers seem to have been particularly vulnerable. Moreover, those children not killed outright were often condemned to early deaths, because the disease destroyed their health and weakened their resistance to other diseases. Southern and mid-Atlantic children also suffered the ravages of another insect-transmitted disease, yellow fever. Probably of African origin, the disease became endemic in the Caribbean and visited devastating epidemics on New York and Philadelphia throughout the eighteenth century and on southern cities well into the nineteenth century (Rutman and Rutman 1976; Cooper and Kiple 1993).

The predominance of infectious disease also shaped the way in which children experienced illness and parents responded to the possibility and reality of infant and child death. In a disease environment like that occupied by colonial children, the experience of illness was frequent and acute, but also short-term. Chronic illness, while not unknown among colonial children, was not very prevalent for the simple fact that those who were born with or developed a long-term chronic or degenerative disease usually soon died from pneumonia or some other acute disease to which their weakened state made them vulnerable. For most of their days, then, colonial children were relatively healthy, if always at risk.

It was the risk rather than the healthiness, however, on which colonial parents seemed to focus most. And with good reason—children who were healthy on Monday could be dead by Friday. Moreover, given the way that infectious diseases were transmitted in colonial America, the risk of losing a child was not spread evenly across families. An infected child would bring home the disease and infect all of his or her siblings. Often they would survive, but sometimes they would not. In 1659, for instance, following what may have been the first epidemic appearance of diphtheria in New England, the Reverend Samuel Danforth penned this stark and simple entry into the records of the First Church of Roxbury: "The Lord sent a general visitation of children by coughs and colds, of which my three children, Sarah, Mary, and Elizabeth Danforth died, all of them in the space of a fortnight" (Duffy 1953).

THE NINETEENTH CENTURY

Our knowledge of infant and child morbidity and mortality patterns is not much better for most of the nineteenth century than it is for the colonial era. Although it is fairly certain that in the last quarter of the century mortality rates among all ages began their steady decline to what they are today, it is not at all clear what they were doing prior to that. Even for many urban areas, death registration continued to be incomplete and often nonexistent prior to the last decade of the century, and birth registration was unreliable well into the twentieth. Consequently, especially for the period before the Civil War, demographic historians have had to rely on such tools of indirect estimation as model life tables, local genealogies, parish records, and various methods of extrapolating from census data. Not surprisingly, a good deal of disagreement has resulted, even in regard to general mortality.

One early study, based on life tables constructed in the mid-nineteenth century, suggests that life expectancy increased steadily through the entire first half of the century as living standards rose. Another, using a variety of data from nineteenth-century Massachusetts, concludes that while mortality among all ages declined during the first third of the century, it rose again in the second third as the effects of industrialization, immigration, and urban growth began to impact on the health of Americans, particularly those living in industrial towns and major cities. A more recent and often-cited study, again focusing primarily on Massachusetts, maintains that after dropping in more urban areas during the late eighteenth century, mortality remained relatively stable up to the Civil War. The most recent studies, pointing to evidence showing that young adult males in the 1850s were smaller in stature than their fathers and grandfathers, hypothesize that the 1830s and 1840s witnessed a significant worsening of the disease environment that compromised the nutritional status of the young and increased mortality among all ages (Vinovskis 1972; Komlos 1996).

Given the lack of certainty concerning the course and levels of overall mortality during the initial two-thirds of the nineteenth century, it is hardly surprising that historians have been reluctant to hazard estimates of the rates and trends of infant and child mortality during the period. Nevertheless, it is both possible and desirable to engage in some informed speculation, especially in regard to the obviously significant question: What impact did early and mid-nineteenth century urbanization, industrialization, and immigration have on the health and survival of American children? One line of speculation has recently been pursued by a group of demographic historians engaging in what they call "anthropometric history"—that is, historical study that bases its analysis on records of the heights and weights of certain populations. Noting that both logic and fragmentary nineteenth-century evidence suggest that the growth of cities in size and number and the increase in internal and foreign migration worked to break down barriers to disease transmission, they posit that the second quarter of the century saw health worsen and mortality rise among the young due to a significant increase in the incidence of infectious disease. As evidence they point to data showing that of the heights of West Point cadets, Union army recruits, Amherst College students, and a few other populations measured over time declined significantly for those born during the 1820s, 1830s, and 1840s. Such a decline in stature suggests that those born in the second quarter of the century received worse nutrition than previous generations. Since the period was one in which per capita production of food in the United States increased, historians have theorized that such a marked decline in nutritional status could only have taken place if there was a significant increase in infectious disease, which can compromise nutrition by impeding absorption or redirecting nutrients away from the building of tissue and toward the fighting of infection (Komlos 1994).

It is also possible to speculate that given their sensitivity to environmental sanitation and population density, the health and survival rates of urban infants and children probably declined during the first half of the century as the inflow of rural Americans and foreign immigrants dramatically increased the number and size of the nation's cities and produced unprecedented levels of overcrowding and nonsanitation. Such certainly was the opinion of mid-nineteenth-century sanitary investigators like Lemuel Shattuck and John Griscom, who compiled and published reports on Boston and New York contending that after declining through the late eighteenth century, mortality rates took a sharp turn upward (Meckel 1990). That city growth was accompanied by a rise in urban infant and child mortality is also the conclusion of a contemporary study exploring the impact of immigration and population density on mortality rates in midcentury Boston. Especially during the decade and a half before the Civil War, the influx of foreign immigrants into the city drove up death rates at all ages and exacted a particularly heavy toll among the young (Meckel 1985).

Interestingly, while the toll was heaviest among the infants and children of the new arrivals, as table 1 shows, it was not dramatically so. One reason for this was that in the mid-nineteenth-century American city, there was little spatial segregation between the classes. It would only be later in the century, when the introduction of horse cars and other transportation innovations allowed the well-off to move beyond walking distance from their places of employment, that the prosperous and the poor ceased to live in close proximity and to experience the same general environmental conditions. Indeed, a close analysis of child mortality rates in Pittsburgh for 1850 concluded that wealth was a relatively weak predictor of which young would live or die (Davis 1993).

That child health and survival in the mid-nineteenth century was not as strongly determined as it is today by family assets is also the conclusion

Table 1
Infant Mortality by Nativity of Parents, Suffolk County, Massachusetts, 1866–1875[a]

Year	IMR[b] Native Parents	IMR[b] One Parent Foreign Born	IMR[b] Both Parents Foreign Born[c]
1866	181.2	188.5	198.7
1867	178.5	185.3	193.3
1868	192.2	201.6	208.4
1869	180.3	184.8	192.4
1870	196.6	204.8	212.4
1871	185.6	184.3	191.4
1872[d]	220.0	235.2	246.7
1873[d]	201.5	216.1	224.8
1874	181.6	188.7	199.9
1875	187.8	209.8	220.4

Source: Secretary of the Commonwealth of Massachusetts, Annual Reports (1866–1875).

[a]Exclusive of stillbirths.

[b]IMR computed as deaths of infants ≤12 months during one year/all births in same year × 1000.

[c]Includes births and deaths designated as of unknown parentage.

[d]The high rates of mortality for 1872 and 1873 were probably in large part due to the small-pox epidemic that ravaged the eastern United States during those years.

of a study of child mortality based on a national sample of 1,600 house-holds matched from the 1850 and 1860 census manuscript schedules. Cal-culating mortality rates on the basis of those children four and under in each family mentioned in the 1850 census who failed to show up in the 1860s census, the study showed that while socioeconomic status influenced the likelihood that a family would lose a child, it did not do so as strongly as region, population density, and number of children. Children in larger families tended to die more often than those in smaller families, most likely because the probability that disease would be introduced into the family increased with each additional family member. Similarly, infants and chil-dren who lived in large cities were almost twice as likely to die in child-hood as their counterparts living in small towns and established rural areas (Steckel 1988).

Somewhat surprisingly, despite its concentration of cities and industry, the Northeast emerged as the healthiest region in the country for children. Just over 13 percent of all northeastern children who reached the age of one failed to celebrate their fifth birthday. The least healthy region was what was then the frontier—Minnesota, Iowa, Missouri, Texas, and the western terri-tories—probably because living conditions were primitive, nutrition poor, and sanitation often bad. Over 21 percent of children aged one to four died, while another 25 to 30 percent probably perished in infancy. Indeed, when death came on the frontier it was as likely to come for an infant or child as it was for all other ages combined. Of the 354 people buried in Leavenworth, Kansas, in 1875 close to 50 percent were children under the age of ten (King 1991). Moreover, it was not just for the children of settlers that the frontier proved deadly during the middle and later decades of the nineteenth century. It was also deadly for the infants and children of the Plains Indian tribes, who came in increasing contact with white Americans after 1840. Within twenty years, the tribes were facing an ecological disaster that took a heavy toll on their children. With their nutritional status compromised by the decreasing availability of buffalo meat and their exposure to whites increasing daily, the tribes were ravaged by a number of epidemics that cut a deadly swathe through their young (Sundstrom 1997).

Although less healthy than the North, the South posed less of a risk to child life than did the frontier, at least for white children. Among the 1860 sample population, only about 16 percent of children aged one to four died, while somewhere less than 25 percent of infants perished. This comparative low risk of death, however, was not enjoyed by the large population of slave infants and children who also inhabited the antebellum South. From the relatively good records that nineteenth-century slave owners kept on slave births, deaths, and physical characteristics like height and weight, scholars have been able to construct a picture of health and survival of slave infants and children that is considerably more accurate than anything we have for white children during the same period. What that picture shows is a deadly childhood, in which 35 percent of all those born failed to reach age one, 48 percent failed to make it to age five, and 57 percent never reached age fifteen. In addition, it seems probable that at least 15 percent of completed pregnancies ended in stillbirth (Steckel 1986).

Given that the health and longevity of adult slaves compared favorably to that of nonslaves, this extremely high rate of slave fetal, infant, and child death—roughly twice that of the free population of the United States—has provoked considerable discussion among demographic historians. One theory offered is that the hard work that slave women did right up to giving birth contributed to stillbirths and deaths in early infancy. Plantation records showing a high proportion of slave infants born at low birth weights lends considerable support to this theory. Work patterns also affected the health of older infants and children. A quick return to work forced slave women early to substitute artificial or mixed feeding for breast-feeding, thereby increasing the risk that their infants would contract and die from gastroenteritis or diarrhea. For those infants who survived, the long absence of their parents at work continued to compromise their health. Slave workers were usually fed in the fields and were provided by their owners with relatively nutritious meals. Not so children, whose diet seems to have consisted in large part of hominy and fat. As a consequence, slave children were nutritionally compromised and highly susceptible to infectious and parasitic diseases. Indeed, plantation records show that slave children were significantly shorter and lighter than their free counterparts and caught up in stature only after they became full-time workers in their early adolescence (Steckel 2000).

With emancipation the health and survival rates of African American infants and children probably improved significantly, although many contemporary public health commentators warned that absent the benign paternalism of the plantation owner, the former slaves and their offspring were doomed to extinction (Meckel 1997). Indeed, records from southern cities, to which many former slaves moved, suggest that while the mortality suffered by African American infants and children was higher than that of their white counterparts, it was considerably lower than what had been common on antebellum plantations (Steckel 2000).

The end of the Civil War did not bring improving health to the children of the rest of the population. Life on the frontier continued to take its toll among children of both white settlers and Native Americans. In the more established regions, infectious and parasitic diseases remained constant threats to the health and survival of the young. The protection offered by rural isolation had all but disappeared as railroads and other modern forms of transportation quickly conveyed disease carriers from place to place. When a worldwide epidemic of cholera entered the United States in 1872, it rapidly moved out of port cities and spread through small towns and rural areas. Not that place ceased to make a difference; it was still healthier for infants and children in rural areas and small towns than it was in the increasingly crowded cores of the nation's cities. Indeed, in the postbellum years, city life and infant and child death came to be closely linked, especially during the hot summer months, when what seemed like epidemics of gastroenteritis and diarrhea would carry off thousands of the urban young. As the *New York Times* editorialized in 1876 after one particularly deadly July week in which over a hundred infants a day had died in Manhattan, "There is no more depressing feature about our American cities than the annual slaughter of little children of which they are the scene" (*New York Times* 1876). Growing public concern with this "annual slaughter of little children" helped precipitate a public health movement to improve infant and child health and survival. Along with a complex amalgam of socioeconomic, environmental, and medical developments at the end of the nineteenth century, that movement started infant and child death rates on the path of decline that they would follow through the twentieth century and into the twenty-first (Meckel 1990).

TWENTIETH CENTURY: DECLINING MORBIDITY AND MORTALITY

As the nineteenth century came to a close and the twentieth century began, infant and child life remained almost as precarious as it had been during the colonial era and nineteenth century. About 6 percent of all children born in turn-of-the-century America failed to survive the first month of their lives, prey most often to complications arising from prematurity, congenital deformities, or birth trauma. Another 7 percent failed to make it to their first birthdays, succumbing to respiratory diseases, or more likely, to any of the variety of gastrointestinal disorders that carried away tens of thousands of American babies each year, especially during the hot summer months. As had been true in the past, early childhood was less risky, though hardly safe. Close to 7 percent of all American children aged one through four who were alive during the first year of the twentieth century were dead by the end of the second. The causes of death among young children were many, but particularly prominent were the infectious diseases that had taken such a deadly toll on children since the nation's early years. Of these, infectious respiratory diseases—particularly pneumonia, croup, influenza, and bronchitis—were the biggest killers, accounting for almost a third of all young child deaths. Indeed, pneumonia alone killed 21 percent of the children aged one to four who died at the turn of the century. Also deadly were the traditional infectious childhood diseases— measles, whooping cough, scarlet fever, and diphtheria—which together were responsible for 23 percent of all young child deaths. These diseases, along with tuberculosis and injuries, were responsible for the bulk of deaths among children five to fifteen (Meckel 1996; Preston and Haines 1991).

As had been true in the colonial era and nineteenth century, not all children in turn-of-the century America faced the same risk of death. City living continued to be dangerous to the health and survival of the young, although the largest American cities were less inimical to child life than moderate-sized cities. This was probably because in large cities such public health measures as filtered water, effective sewerage and garbage removal, and various health education programs were earliest implemented. Region also continued to make a difference. But by 1900, New England, with its concentration of industrial towns and its overall population density, had become the least healthy section of the country for the young. Indeed, children in the Midwest had close to a 30 percent better chance of surviving than did children in New England. The importance of family economic status seems to have been somewhat greater in 1900 than it was in 1850, probably because wealth allowed families to escape the unsanitary urban environment and build houses in the less crowded and more salubrious suburbs that were beginning to ring American cities. Race also continued to be a major, perhaps *the* major, determinant of higher rates of death and disease among some children than others. As the century began, African American children were twice as likely to die before reaching five than were white children (Preston and Haines 1991).

Of course, most American children at the beginning of the century survived to reach adulthood. But for a significant proportion of those who did, childhood was marred by frequent illness, physical handicap, and chronic pain. Although data on turn-of-the century levels of disease and incapacitation are not abundant, what does exist suggests that childhood a hundred years ago was far more compromised than it is today by frequent illness, physical discomfort, and disability. Every year uncounted numbers of infants were condemned to lives as partial invalids by congenital deformity or birth trauma. Children who were blind or deaf—from infection or accident—were common. So too were children whose frames were stunted or twisted from rickets, scoliosis, or tuberculosis or whose hearts had been damaged by a bout with diphtheria or scarlet fever. Also common were children who hobbled about on crutches because of a crippling accident or because they had suffered partial paralysis as a result of poliomyelitis, a disease that was beginning to make its presence felt and would soon replace diphtheria as the most terrifying childhood scourge. Less terrifying but almost universal was pain and discomfort from a variety of chronic health problems. Among school-aged children, bacterial and parasitic skin and scalp diseases were close to endemic; discharge from eye, ear, and sinus infections was so common that it often did not occasion comment; and ongoing mouth and tooth pain from rotting teeth was considered a normal part of childhood. Indeed, records from periodic dental exams given to school children during the first decade of the century reveal that upward of 80 percent of those examined had significant dental carries (Meckel 2002).

Against these diseases and deformities, there were few weapons available. Late-nineteenth-century advances in diagnostic technology and in the emerging science of bacteriology produced better understanding of the etiology and physiology of disease, but they did not significantly increase the ability of health care providers to combat disease. Only one effective chemotherapy existed in 1900—diphtheria antitoxin. Hence, physicians continued to rely on the drugs they had used through much of the nineteenth century: digitalis, quinine, and opium derivatives. Indeed, although they were beginning to grasp prophylaxis and were on the threshold of a revolution in understanding and practice, even the best educated and trained turn-of-the-century physicians could seem helpless in the face of disease. Not untypical was the experience of Abraham and Mary Putnam Jacoby. Both were eminent physicians—he the most respected pediatrician in America and she the first woman admitted to membership in the New York Academy of Medicine. Although both considered themselves experts in the management of diphtheria, they were powerless to prevent the death of one of their own children from the disease (Hammonds 1999).

One hundred years later, at the beginning of the twenty-first century, barely seven-tenths of 1 percent of all children born in the United States fail to reach age one, and less than nine-tenths of 1 percent fail to make it to age twenty (FIFCFS 2001). Although infant and child death is certainly not unheard of, it has become infrequent enough to be considered a tragic abnormality. This dramatic reduction in mortality among children occurred within the context of an overall decline during the century in the death rates of Americans of all ages and as part of an epidemiologic transition in which chronic and degenerative diseases supplanted infectious disease as the major killers of Americans. Although the late-twentieth-century resurgence of tuberculosis and the appearance of AIDS, Lyme disease, and some deadly disorders caused by new strains of streptococcal and E. coli bacteria offer vivid reminders that the microbial threat to health in the United States has not been banished, infectious disease in general is no longer the handmaiden of death. This is particularly true of the young, for whom infectious disease is not the mass killer it was earlier in the century. Although children still die from infectious disease, they do so extremely rarely.

VARIATIONS IN RATES AND TRENDS

As was the case with mortality among other American age groups, infant and child mortality rates began their decline to present-day levels sometime in the last two decades of the nineteenth century. Probably beginning to decline first in rural areas, they fell fastest and farthest in the nation's largest cities. In New York City, for instance, infant mortality during the mid-1880s stood at a shockingly high 25 percent. By 1900, it had dropped to just over 18 percent and by 1915 to less than 10 percent (table 2). Similar though less dramatic declines occurred in Boston, Philadelphia, Chicago, and other major American cities, driven in large part by a concurrent drop in the incidence and seriousness of summer gastroenteric disorders among infants. Beginning to fade in the 1890s, the summer diarrheal epidemics that had plagued American urban infants since the eighteenth century had all but disappeared by the 1920s (Cheney 1984). Aside from reducing infant mortality, this disappearance of summer gastroenteric disorders contributed to a shift in the seasonal distribution of deaths among the young. Where in 1900 roughly an equal number of infant and child deaths occurred during the warm and cold months, now far more occur in fall and winter.

While the mortality of infants and children dropped relentlessly during the twentieth century, it did not do so uniformly over time. Indeed, the overall decline of mortality among the young was marked by some short-term fluctuations and reversals and by more rapid declines in some periods than others. Unlike the middle-aged and elderly, for whom mortality declined most sharply in the middle and last thirds of the century, children experienced their greatest improvement in life expectancy before 1930, with gains

Table 2
Infant Mortality in New York City,[a] 1885–1919

Year	Births[b]	Deaths <1 year[c]	Infant Mortality Rate[d]
1885	37,543	9,303	247.8
1890	46,176	10,288	222.8
1900	90,801	16,627	183.1
1905	115,422	16498	142.9
1910	135,873	16,215	119.3
1915	144,138	13,866	96.2
1919	133,027	10,699	80.4

Source: Ernst Meyer. 1921. *Infant Mortality in New York City: A Study of the Results Accomplished by Infant Life-Saving Agencies, 1885–1920.* New York: Rockefeller Foundation International Health Board, 130 (facing).

[a]Manhattan and the Bronx.
[b]Estimated, not recorded births. Estimates based on New York City Health Department assessment that in 1885 recorded deaths were 20 percent less than actual births, in 1890 15 percent less, in 1900 10 percent less, in 1910 5 percent less, and in 1919 2 percent less.
[c]Exclusive of stillbirths.
[d]Infant mortality rates computed as deaths of infants ≤12 months during one year/all births in same year x 1000. The rates here have been recalculated to correct original compiler's mathematical errors.

ranging from just under 60 percent for those aged five through fourteen to over 70 percent for those aged one to four. The one exception to this pattern has been the mortality of neonates—that is, of those under one month. While the mortality of older infants fell rapidly during the first third of the century and has been relatively stable since midcentury, that among neonates has dropped just as fast at the end of the century as at the beginning (Meckel 1996).

Although all groups of American infants and children enjoyed the twentieth-century decline in mortality, they did not do so equally. As with so many other social benefits, improving health among the young during the twentieth century has correlated closely with socioeconomic status. Moreover, the strength of that correlation may have increased over the course of the century, as the quality of medical care improved and thus as the ability to purchase it had an ever greater impact on health (table 3). Similarly, as medical care and advice have improved in effectiveness, certain characteristics associated with higher economic status—most notably maternal education, a commitment to healthy behaviors, and knowledge of and willingness to utilize available health services—have become much more important in determining levels of health and survival among the young. For instance, both family income and maternal education correlate strongly with

Table 3
Infant, Neonatal, and Post-Neonatal Mortality by Race, 1990–1999

Year	Infant Mortality[a]			Neonatal Mortality[b]			Post-neonatal Mortality[c]		
	All	White	Black[e]	All	White	Black	All	White	Black
1990	9.2	7.6	18.0	5.8	4.8	11.6	3.4	2.8	6.7
1995	7.6	6.3	15.1	4.9	4.1	9.8	2.7	2.2	5.3
1999	7.1	5.8	14.6	4.7	3.9	9.8	2.3	1.9	4.8

Source: National Center for Health Statistics. 2001. *Health, United States, 2001*. Hyattsville, Md., table 23.

[a]Infant mortality rates computed as deaths of infants ≤12 months during one year/all births in same year × 1000.
[b]Neonatal mortality rates computed as deaths of infants ≤28 days during one year/all births in same year × 1000.
[c]Post-neonatal mortality rates computed as deaths of infants >28 days but ≤12 months during one year/all births in same year × 1000.

"White" designates infants born of a white mother.
"Black" designates infants born of a black mother.

the likelihood that a pregnant woman will seek first-term prenatal care and that new parents will have their child vaccinated (Children's Defense Fund 1994).

Race has also been a significant determinant of the rate and extent that mortality and morbidity declined among the young in the twentieth century. In 1915, mortality among infants classified as nonwhite was 1.8 times that of their white counterparts (table 4). Although the death rates of both groups have dropped dramatically through the century, the disadvantage has persisted and may even have grown. In 1999 infant mortality among blacks was 2.5 times higher than among whites. Among Native Americans it was 2.3 times higher. Race also is a factor at other ages. Black children aged one through four die at twice the rate white children that age do; and Native American children die at 1.7 times the white rate.

CHANGING CAUSES OF DEATH

Closely connected to the decline in mortality among the young in the twentieth century have been three major changes in the leading causes of death among infants and children. The first change has been a dramatic drop in both the number and proportion of child deaths caused by infectious disease. The second has been a corresponding increase in the proportion, if not the number, of child deaths from chronic and degenerative

Table 4
Death Rates[a] by Age, Sex, and Race/Ethnicity, 1999

| Age | 1–4 | | 5–14 | | 15–24 | |
Race/ethnicity	Male	Female	Male	Female	Male	Female
White	33.9	27.4	20.3	14.9	104.9	58.4
Black	66.0	51.5	34.6	22.6	185.6	60.1
Indian/Eskimo	59.4	43.1	23.1	21.7	218.5	67.5
Asian/Pacific Islander	26.6	19.4	12.9	11.5	58.7	29.1
Hispanic	34.3	29.8	19.4	14.4	124.9	36.4

Source: National Center for Health Statistics. 2001. *Health, United States, 2001*. Hyattsville, Md., table 36.

[a]Death rates computed as number of deaths in age group during 1999/100,000 living in that age group in same year.

diseases and from external causes—that is, from accidents, injuries, homicide, and suicide. The third has been an increase in the proportion of infant mortality attributable to congenital malformations and anomalies, prematurity, low birthweight, and other so-called diseases of early infancy, as well as a corresponding decrease in the proportion of infant mortality caused by infectious gastrointestinal and respiratory diseases.

In 1900, infectious gastrointestinal and respiratory diseases killed close to half of all infants who died that year. Pneumonia was the leading killer of children aged one to four and diphtheria that of children five through fourteen. Other infectious diseases also caused large numbers of deaths among the young. Measles, whooping cough, scarlet fever, meningitis, and the various respiratory diseases cut down thousands of children aged one to fourteen. Indeed, infectious disease accounted for over 60 percent of all deaths of children less than fifteen (Preston and Haines 1991).

Today, deaths of American infants from gastrointestinal disease are exceedingly rare, and the proportion of infant deaths caused by infectious respiratory diseases has shrunk from close to 20 percent to under 2 percent. The biggest killers of infants today are congenital anomalies, disorders related to prematurity and low birthweight, and sudden infant death syndrome (SIDS). This does not mean, however, that deaths from these causes are on the rise. Far more infants in both the distant and near past died from congenital anomalies and disorders related to prematurity and low birthweight than do today. Indeed, since the late 1960s, the death rates from both sets of problems have declined quite significantly. Similarly, although deaths were not attributed to SIDS prior to the last quarter of the twentieth century, that is only because the syndrome was not given a name until then. As both medical and popular literature attest, infants have been dying inexplicably in their sleep for centuries. Moreover, while SIDS remains the biggest cause of post-neonatal infant deaths, its rate is barely 65 percent of what it was in 1980 (Anderton, Barrett, and Bogue 1997).

Infectious disease also accounts for only a tiny fraction of the deaths suffered by children one through fourteen. Of all the many infectious diseases that threatened and took the lives of young and older children at the beginning of the century, only pneumonia and influenza remain significant, though much less so than they were. If a child dies today, it is more likely that it will be from birth defects, cancer, or heart disease than from an infectious disease (table 5). Most likely, though, death will come from an external cause. Despite real success during the last thirty years in reducing the number of child deaths from accidents, 39 percent of all children aged one through fourteen who died in 1999 did so from unintentional injuries. Even more disturbing is that an additional 8 percent of all children who died that year were either murdered or took their own lives.

Table 5
Leading Causes of Death by Age Group, 1900 and 1999

1900	1999
Less than 1 year of age	
1. Gastrointestinal diseases	1. Congenital Anomalies
2. Pneumonia and Influenza	2. Sudden Infant Death Syndrome (SIDS)
3. Prematurity	3. Respiratory Distress Syndrome
4. Atrophy/Debility	4. Prematurity and Low Birthweight
5. Convulsions	5. Maternal Complications of Pregnancy
Ages 1 through 4	
1. Pneumonia and Influenza	1. Accidental Injuries
2. Gastrointestinal Diseases	2. Congenital Anomalies
3. Diphtheria	3. Malignant Neoplasm
4. Bronchitis	4. Heart Diseases
5. Measles	5. Homicide
Ages 5 through 14	
1. Diphtheria	1. Accidental Injuries
2. Accidental Injuries	2. Congenital Anomalies
3. Pneumonia and Influenza	3. Malignant Neoplasm
4. Gastrointestinal Diseases	4. Homicide
5. Scarlet Fever	5. Heart Diseases

Sources: Samuel H. Preston, and Michael R. Haines. 1991. *Fatal Years: Child Mortality in Late Nineteenth-Century America* (Princeton, N.J.: Princeton University Press), 4; National Center for Health Statistics. 2001. *Health, United States, 2001*. Hyattsville, Md., table 33.

ENGINES OF CHANGE

Behind the dramatic twentieth-century reduction of mortality among American infants and children and the concurrent drop in the incidence and fatality of infectious disease were a wide array of socioeconomic, eco-biological, behavioral, political and technological and scientific developments. In the first third of the century, declining fertility and better nutrition and housing, accompanying a rising standard of living, contributed significantly to the reduction of disease and death among infants and children. So too did environmental improvements, especially in cities, brought about by the construction of water supply and sewerage systems and the implementation of effective refuse removal. Also crucial was the work of public health officials and their allies in social work and medicine in combating the transmission of diseases among school children, in controlling milk-borne diseases, and in educating the public in the basics of preventive, infant, and child hygiene.

For many of the same reasons that they declined in the first third of the century, mortality and morbidity among infants and children continued to drop in the second and third. But beginning in the 1930s, the development and application of specific medical interventions and technologies played an increasingly important role. The perfection of effective fluid and electrolyte therapy to combat acidosis and dehydration in infants; the development and dissemination of vaccines providing immunity against traditional killers like pertussis, measles, and polio; the discovery and employ of sulfonamides and antibiotics to reduce fatalities from bacterial infections; the increasingly sophisticated use of vitamins and minerals to aid metabolism and combat such childhood scourges as rickets, pellagra, and pernicious anemia; and the design and implementation of surgical, therapeutic, and intensive care techniques to correct congenital deformities and to counter the risks faced by premature and low-birthweight infants—all have worked together to reduce the likelihood that an American childhood will be scarred by disease or ended prematurely by death.

A HEALTHIER CHILDHOOD?

Children die far less often today than they did in the past—but are they healthier? While common sense would argue that they are, some epidemiologists and historical demographers speculate that declining mortality and episodes of acute sickness have been accompanied by a rise in the percentage of children alive at a particular time who suffer long-term chronic or degenerative disease or serious physical incapacitation from birth defects or shortened gestation. In the past, they note, children were sick for short periods of time and either recovered or died. Today, modern medicine has allowed children to be sick, or at least incapacitated, for decades at a time.

Hence it may be that at a given moment more children are sick today than in the past (Riley 1989).

There is also considerable evidence that certain chronic conditions, particularly asthma and diabetes, are on the rise among American children. While the causes of this rise remain uncertain, many researchers have connected the growing incidence among children of asthma to worsening environmental pollution and that of diabetes to what some in the health community see as a mounting epidemic of childhood obesity. Moreover, some health researchers speculate that while the traditional childhood diseases have only a fraction of the impact they used to on children's health, their place has been taken by a set of "new morbidities" that include mental and emotional problems plus a range of such health-destroying behaviors as substance abuse and promiscuous, early, and unprotected sexual activity (FIFCFS 2001).

While such speculation might have some basis, it is also hard to deny that American infants and children today live in environments in which biological and other threats to survival are far fewer and less deadly than they were in the past. Both the decline in the incidence and deadliness of infectious disease and the overall decline in mortality among the young suggest that contemporary children who make it into adulthood do so having experienced only a fraction of the acute disease episodes that were routine for children in the past. Thanks to an array of surgical, dental, medical, and pharmaceutical innovations, children also live with far less day-to-day pain and discomfort than they did in the past. One need not be Whiggish about the transformation in childhood that this represents or blind to the inequalities in child health that persist to recognize just how profound that transformation has been.

WORKS CITED

Alter, George. 1997. "Infant Mortality in the United States and Canada." In *Infant and Child Mortality in the Past*. Edited by Alain Bideau, Bertrand Desjardins, and Hector Perez Brignoli, 91–108. Oxford: Clarendon.

Anderton, Douglas L., Richard E. Barrett, and Donald J. Bogue. 1997. *The Population of the United States*. 3rd ed. New York: Free Press.

Archer, Richard. 1990. "New England Mosaic: A Demographic Analysis of the Seventeenth Century." *William and Mary Quarterly* 47: 477–501.

Calhoun, Arthur. 1917. *A Social History of the American Family from Colonial Times to the Present*. Cleveland: Arthur H. Clarke.

Cheney, Rose A. 1984. "Seasonal Aspects of Infant and Child Mortality: Philadelphia 1865-1920." *Journal of Interdisciplinary History* 14: 561–85.

Children's Defense Fund. 1994. *Wasting America's Future: The Children's Defense Fund Report on the Costs of Child Poverty*. Boston: Beacon Press.

Cook, Sherburne. 1997. "The Significance of Disease in the Extinction of the New England Indians." In *Biological Consequences of European Expansion, 1450–1800*.

Edited by Kenneth Kiple and Stephen Beck, 251–74. Brookfield, Vt.: Ashgate/Variorum.

Cooper, Donald B., and Kenneth F. Kiple. 1993. "Yellow Fever." In *The Cambridge World History of Human Disease*. Edited by Kenneth F. Kiple. Cambridge: Cambridge University Press.

Davis, Eric Leiff. 1993. "The Era of the Common Child: Egalitarian Death in Antebellum America." *Mid-America* 75: 135–63.

Demos, John. 1970. *A Little Commonwealth: Family Life in Plymouth Colony*. New York: Oxford University Press.

Duffy, John. 1953. *Epidemics in Colonial America*. Baton Rouge: Louisiana State University Press.

———. 1997. "Smallpox and the Indians in the American Colonies." In *Biological Consequences of European Expansion, 1450–1800*. Edited by Kenneth Kiple and Stephen Beck, 233–50. Brookfield, Vt.: Ashgate/Variorum.

Earle, Alice Morse. 1899. *Child Life in Colonial Days*. New York: Macmillan.

Federal Interagency Forum on Child and Family Statistics (FIFCFS). 2001. *America's Children: Key National Indicators of Wellbeing, 2001*. Washington, D.C.: U.S. Government Printing Office.

Fingerhut, Lois, and Joel Kleinman.1989. *Trends and Current Status in Childhood Mortality*. Washington, D.C.: National Center for Health Statistics.

Greven, Philip. 1970. *Four Generations: Population, Land, and Family in Colonial Andover*. Ithaca, N.Y.: Cornell University Press.

Hammonds, Evelynn Maxine. 1999. *Childhood's Deadly Scourge: The Campaign to Control Diphtheria in New York City, 1880–1930*. Baltimore: Johns Hopkins University Press.

King, Charles R. 1991. "Childhood Death: The Health Care of Children on the Kansas Frontier." *Kansas History* 14: 26–36.

Komlos, John, ed. 1994. *Stature, Living Standards, and Economic Development: Essays in Anthropometric History*. Chicago: University of Chicago Press.

———. 1996. "Anomalies in Economic History: Toward a Resolution of the 'Antebellum Puzzle.'" *Journal of Economic History* 56: 202–14.

Kulikoff, Allan. 1986. *Tobacco and Slaves: The Development of Southern Cultures in the Chesapeake, 1680–1800*. Chapel Hill: University of North Carolina Press.

Kunitz, Stephen J. 1984. "Mortality Change in America, 1620–1920." *Human Biology* 56: 569–82.

Meckel, Richard A. 1985. "Immigration, Mortality, and Population Growth, 1840–1880." *Journal of Interdisciplinary History* 15: 393–417.

———. 1990. *Save the Babies: American Public Health Reform and the Prevention of Infant Mortality 1850–1929*. Baltimore: Johns Hopkins University Press; Ann Arbor: University of Michigan Press.

———. 1996. "Health and Disease." In *Encyclopedia of the United States in the Twentieth Century*, vol. 2. Edited by Stanley I. Kutler et al. New York: Charles Scribner's Sons.

———. 1997. "Racialism and Infant Death: Late Nineteenth and Early Twentieth Century Socio-Medical Discourses on African American Infant Mortality." In *Ethnicity and Health: Historical and Contemporary Perspectives*. Edited by Lara Marks and Michael Worboys, 70–92. London: Routledge.

———. 2002. "Delivering Oral Health Services to Children in the Past: The Rise and Fall of Children's Dental Clinics." *Ambulatory Pediatrics.*

National Center for Health Statistics. 2001. *Health, United States, 2001.* Hyattsville, Md.: Author.

New York Times. 1876. July 19, 4.

Norton, Susan. 1971. "Population Growth in Colonial America: A Study of Ipswich, Massachusetts." *Population Studies* 25: 318–44.

Preston, Samuel H., and Michael R. Haines. 1991. *Fatal Years: Child Mortality in Late Nineteenth-Century America.* Princeton, N.J.: Princeton University Press.

Riley, James C. 1989. *Sickness, Recovery, and Death: A History and Forecast of Ill Health.* Iowa City: University of Iowa Press.

Rutman, Darrett B., and Anita H. Rutman. 1976. "Of Agues and Fevers: Malaria in the Early Chesapeake." *William and Mary Quarterly* 33: 31–60.

Slater, Peter Gregg. 1977. *Children in the New England Mind: In Death and in Life.* Hamden, Conn.: Archon Books.

Smith, Daniel B. 1978. "Mortality and Family in the Colonial Chesapeake." *Journal of Interdisciplinary History* 8: 403–27.

Steckel, Richard. 1986. "A Dreadful Childhood: The Excess Mortality of American Slaves." *Social Science History* 10: 427–65.

———. 1988. "The Health and Welfare of Women and Children 1850–1860." *Journal of Economic History* 48: 333–45.

———. 2000. "The African American Population of the United States, 1790–1920." In *A Population History of North America.* Edited by Michael R. Haines and Richard H. Steckel, 483–528. New York: Cambridge University Press.

Sundstrom, Linea. 1997. "Smallpox Used Them Up: References to Epidemic Disease in Northern Plains Winter Counts." *Ethnohistory* 44: 305–43.

Vinovskis, Maris. 1972. "Mortality Rates and Trends in Massachusetts before 1860." *Journal of Economic History* 32: 184–213.

———. 1976. "Angels Heads and Weeping Willows: Death in Early America." *Proceedings of the American Antiquarian Society* 86: 273–302.

2 Stories of Childhood Health and Disease

Heather Munro Prescott

Stories about child health and disease give us insight into the social milieu in which they were written. They can tell us much about the state of medical knowledge at the time, how a particular historical era viewed childhood as a life stage, and what values the society hoped to transmit to children and adolescents. Sometimes these stories reflect the author's subjective experience of childhood illness, either as child, parent, or other caregiver. In other cases, the image of the sick and suffering child is used as a metaphor for larger social ills. Historically, high rates of child illness and death prompted culturally sanctioned responses, although these responses have varied considerably over time. In early America, narratives of children's experiences with disease and death were closely linked with notions of Christian piety and virtue. Although stories of child health and disease gradually became more secular in the late nineteenth and twentieth centuries, quasi-religious themes of recovery and redemption were present in both fictional and nonfictional descriptions of childhood illness well into the twentieth century. As rates of child illness and mortality declined in the mid-twentieth century, public discussion of child sickness and death became less common, particularly in literature aimed at children and adolescents. More recently, stories of child health and disease have reappeared as part of a "new realism" in child and adult literature. These stories provide children and parents alike with realistic depictions of various illnesses and of how to cope with them.

COLONIAL ERA

In her famous poem "In Memory of My Dear Grandchild Elizabeth Bradstreet" (1699), Anne Bradstreet wrote the following lament:

> How oft with disappointment have I met
> When I on fading things my hopes have set.

Anne Bradstreet's ode to her deceased grandchild reflected an experience common to many colonial Americans. Although Richard Meckel observes in his essay in this volume that infant and child mortality was not as great as originally supposed and that child mortality varied considerably by time period, region, population density, and race, it is clear from literary sources of this period that parents tended to fear the worst when it came to infant and child mortality. Diseases struck without warning or apparent reason and could wipe out all of a family's offspring in a single epidemic. In his *Right Thoughts in Sad Hours* (1689), Boston minister Cotton Mather (1663–1728), who saw nine of his fifteen children die before reaching the age of five, reminded parents that "a dead child is a sight no more surprising than a broken pitcher, or a blasted flower" (Murray 1998).

Historians have debated how rates of infant and child mortality affected early American views of children and childhood as a life stage. Some historians, drawing on the work of French historian Philippe Ariès, have argued that the modern concept of childhood could not develop until infant and child mortality were reduced enough to allow parents to make an intense emotional investment in each individual child. Instead of viewing childhood as a life stage deserving special protections, colonial Americans considered children "miniature adults" who had to grow up quickly in a harsh environment (Ariès 1962; Morgan 1966). Others have suggested that despite the brutal reality of child mortality, early Americans cherished their children and invested much time and energy in children's religious education, out of parental love and concern (Stannard 1974; Demos 1970; Slater 1977). Though Cotton Mather, who saw many of his siblings and children die in infancy, acknowledged that childhood death was exceedingly common, he also spoke of his children with great tenderness, likening the loss of a child to the tearing off of a limb (Avery 1994).

It is clear from stories of child illness and death from this time period that colonial experiences and views of childhood differed considerably from those of today. In an era before modern medical technologies, the possibility of one's own death or that of a close relative was an ever-present one. In addition, religious doctrine at this time emphasized the innate sinfulness of children and the need for parents to suppress their children's natural depravity by instructing them in biblical principles from an early age. Colonial Americans therefore believed that children should be presented with the reality of death and its theological implications as soon as they were old enough to pay attention to adult instruction (Stannard 1974; Mintz and Kellogg 1988; Murray 1998).

This sensibility is apparent in one of the most widely read children's books in colonial America, James Janeway's *A Token for Children, Being an Exact Account of the Conversion, Holy and Exemplary Lives and Joyful Deaths of Several Young Children* (1671). The first book in colonial America to tell the experiences of children themselves, the book illustrated for children and adults alike the importance of adopting pious and virtuous habits early in life. Janeway's book prompted similar sentiments in colonial children. William Godwin (1756–1836) recalled that "I felt as if I were willing to die with them if I could with equal success, engage the admiration of my friends and mankind." Eleven-year-old Hannah Hill of Philadelphia was so inspired by Janeway's writings that she left instructions for her last words to be published as *A Legacy for Children, being some of the last expressions and dying sayings of Hannah Hill, Jnr. Of the City of Philadelphia* (1714). Although this theological framework would eventually disappear, this image of the virtuous dying child, meant to serve as an example of good behavior for living children, would remain a fixture of both religious and secular writings about child health and illness for many years to come (Avery 1994).

THE EARLY REPUBLIC AND THE NINETEENTH CENTURY

During the late eighteenth and early nineteenth centuries, new views about childhood emerged that would have a great impact on stories of child health and illness. Philosophical tracts on childhood and child rearing, most notably Jean-Jacques Rousseau's *Emile* (1762), challenged Puritan doctrine on the innate depravity of children and instead proclaimed the child's natural innocence and purity. Children and childhood played a central role in the ideology of the new republic, which placed a great emphasis on universal education and nurture of the young (Mintz and Kellogg 1988). Reflecting this new view of childhood, children's gravestones were frequently marked with angels or animal figures symbolizing children's closeness to things natural and pure. An infant's gravestone from 1784 read:

> A spotless life my coffin is,
>
> And innocence my shroud. . . .
>
> And tho' deny'd God's house on Earth,
>
> I tread his courts in Heaven. (Brewer 1984)

Likewise, in a story from her *Juvenile Miscellany,* published in 1826, Lydia Child describes the life of Emily Waters, "a good affectionate girl who likes to play." When Emily's baby sister dies, her mother tells her that the baby "is happy now and will never more have pain or sickness" (Avery 1994).

At the same time, religion was still an important component of American national identity; the early years of the republic witnessed a nationwide religious revival known as the Second Great Awakening. In order to instruct the young in proper religious principles, various congregations started Sunday schools beginning in the 1790s. Like their English forerunners, these schools were originally intended to provide education to working children who could not attend regular public school sessions. By the early 1800s Sunday schools had shifted toward disseminating an evangelical Christian message to all children. In 1824, over 720 Sunday schools were unified under the American Sunday School Union, which soon began publishing religious tracts and stories for children. As in the colonial period, Sunday school stories such as *The Dairyman's Daughter* and *Light on Little Graves* used child illness and death as catalysts for religious conversion and piety in young and old alike. Even books that were not explicitly religious contained images of "child redeemers" whose suffering inspired others to embrace morally upstanding behavior (Murray 1998).

The Second Great Awakening coincided and was intertwined with other social movements of the early nineteenth century, most notably temperance, abolition, and health reform. White, middle-class Americans in the early nineteenth century became increasingly concerned about the impact of various developments, including industrialization, westward expansion, immigration, the spread of slavery, and growing class disparities. Fears that traditional American values were being lost amid a sea of disturbing social changes prompted middle-class reformers to apply the message of moral perfection contained within evangelical Christianity to various social institutions. Belief in the natural innocence and malleability of children led reformers to target many of their messages for a young audience. Themes of social improvement and moral uplift appeared frequently in children's books, magazine stories, and advice manuals that were written during the early nineteenth century. Temperance messages were especially prevalent in children's literature of this period. The popular children's periodical *The Youth's Companion*, first published in 1826, frequently carried stories about the dangers of alcohol. Temperance stories typically claimed that the "road to ruin" frequently began in childhood when parents indulged their children's fondness for sweets and other unhealthy foods. *The Glass of Whiskey* (1825), published by the American Sunday School Union, tells the story of young Hugh, who first develops a taste for alcohol at age six when given a toddy sprinkled with sugar and nutmeg. Hugh soon becomes addicted and succumbs to an early death after drinking an entire jug of rum found in a closet (Murray 1998). Pro-temperance literature frequently used the image of a sick or dying child as a plot device that leads adults to give up drinking and other bad habits. In *Ten Nights in a Bar-Room and What I Saw There* (1854), Timothy Shay Arthur showed how the love and forgiveness of Joe's sick daughter Mary causes Joe to overcome the "evil influences that were getting possession of even his external senses" (Sanchez-Eppler 1995).

Abolitionist literature drew on sentimental visions of sick or dying children also in order to convey the emotional pain inflicted by slavery. The most renowned pro-abolitionist novel, *Uncle Tom's Cabin, or Life Among the Lowly* (1853), depicts the angelic death of Little Evangeline St. Clare. The novel was inspired by Harriet Beecher Stowe's personal anguish following the death of her beloved son Charley during the cholera epidemic of 1848–49. In a letter to Elizabeth Cabot Follen in 1852, Stowe wrote that it was on Charley's "dying bed and at his grave that I learned what a poor slave mother may feel when her child is torn away from her. In those depths of sorrow which seemed to me immeasurable, it was my only prayer to God that such anguish might not be suffered in vain" (Hedrick 1994).

The experiences of real slave mothers are harder to uncover, since few left behind written records, but it is clear from mortality statistics that they experienced greater loss of children than did white women. Nearly half of all slave children died during their first year, a rate that was twice as high as that for white infants. Moreover, slave women found it difficult to care for sick children because of their work responsibilities. The emotional trauma of losing a parent to death or relocation could precipitate illness in a child. One former slave interviewed during the Great Depression recalled that when his mother was sold away, the "cruel separation brought on a fit of sickness, from which they did not expect I would recover" (Abel 2000).

Images of suffering children were also used to raise public support for public health reforms affecting children directly. By the mid-nineteenth century, there was a growing concern among middle-class reformers in many Western nations that the conditions of the industrial city were responsible for persistently high rates of infant and child mortality, especially among the urban immigrant poor (Meckel 1998). The English writer Charles Dickens, whose stories enjoyed widespread popularity on both sides of the Atlantic, provided the model for this genre with such classic characters as Tiny Tim in *A Christmas Carol* (1843) and Little Nell in *Old Curiosity Shop* (1840). American reformers used similar images to evoke sympathy for the plight of impoverished urban children. For example, in *Poor and Proud* (1858), William Taylor Adams told the woeful tale of eleven-year-old Katy Redburn, who tries to provide for herself and her consumptive mother amid evil landlords and other heartless villains in her South Boston neighborhood (Adams 1858).

However, there were conflicting views within American literature about the poor and their problems. Even authors who supported reforms to help the underprivileged tended to emphasize individual behavior and typically made distinctions between the "worthy" poor, who adopted proper middle-class health practices, and the "unworthy" poor, who refused to give up drinking and other "bad" habits (Meckel 1998). According to historian Martha

Verbrugge, health reform during this period was a "translation of middle-class ideology into physiological terms"; that ideology emphasized such middle-class norms as moderation, self-control, and persistence (Verbrugge 1988). This message of individual responsibility for health is especially apparent in the work of Horatio Alger, whose stories of poor but noble working boys reinforced American notions of personal responsibility and self-improvement. The young eponymous heroes of books like *Ragged Dick* (1868) and *Paul the Peddler* (1871) achieve personal success through a mixture of determination, luck, and above all, avoidance of such risks to health and morality as drinking, smoking, and prostitution (Avery 1994; Murray 1998).

By the mid-nineteenth century, the market for children's stories was becoming increasingly segmented by gender, and authors were writing stories specifically aimed at either girls or boys. Novels and stories for girls were part of a larger literary tradition of fiction writing by and for women that flourished during the nineteenth century. Periodicals, novels, poems, essays, and sermons contributed to a "Cult of True Womanhood" that glorified women as more pious, pure, domestic, and submissive than men, and that touted women's role as an uplifting social influence within the home and in society as a whole (Welter 1966). Women writers at this time built careers on female readers' eagerness for advice literature and fiction that portrayed women's roles in a positive light (Douglas 1977). Like Stowe, female writers frequently drew on their own experiences with sickness and loss of children. The prevalence of childhood illness and death in Victorian literature reflected persistently high rates of child morbidity and mortality. Even though improvements in diet and medical care had improved mortality rates, factors of increasing immigration, urban crowding, and poor sanitation meant that nearly a quarter of all children died before reaching adolescence (Meckel 1998).

In response to this grim reality, a body of "consolation literature" encouraged women to see themselves as part of a "sisterhood of suffering" that helped women transcend their own anguish by linking them to others who shared similar experiences (Abel 2000). According to Stowe's biographer Joan Hedrick, Stowe's works were part of "an informal priesthood of women who have suffered," a response in part to high rates of infant and child mortality (Hedrick 1994). Beginning in the 1860s, the new medium of photography provided another avenue through which women and other family members could publicly express their grief. Postmortem photography became a popular tradition during the second half of the nineteenth century. According to Eleanor Brown, like consolation literature, postmortem photographs of departed children "promoted emotional healing through the complex ritual of grieving and the Victorian public acceptance of death" (Brown 1997).

A woman's induction into this sisterhood of suffering often began during late childhood or adolescence, as girls were called upon to care for younger siblings and other family members during illness. This sense of familial obligation was felt even by girls who left home to attend school or work for wages. In a letter to her mother, fourteen-year-old Eliza Southgate wrote upon hearing of her siblings' illness, "I am very sorry for your trouble, and sympathize with you in it. I now regret being from home, more than ever, for I think I might be of service to you now the children are sick" (Bowne 1887). Susan Warner's extremely popular children's book *The Wide, Wide World* (1852), sales of which exceeded even those of *Uncle Tom's Cabin*, describes young Ellen Montgomery's intense emotional suffering and abrupt transition to womanhood upon the death of her mother from tuberculosis (Warner 1852/1987). Novels and stories written for girls at this time often contained heroines whose illnesses led them to adopt appropriately feminine behavior.

The following passage from Louisa May Alcott's classic novel *Little Women* is the best-known example of how the illness of a close family member inspires young women to become more virtuous and feminine. Alcott vividly described the suffering of young Beth March from scarlet fever and the impact her illness has on the rest of the March family and their friends and neighbors: "How dark the days seemed now, how sad and lonely the house, and how heavy were the hearts of the sisters as they worked and waited, while the shadow of death hovered over the once happy home." Older sister Jo "devoted herself to Beth day and night, not a hard task, for Beth was very patient, and bore her pain uncomplainingly as long as she could control herself." As Beth hovers between life and death, her sisters vow to become more virtuous young women:

> The girls never forgot that night, for no sleep came to them as they kept their watch, with that dreadful sense of powerlessness which comes to us in hours like those.
>
> "If God spares Beth, I never will complain again," whispered Meg earnestly.
>
> "If God spares Beth, I'll try to love and serve Him all my life," answered Jo, with equal fervor.
>
> "I wish I had no heart, it aches so," sighed Meg, after a pause.
>
> "If life is often as hard as this, I don't see how we ever shall get through it," added her sister despondently.

Beth survives this initial illness, but her health is permanently weakened. Later in the novel, Beth and her family "cheerfully" accept the inevitability of her early death: "With tears and prayers and tender hands, Mother and sisters made her ready for the long sleep that pain would never mar again, seeing with grateful eyes the beautiful serenity that soon replaced the pathetic patience that had wrung their hearts so long, and feeling with reverent joy that to their darling death was a benignant angel, not a phantom full of dread" (Alcott 1869).

Similarly, in *What Katy Did* (1872), Susan Coolidge shows how a serious back injury and convalescence forced Katy to give up her selfish ways and devote herself to the care of others (Murray 1998). Female characters who overstepped boundaries of proper feminine decorum could risk illness or even death. For example, in the Massachusetts Sabbath School Society book *The Governess* (1849), young Julia spends the night dancing at a ball, catches a cold, and upon her deathbed chastises her mother for allowing her to spend the evening on frivolous pursuits (Avery 1994).

Illness and suffering were not the only themes in girls' stories; there were also tales of robust girls whose healthful behavior was meant to serve as a model for other children. Images of thriving children living in idyllic rural surroundings became increasingly prevalent by midcentury, especially after the Civil War, and provided a counterpoint to disturbing stories of urban decay and diseased foreigners crowding into America's large cities. Charles Loring Brace, founder of the Children's Aid Society in New York and author of *The Dangerous Classes of New York* (1872), argued that the urban environment was a poisonous one for its inhabitants, particularly the young. Children raised in such toxic conditions, Brace argued, resembled a species of "street rats" who "gnawed away at the foundations of society and scampered when light was brought near them." Brace, however, offered a more optimistic portrait of the "dangerous classes" than did other critics of urban America at this time, claiming that the deviant behavior of slum children was a product of their environment, not hereditary weakness (Burns 1988).

At the same time, medical warnings about the dangers of "overcivilization" were becoming increasingly common. The neurologist George Miller Beard warned in 1881 that too much sedentary indoor work and too little outdoor exercise was taking a toll on the white middle classes, especially the young (Lears 1981; Burbick, 1994). Warnings about the dangers of intellectual work were particularly stringent in the case of girls. In his book *Sex in Education, or a Fair Chance for the Girls* (1874), the Harvard medical professor Dr. Edward H. Clarke argued that "brain-work" and menstruation were incompatible. Education of girls during the critical period of reproductive development, Clarke argued, would irreparably damage their reproductive organs and eventually lead to the extinction of the white middle classes. Some critics used this argument to criticize all efforts to educate girls and women. Others argued that the problem could be solved by balancing brain work with healthy outdoor activities (Verbrugge 1988).

One of the best-known children's books depicting the healing power of nature is Swiss-born author Johanna Spyri's *Heidi* (1884). The story centers around a young orphan sent to live with her grandfather in the Swiss Alps. Originally put off by her grandfather's gruff manner, Heidi comes to love life in the countryside. Several years later, Heidi's Aunt Detie reclaims the child and brings her to Frankfurt as a companion to her invalid cousin Klara.

Heidi soon becomes homesick and convinces her aunt to send her and Klara back to the Swiss countryside. It is here, in a setting of plenty of fresh air, sunshine, and wholesome food, that Klara overcomes her illness and regains her ability to walk (Spyri 1884).

Occasionally, such literature challenged established gender roles for girls. The best-known example is the character Jo March in *Little Women;* in her vigorous athleticism she contrasts starkly with her invalid sister Beth (Alcott 1869). Likewise, in her novel *Meadowbrook* (1857), Mary J. Holmes described nine-year-old tomboy Rosa Lee, who likes jumping from the hayloft, swinging on gates, climbing trees, and other unladylike pursuits. Rather than meeting an untimely death, Rosa Lee grows up to be a successful schoolteacher and marries a refined, intelligent, wealthy young man (Cogan 1989). In their autobiographies women who grew up in the nineteenth century commonly recommended outdoor activities for girls, especially those who were sickly or frail. The doctor of Carolyn Briggs of Northhampton, Massachusetts, believed her at risk for consumption and recommended that she live "out of doors as much as possible, without regard to weather." However, even these rugged tomboys are eventually domesticated and, while never surrendering their love of the outdoors, accept traditional roles of wife and mother (MacLeod 1994).

Stories written for boys were even more likely to draw upon rural motifs and the healing power of nature. Authors of such works argued that Victorian fiction, much like the female-dominated Victorian home, "feminized" boys and failed to give them appropriate masculine role models. Authors of boys' stories, therefore, increasingly rejected the moral didacticism of Sunday school literature in favor of tales of rugged individualism (Burns 1988; Murray 1998). The most famous exemplar of this genre was Mark Twain, who wrote parodies of Sunday school stories for popular newspapers. In "The Story of the Bad Little Boy That Bore a Charmed Life" (1865) and "The Story of the Good Little Boy Who Did Not Prosper" (1870), Twain lampooned the formulaic Sunday school story and reversed the outcomes. The bad boy lies and pulls pranks on his family and friends but is never punished, nor does he undergo religious conversion or die. Conversely, the good little boy is wrongly accused of theft and is unable to convince adults otherwise despite martyrlike good behavior. Twain later expanded these themes in his classic novels *Tom Sawyer* (1876) and *The Adventures of Huckleberry Finn* (1885), both of which showed how boys could thwart the "feminized" culture of traditional Christian piety. The hero of the latter novel even self-consciously mocks the Victorian convention of the innocent dead child by faking his own death and watching the grief-stricken mourners at his "funeral" (Murray 1998). Nevertheless, Victorian conventions linking death and illness with religious redemption and moral awakening persisted well into the next century.

THE TWENTIETH CENTURY

At the beginning of the twentieth century, sentimentalized orphans and sick children remained stock characters in children's fiction. Frances Hodgson Burnett's classic book *The Secret Garden* (1911) tells the tale of two cousins, Mary Lennox and Colin Craven, who suffer from health problems and who have been orphaned or abandoned by their parents. Both characters manage to heal themselves through their dedication to restoring the "secret garden" kept by Colin's departed mother, eventually softening the hearts of the adults around them (Murray 1998). Gene Stratton-Porter's popular series of novels for children, including *Freckles* (1904) and *A Girl of the Limberlost* (1911), also stressed the healing and transformative power of nature. In Eleanor Porter's *Pollyanna* (1913), the title heroine is seriously injured in an auto accident and is forced to spend months in bed recuperating. Rather than mope, Pollyanna plays her "gladness game"; rather than feeling disappointed or unhappy she focuses on the good aspects of her life. Pollyanna eventually recovers and along the way converts her friends and relatives to a positive way of thinking (Murray 1998).

Frequently these stories reflected the serious health risks faced by many children, even those from privileged circumstances, at the turn of the century. For example, Inez Irwin's series of children's books, starting with *Maida's Little Shop* (1910), told the story of Maida, who despite having everything her wealthy father can buy her, suffers from poor health and is unable to walk. Maida eventually regains the use of her legs following an operation by a renowned German specialist but remains listless until her father buys her a shop for which to care. There, activity and interaction with her peers restore Maida to health and happiness. The adventures of Maida and her friends continued through a series of books, all of which described the positive impact of productive activity on child health.

Narratives of child illness and death carried over into a new medium that appeared at the turn of the century—motion pictures. Many early films were adapted versions of classic children's books and stories. Other films drew upon the tradition of Victorian melodrama to create new tales featuring child victims. The acclaimed director D. W. Griffith was the undisputed master of this genre. In films such as *Broken Blossoms, Orphans of the Storm,* and *Way Down East,* Griffith displayed familiar images of children victimized by cruelty, disease, and early death (Jennings 1980).

At the same time, children's books and stories increasingly reflected developments in scientific medicine and public health. Reformers in this period disseminated printed literature, photographic studies, and documentary films to educate the public about child health matters and to foster support for child health and welfare reforms. Photojournalists such as Jacob Riis and Lewis Hine published photographic essays and gave lantern-slide presentations that depicted the dismal living conditions endured by the nation's poorer classes and the terrible toll these circumstances took on child health. Various state, local, and national public health organizations, such as the U.S. Children's Bureau, the American Association for the Study and Prevention of Infant Mortality, and the National Association for the Study and Prevention of Tuberculosis, also disseminated narratives and photographs. These stories were intended to educate the public about child health issues, stimulate reform, and promote donations for various child health causes. Frequently these organizations used photographs and personal testimony of young sufferers to gain public sympathy and donations for their causes (Golden 1996).

Public health organizations also produced a wealth of literature and imagery for children. The Child Health Organization of America (CHO), established by the New York Academy of Medicine in 1918, played a leading role in creating age-appropriate stories, plays, and games containing public health tips. These stories used amusing characters, such as "Cho-Cho the Health Clown" and "Professor Happy," and employed fantasy settings to make their messages appealing to young audiences. In *Cho-Cho and the Health Fairy* (1920), Eleanor Glendower Griffith borrowed plot devices from children's classics such as *Peter Pan* and *The Wizard of Oz* to show how children can help the Health Fairy rebuild her house of health, destroyed by an evil witch (Griffith 1920). The CHO even encouraged children and teachers to write their own health plays and stories. In such tales as "The Wizardry of Milk" and "The Pied Piper of Health," pupils in the public schools of New York City showed their classmates the joys and wonders that sprang from adopting proper health habits (Child Health Organization of America 1921).

Stories by and for child sufferers also started to appear during this period. Among the most prolific were those written by children and adolescents who were residents of sanatoriums for treatment of tuberculosis. Going to a sanatorium meant separation from parents and friends. These institutions helped children adapt to their strange surroundings by providing games and activities, including writing poems and stories about their illness experiences. Young residents of the Pennsylvania State Tuberculosis Sanatorium contributed regularly to *Spunk*, a newsletter by and for the institution's patients. Children's writings tended to be lighthearted, emphasizing the fun activities the facility provided for young patients. However, occasionally a child author would express feelings of homesickness and frustration, as in the following "Children's Song:"

> I spent five years at Mont Alto
> And five more years have I to stay
> For knocking off a piece of my lung
> And leaving the other part decay.
> Sad and lonely,
> Sitting in the cure chair all alone, alone;
> Thinking of the days that I spent up here,
> And the hours when I was home.

Stories about how to prevent and treat tuberculosis extended beyond the sanitorium walls. In the 1910s, the National Tuberculosis Association began a program of health instruction in the public schools, enlisting children in a "modern health crusade" against tuberculosis. Children participated in the "battle" against tuberculosis by buying and selling Easter Seals; by performing "health chores" such as brushing teeth, getting adequate sleep, and eating nourishing food; and by participating in "health pageants" that demonstrated the habits conducive to good health. The NTA designed instructional booklets with children's interests in mind, employing cartoon characters like "Tommy Tubercle" and "Huber the Tuber" to engage children's attention (Feldberg 1995).

Messages about how to prevent disease even carried over into mainstream fiction for children. For example, Margery Williams' *The Velveteen Rabbit* (1922) depicts a child's bout with scarlet fever, after which the Boy's nursery is disinfected and all belongings discarded, including his beloved toy. The story ends happily for the velveteen rabbit, however, when the nursery magic Fairy turns the toy into a real rabbit (Williams 1922).

The reform activity of the early twentieth century culminated in a view of childhood that required that children be sheltered from the unpleasant aspects of the adult world. This attitude was reflected in the children's literature of the 1920s and 1930s, which tended to avoid harsh social realities caused by war and economic uncertainty (Murray 1998). Authors frequently set their stories in a romanticized, rural past and touted the healthful benefits of the honest, simple lifestyles of the country's ancestors. The theme of rugged country living as an antidote to modern ills was most prevalent in stories for boys. Books like Bertha and Ernest Cobb's *Dan's Boy* and Arthur Pier's prep-school novels depicted the benefits of sports and healthy living in developing manly character in boys. Girls' stories also tended to advocate developing strong, healthy bodies. Carol Brink's popular novel *Caddie Woodlawn* (1935) depicted the life of a young girl growing up in frontier Wisconsin during the 1860s. Caddie is allowed to run free and play alongside her brothers because her father hopes that outdoor living will improve her fragile health. However, like many Victorian heroines, Caddie eventually has to rein in her tomboyish ways and become a "true woman" (MacLeod 1994).

Laura Ingalls Wilder's immensely popular "Little House" series of novels also depicted the moral and physical benefits of frontier life. Wilder and her daughter Rose Wilder Lane, who helped edit the novels, were both opposed to the economic-recovery programs proposed under President Roosevelt's New Deal, and their novels showed how a frontier family could overcome any adversity without government "meddling." *By the Shores of Silver Lake* (1939) even introduced the theme of a young person's illness as a catalyst for a character's self-improvement. In the novel, Mary Ingalls is left blind after a bout with scarlet fever. This incident forces young Laura to grow up quickly and begin teaching school to supplement the family's meager income (Murray 1998).

Stories about child illness written by and for adults tended to be more realistic and were aimed at finding solutions to specific social ills affecting children. In his magazine *True Stories*, Bernarr Macfadden published brutally honest stories about mothers who had lost infants and children to preventable diseases and accidents (Simonds and Rothman 1992). During the 1930s and early 1940s, proponents of the New Deal reforms drew upon images of suffering children to promote their reform efforts on behalf of child health and welfare. Documentary photographs by Dorothea Lange and Walker Evans showed the devastating effects of hard economic times on the health of the nation's young (Higonnet 1998). Letters from desperate parents to the Children's Bureau and to President and Mrs. Franklin Delano Roosevelt indicated the inadequacies of the private health care system and the need for the government to take a stronger role in providing medical care for its neediest citizens (Abel 2000). Motion pictures featuring prominent healers and hospital settings, such as *The Story of Louis Pasteur* (1936) and *Dr. Ehrlich's Magic Bullet* (1940), showed the impact that modern medical triumphs had on many deadly diseases, especially those affecting children. Yet some stories were ambivalent about the role of doctors, suggesting that medical authority came at a price. In his short story "The Use of Force" (1938), William Carlos Williams, who was a physician as well as a writer, shows a protracted battle between a doctor and a recalcitrant little girl. The story nicely captures the terror that children felt in facing doctors, as well as the brutal lengths to which doctors felt obliged to go to get accurate diagnoses from child patients. Although the doctor says to himself that the girl must be "protected against her own idiocy" and that "others must be protected against her," he also feels a powerful sense of "adult shame" in using physical force to examine the girl's throat.

By the 1940s, advances in disease prevention and medical therapeutics caused a dramatic reduction in child deaths from infectious diseases. Consequently, stories about child illness in the 1940s and 1950s focused on lingering deadly scourges, most notably polio. Polio epidemics swept the country in the 1940s and 1950s, and the personal testimony of the disease's victims was used to inspire donations to the March of Dimes. Polio survivors and their parents published autobiographical and biographical accounts as a way of dealing with the anguish the disease caused them, as well as of instructing other sufferers in how to adjust to the physical limitations the disease caused. As Daniel Wilson observes in his study of these polio narratives, almost all of these personal stories were "structured as accounts of triumph over adversity" that served to educate a polio sufferer in how to be a "good handicapped person." Letters of polio patients to President Roosevelt suggest that feelings of depression and anger were common among sufferers, but these emotions were rarely expressed in published testimony of polio patients. Instead, published accounts tended to shun bitterness and disappointment and to favor upbeat, inspirational stories of personal triumph over disability. For example, in *No Time for Tears*, Charles H. Andrews described his ten-year-old son Charlie's eagerness to comply with medical therapy (Wilson, 1994).

> "Charlie," she [the therapist] said, "you want to be completely well again, don't you?"
>
> "Yes ma'am, I sure do. I want to go to summer camp next year."
>
> "All right then. Whatever I tell you to do, you must do. And work, work all the time. Can I count on you to co-operate with me?"
>
> "Gosh," he spilled out, "I'll do anything." (Andrews, 1951)

In the 1940s and 1950s stories of child illness also drew attention to a disease that had previously been overshadowed by infectious diseases—cancer. During the late 1940s, popular accounts of cancer increasingly showed child victims of the disease and played up the risk of this disease in childhood. As in the past, child victims were used to drum up public sympathy and donations to scientific research. The appearance of twelve-year-old "Jimmy" on the popular radio program "Truth or Consequences" on May 22, 1948, helped raise public awareness of the disease and created a philanthropic organization, the Jimmy Fund, dedicated to scientific research on childhood cancers. Like polio narratives, personal accounts of childhood cancer emphasized personal triumph and bravery in the face of disease, even impending death. In his best-selling memoir *Death Be Not Proud* (1949), John Gunther told the inspirational story of his teenage son Johnny's courageous struggle with brain cancer, showing that his son "did not die like a vegetable. He died like a man, with perfect dignity." Like earlier stories of child death, the memoir served as a way to process the author's own grief, as well as give other parents advice on how to deal with the tragic loss of a child (Gunther 1949).

Fiction for children during the 1940s and 1950s was largely silent on issues of illness and death. In the aftermath of World War II and because of the uncertainty created by the Cold War, authors of children's books tended to treat childhood as a carefree time and to steer clear of disturbing topics that might upset young readers. When the subject of death was discussed, it was usually transferred to the animal worlds, as in E. B. White's *Charlotte's Web* (1954).

Since the 1960s, children's fiction has emulated larger cultural shifts and increasingly deals with serious social issues affecting the nation. The precursor for what became known as the "problem" young-adult novel was J. D. Salinger's *The Catcher in the Rye* (1951), which described adolescent anomie and emotional problems in frank terms. Salinger's book paved the way for a new realism in young adult and children's novels of the 1960s and

1970s. Novels such as Paul Zindel's *My Darling, My Hamburger* (1969), Alice Childress's *A Hero Ain't Nothin' but a Sandwich* (1973), and Joanne Greenberg's *I Never Promised You a Rose Garden* (1977) dealt with such serious health issues as substance abuse, pregnancy, sexually transmitted diseases, and mental illness. Judy Blume's series of novels for preteens candidly portrayed issues regarding adolescent health and maturation. *Are You There God? It's Me, Margaret* (1970) depicted a young teenage girl's anxieties about developing breasts, menstruation, and emerging sexual feelings. *Deenie* (1973) tells the story of a thirteen-year-old girl with scoliosis, while *Blubber* (1974) describes a young boy's struggle with obesity.

Memoirs of child illness have also appeared with growing frequency since the 1960s, and they give testimonies that were less saccarine than were the memoirs of earlier eras. In his book *The Long Walk Home* (1964), Leonard Kriegel reflects on the anguish he felt as a teenage polio patient:

> At first, the war was between Mr. Thompson and me. Mr. Thompson was the therapist in charge of rehabilitation, and he coddled me with the textbooks that told him to ascribe to fear my refusal to cooperate with his desires. But it wasn't fear. It was hatred, hatred of what they were trying to make of me, and I knew it . . . I refused to think of it as walking. I thought of it as necessity, as doing what they wanted me to do. I was meeting them halfway, but at the same time I was matching my will against theirs, my knuckle-down boyhood shrewdness against their closed-fist adult power. I never took more than five or six steps. (Kriegel 1964/ Wilson 1994)

This new realism also extended to the subject of child death and became part of a larger trend toward removing the taboo regarding discussions of death and dying. In 1969, psychiatrist Elizabeth Kubler-Ross published *On Death and Dying*, which claimed that suppressing acknowledgment of death was emotionally unhealthy and described stages that the grieving needed to go through to reach a healthy psychological state. Kubler-Ross's book paved the way for a surge of consolation literature aimed at parents who lost children and infants (Simonds and Rothman 1992). Literature for children and adolescents also reflected this new honesty about death. Young-adult books such as Mary Luther Call's *Where the Lilies Bloom* (1969), Grover Ezell's *Grover*, and Bill and Vera Cleavers's *Ellen Grae* (1967) show children and adolescents overcoming the illnesses and deaths of parents and siblings (Murray 1998).

Realistic stories about child and adolescent health problems also appeared in television shows and motion pictures. Most notable is ABC's popular series of after-school specials, which began in the early 1970s, which presented stories on controversial issues suggested by such titles as "The Boy Who Drank Too Much," "Please Don't Hit Me, Mom," "Stoned," and, most recently, "Just a Regular Kid: An AIDS Story." Popular films, such as *Ordinary People* (1980), *The Best Little Girl in the World* (1981), *Lorenzo's Oil* (1993), and

Girl, Interrupted (2000), also gave realistic depictions of serious mental and physical health problems affecting children and adolescents.

Today, fictional and nonfictional accounts of child and adolescent disease and death have become so common that they now serve as guides for parents and children on how to deal with serious illnesses, as well as the normal aspects of growing up. Children and adolescents suffering from cancer can read fictional accounts of this illness in Alice Bach's *Waiting for Johnny Miracle* (1980) or Cherie Bennett's *Zink* (1999). Young sufferers of AIDS can find inspiration in Ryan White's memoir *My Own Story* (1991). Children and adolescents with chronic illnesses can find fictional representations of their diseases—such as Willo Davis Roberts's *Sugar Isn't Everything* (1987), which describes a young girl's struggle to come to terms with diabetes. In addition, parents and children can turn to forums and chat rooms on the World Wide Web to read and share stories about personal experiences with particular illnesses. Like the consolation literature of an earlier era, these stories help parents and children cope with illness and death by linking them to fellow sufferers.

WORKS CITED

Abel, Emily K. 2000. *Hearts of Wisdom: American Women Caring for Kin, 1850–1940.* Cambridge, Mass.: Harvard University Press.

Adams, William Taylor (Oliver Optic). 1858. *Poor and Proud; Or, the Fortunes of Katy Redburn, a Story for Young Folks.* Chicago: W. B. Conkey.

Alcott, Louisa May. 1869. *Little Women.* E-text at etext.lib.virginia.edu/toc/modeng/ public/AlcLitt.html.

Andrews, Charles H. 1951. *No Time for Tears.* Garden City, N.Y.: Doubleday.

Ariès, Philippe. 1962. *Centuries of Childhood: A Social History of Family Life.* New York: Random House.

Avery, Gillian. 1994. *Behold the Child: American Children and Their Books 1621–1922.* Baltimore: Johns Hopkins University Press.

Bowne, Eliza Southgate. 1887. *A Girl's Life Eighty Years Ago: Selections from the Letter of Eliza Southgate Bowne.* New York: Charles Scribner's Sons.

Brewer, Priscilla. 1984. "The Little Citizen: Images of Children in Early Nineteenth-Century America." *Journal of American Culture* 7: 45–62.

Brown, Eleanor. 1997. "Victorian Visual Memory and the 'Departed' Child." *Archivist* 115: 22–31.

Burbick, Joan. 1994. *Healing the Republic: The Language of Health and the Culture of Nationalism in Nineteenth-Century America.* New York: Cambridge University Press.

Burns, Sarah. 1988. "Barefoot Boys and Other Country Children: Sentiment and Ideology in Nineteenth-Century American Art." *American Art Journal* 20: 25–50.

Child Health Organization of America. 1921. *Health Plays for School Children as Developed by Teachers and Pupils of the Public Schools in Greater New York.* New York: Author.

Cogan, Frances B. 1989. *All-American Girl: The Ideal of Real Womanhood in Mid-Nineteenth Century America.* Athens: University of Georgia Press.

Demos, John. 1970. *A Little Commonwealth: Family Life in Plymouth Colony.* New York: Oxford University Press.

Douglas, Ann. 1977. *The Feminization of American Culture.* New York: Alfred A. Knopf.

Feldberg, Georgina D. 1995. *Disease and Class: Tuberculosis and the Shaping of North American Society.* New Brunswick, N.J.: Rutgers University Press.

Golden, Janet. 1996. "The Iconography of Child Public Health: Between Medicine and Reform." *Caduceus* 12: 55–72.

Griffith, Eleanor Glendower. 1920. *Cho-Cho and the Health Fairy.* New York: Child Health Organization of America.

Gunther, John. 1949. *Death Be Not Proud.* New York: Modern Library.

Hedrick, Joan D. 1994. *Harriet Beecher Stowe: A Life.* New York: Oxford University Press.

Higonnet, Anne. 1998. *Pictures of Innocence: The History and Crisis of Ideal Childhood.* New York: Thames and Hudson.

Jennings, Wade. 1980. "Images of Children in American Film." *Indiana Social Studies Quarterly* 33, no. 2: 85–92.

Kriegel, Leonard. 1964. *The Long Walk Home.* New York: Appleton Century.

Lears, T. J. Jackson. 1981. *No Place of Grace: Antimodernism and the Transformation of American Culture.* New York: Pantheon Books.

MacLeod, Anne Scott. 1994. *American Childhood: Essays on Children's Literature of the Nineteenth and Twentieth Centuries.* Athens: University of Georgia Press.

Meckel, Richard A. 1998. *Save the Babies: American Public Health Reform and the Prevention of Infant Mortality, 1850–1929.* Ann Arbor: University of Michigan Press.

Mintz, Steven, and Susan Kellogg. 1988. *Domestic Revolutions: A Social History of American Family Life.* New York: Free Press.

Morgan, Edmund S. 1966. *The Puritan Family: Religion and Domestic Relations in Seventeenth-Century New England.* New York: Harper & Row.

Murray, Gail S. 1998. *American Children's Literature and the Construction of Childhood.* New York: Twayne.

Sanchez-Eppler, Karen. 1995. "Temperance in the Bed of a Child: Incest and Social Order in Nineteenth-Century America." *American Quarterly* 47: 1–33.

Simonds, Wendy, and Barbara Katz Rothman. 1992. *Centuries of Solace: Expressions of Maternal Grief in Popular Literature.* Philadelphia: Temple University Press.

Slater, Peter. 1977. *Children in the New England Mind.* Hamden, Conn.: Archon Books.

Spyri, Johanna. 1884. *Heidi.* E-text at etext.lib.virginia.edu/toc/modeng/public/SpyHeid.html.

Stannard, David E. 1974. "Death and the Puritan Child." *American Quarterly* 26: 456–76.

Stowe, Harriet Beecher. 1853. *Uncle Tom's Cabin, or Life Among the Lowly.* Boston: John P. Jewett; Cleveland: Jewett, Proctor, and Worthington.

Tannenbaum, Rebecca J. 2002. *The Healer's Calling: Women and Medicine in Early New England.* Ithaca, N.Y.: Cornell University Press.

Verbrugge, Martha H. 1988. *Able-Bodied Womanhood: Personal Health and Social Change in Nineteenth-Century Boston.* New York: Oxford University Press.

Warner, Susan. 1852/1987. *The Wide, Wide World.* Afterword by Jane Tompkins. New York: Feminist Press.

Welter, Barbara. 1966. "The Cult of True Womanhood, 1820–1860." *American Quarterly* 18: 131–75.

Williams, Margery. 1922. *The Velveteen Rabbit, or How Toys Become Real.* New York: Alfred A. Knopf.

Wilmer, Harry A. 1942. *Huber the Tuber: A Story of Tuberculosis.* New York: National Tuberculosis Association.

Wilson, Daniel. 1994. "Covenants of Work and Grace: Themes of Recovery and Redemption in Polio Narratives." *Literature and Medicine* 13, no. 1: 22–41.

3 A Sound Mind for the Child's Body: The Mental Health of Children and Youth

Kathleen Jones

As used today, childhood "mental health" and "mental illness" refer to the two ends of a continuum along which medical and psychological experts trace deviation from accepted conventions of age-specific feelings and actions. At one end are extreme psychopathologies, such as childhood schizophrenia, autism, and bipolar disorder; at the other are what science and society have defined as normal and age appropriate. In between is a broad and continually expanding collection of mental states, emotions, and behaviors judged to be deviant to a lesser or greater degree. It has not always been like this. Prior to the second half of the nineteenth century, there was little medical or popular recognition of mental and emotional disorders in children. This was not, however, because children did not engage in deviant or erratic behaviors or exhibit symptoms of mental or emotional problems. Rather, it was because earlier Americans tended to locate the causes of those behaviors in regions other than the medical.

COLONIAL ERA INTERPRETATIONS OF ERRATIC AND DEVIANT CHILD BEHAVIOR

From a variety of sources we know that there were many instances of child and adolescent behavior in colonial America that today would be associated with mental disorders. Sixteen-year-old Elizabeth Knapp suffered seizures in the fall of 1671 and threatened suicide several times (Kushner 1989). In 1692 a group of adolescent girls in Salem, Massachusetts, barked, mewed, spoke gibberish, screamed, and leaped on tables or crawled beneath them. Other children were reported to have fits, act crazed for no apparent reason, or attack parents and masters with no provocation (Sommerville 1982).

Colonial Americans recognized and often condemned these behaviors as aberrant but did not generally consider them signs of mental illness. More likely, influenced by a powerful religious heritage that offered supernatural explanations of natural phenomena, they attributed these behaviors to satanic influence.

Colonial Americans also interpreted the erratic and deviant behavior of children within the context of prevailing conceptions of child development. Especially among the more strictly religious, the notion that children were essentially innocent and good had not yet taken hold. Indeed, children were often described as subhuman and bestial, governed by appetites and passions rather than reason. Child rearing involved nurturing reason while taming appetites and passions, and bridling the will. Erratic and deviant behavior was thus considered less a sign of mental illness than a lack of training and self-control.

The tendency not to associate deviant child behavior with mental or emotional disorders continued into the early nineteenth century, despite an efflorescence of medical interest and writing on the brain and its workings. Benjamin Rush, arguably the nation's best-known physician of the time, contended in his *Medical Inquiries and Observations upon the Diseases of the Mind* (1812) that mental illness was exceedingly rare among the young, noting that he had seen but four cases in thirty years. Although not ruling out the possibility that children could "go mad," he suggested that the physical conditions which produced mental illness rarely were present before age twenty (Rush 1981).

DEVELOPMENT AND DEVIANCE IN NINETEENTH-CENTURY AMERICA

By the middle third of the nineteenth century, Rush's views on the child's immunity to mental disease were being challenged, particularly by alienists, the physicians in charge of mental asylums. For alienists of this era, sanity, like physical health, represented balance, and mental illnesses, like somatic illnesses, were precipitated by psychological and environmental factors interacting with the constitution of an individual to disrupt physical or mental harmony. In practice these ideas meant that most insanity appeared to be the result of individual volition—lifestyle choices that included immoral behavior, unsatisfactory living conditions, or failure to excise unnatural stresses. In such a scheme, training in self-control and right living became key to both prevention and treatment of insanity (Grob 1994).

Prevention led the alienists straight to childhood; as they examined the lives of their adult patients, alienists found that the insane often shared two patterns of "defective training" in early life—insane adults had been youthful masturbators or had been intellectually precocious. If continued over long periods of time, masturbation made boys unwilling to work, impudent toward their parents, and morbidly depressed; it could ultimately result in a form of "masturbatory insanity." Men of upstanding character were expected to control their sexual appetites; boys who did not learn during adolescence to master these urges would become social and economic failures as adults and candidates for insanity. Consequently, alienists warned parents and young people of the dangers of "self-pollution" (Neuman 1975).

Alienists also cautioned parents about the dangers of "overeducation" or precocity (Kett 1978). Parents and teachers who pushed too much schooling at too early an age could cause young people, especially young girls, to reel from mental shock. Excessive intellectual exertion seemed to tax the young girl's brain to such an extent that if not stopped, the nervousness that resulted could progress to the female disease of "hysteria," with symptoms of fits, paralysis, and depression (Smith-Rosenberg 1972). The claims made by alienists that educating girls ruined their physical and mental health contributed to the nineteenth-century debate over women's rights to higher education. Just as boys who masturbated risked becoming failures as men, overly educated girls risked becoming so mentally unstable they would be unable to fulfill their domestic duties as wives and mothers. To be sure, symptoms of masturbation and precocity could be found in both genders. More important, however, both behaviors equated sanity with new middle-class family roles, and each reinforced a connection between character training by parents and the emotional health of children.

When alienists wrote about masturbation and overeducation they envisioned youngsters in white families dominated by "moral mothers," the social role assigned to middle-class women whose primary responsibility was child rearing. African American youngsters, especially those living in southern states as slaves, did not figure in the discussion. Although slaveholders were well aware of the physical ailments of their property, they generally agreed that slaves rarely became insane, because the simple lifestyle of slavery protected slaves from "mental excitement." While nineteenth-century southerners thought madness was limited to the white race, recent historians have drawn attention to slavery's potential for psychologically damaging the slave child's mind. Joseph Illick suggests that African American children may have been more fearful and may have been unable to develop feelings of self-esteem because as slaves they were separated at an early age from their mothers. In contrast, Wilma King and Marie Jenkins Schwartz argue that parents were a forceful presence in the slave child's life, negotiating with owners if a child refused to follow orders and fostering feelings of self-worth despite the imperative to observe courtesies demanded by white owners (Illick 2002; King 1995; Schwartz 2000). Their debate hinges on current perceptions of African American family life and recent psychological theory concerning the degree to which a young child's separation from its mother has a negative impact on emotional development. It cannot be disputed, however that racist attitudes detrimentally affected perceptions of the slave child's intellectual and emotional development. This child and its Anglo-Saxon counterpart were forced to live in different psychological universes.

By midcentury the treatment of mental illness often meant care in an asylum, either a private hospital or one of the new state-supported institutions that began to appear during the first half of the nineteenth century. Few children, however, were admitted to asylums. In his study of mental health policies in the United States, Gerald Grob concluded that the "overwhelming majority" of the patients in nineteenth-century asylums were between the ages of twenty and fifty (Grob 1994, 82). Clearly the alienists who founded the new specialty of psychiatry had little direct contact with children, an omission apparent in the dearth of case studies of childhood insanity in mid-nineteenth-century psychiatric publications. Most likely alienists treated so few children because families, who dictated the terms of asylum admissions, either did not recognize symptoms in the young or were not sufficiently troubled by childhood behavior to seek alternatives to family care. They may also have interpreted the behavior not as a symptom of mental illness but as evidence of "idiocy," for which separate residential educational institutions were also established as part of the nineteenth-century asylum-building mania.

Mental retardation was scarcely a new problem in the early nineteenth century. As the historian James Trent concludes, "all postrevolutionary Americans knew feebleminded people" and found ways to incorporate them into families and communities (Trent 1994). Before the use of intelligence tests made possible fine gradations of mental aptitude, the symptoms of mental retardation and mental illness were not so easily distinguishable, especially when seen in children.

The first generation of alienists and superintendents of institutions for the feebleminded defined "idiocy" as the absence of will and set out to train pupils in self-control, much as moral mothers were expected to rear children without mental defects. Edward Seguin developed the methods that shaped the first American "schools" for children with mental retardation. The schools claimed a high success rate; students reputedly "graduated" to assume productive roles in their families and communities. These early schools were small and selective, which accounted in part for their successes. After the Civil War schools became larger, admitted pupils with a greater range of aptitudes, hired physicians as superintendents, and began to focus more on custodial functions and less on education (Trent 1994; Tyor and Bell 1984).

These changes also resulted from new ways of thinking about idiocy. The second generation of superintendents, those who took charge after the 1860s, viewed idiocy as a permanent problem of faulty inheritance rather than an absence of will curable through a program of education. As part of this new construction, traits such as alcoholism, poverty, insanity, sexual immorality, delinquency, and idiocy were thought to be passed from generation to generation, causing the feebleminded (as they were now sometimes called) to be more feared than indulged, as they had been in colonial communities. With fear came the idea of permanent institutionalization, to protect the feebleminded from a society into which they could never fit, and to protect society from the burden of another generation of feebleminded children. During the first years of the twentieth century, these hereditarian ideas, called "eugenics," or the "science of human breeding," led many state legislatures to institute programs of involuntary sterilization for the institutionalized feebleminded (Trent 1994).

The training schools gathered in one place large numbers of unmanageable children. This grouping made it possible for administrators increasingly trained in medicine rather than education to observe different patterns and classify symptoms into discrete disease entities. Such differential diagnosis was a first step toward medical identification of mental illness among the young.

As mid-nineteenth-century physicians began to devise unique categories of child mental illness, they did so first from within the population of idiots. Isaac Kerlin, the physician-superintendent of the Pennsylvania Training School for Feeble-Minded Children, identified a group of children who were not feebleminded yet whose parents had turned to Kerlin's school because something seemed amiss in their mental makeup. Tom was an "incorrigible boy," and Anne left her mother "flushed with exasperation." The descriptions bore a close resemblance to delinquency or poor training, and at first he called them "moral idiots." Kerlin, however, found the behaviors consistent with ideas about mental illness and proposed a new diagnosis, "juvenile affective insanity," to distinguish illness from badness. Although Kerlin's article included Anne as an example, the diagnosis was applied almost entirely to boys (Kerlin 1879, 611; Trent 1994).

How did these medical developments change the lives of nineteenth-century parents and children? Historians have had little to say on this subject. For middle-class parents the alienists' cautionary tales of mental collapse due to faulty training may have caused more vigilance, more effort to instill habits of sexual restraint. For middle-class children there were new opportunities and new institutions. Despite the warnings of some physicians, educational opportunities for young women increased dramatically after the Civil War. The residual effect of the fears about precocity may have contributed to the use of a modified curriculum for female students. Boys and girls—orphans, delinquents, and idiots—were now housed in separate institutions solely for young people, where they were usually subjected to rigorous regimens of training. In these settings relationships with peers probably assumed more importance than they had in institutions housing all generations (such as almshouses). The availability of age-specific institutions also increased the likelihood that parents of a difficult child would take steps to remove the child from the family, a step that superintendents of training schools usually encouraged. For young people with emotional, behavioral, and mental aptitude problems, living in an institution had become much more common by the end of the nineteenth century.

"Juvenile affective insanity" was one of several new categories of child mental illness to appear in the medical literature at the end of the nineteenth century. "Childhood hysteria" was another (Mills 1891), "anorexia nervosa" yet a third (Brumberg 1988). Taken together, they suggest that medical professionals had overthrown the belief that a child's mind was immune to insanity. Indeed, the mind of the child came to be seen as an extremely complex mechanism deserving of further scientific and medical research. Developments in medicine and in the new discipline of psychology shaped this professional interest in the insanities of childhood. What opened the door to this interest, however, was the belief in the fragile innocence and malleability of the child's mind, a malleability that parental training (or surrogate parental training in institutions) could preserve and nurture to a fine and healthy adulthood.

SPECIALIZING IN THE CHILD, 1880s–1940s: CLINICAL TREATMENT FOR EMOTIONAL AND BEHAVIORAL PROBLEMS

The years from the 1880s to the 1940s were pivotal ones for the development of professional interest in child mental illness. Child health became the focus of a new medical specialty—pediatrics. Disorders of the child's mind began to interest specialists in neurology. New theoretical developments in their discipline led psychologists to study the process of intellectual development in the child. The problem of juvenile delinquency drew psychiatric professionals to support child welfare advocates in their efforts to understand why some children repeatedly broke the law. Finally, the Freudian invasion of American psychiatry reformulated the meaning and significance of the emotional lives of young people. Identification of new diseases, debates about causation, studies of treatment programs, creation of new institutions, emergence of new professions concerned specifically with the mental health of the child, and the popularization of expert knowledge all combined during these decades to generate tremendous sensitivity to the emotional contexts for the behavioral problems of children and adolescents.

The medical and psychological professionals responsible for these developments worked within a culture that worshipped medicine and the biological sciences. By the end of the nineteenth century Americans were enthusiastic about the Darwinian theory of evolution, the biological doctrine of "survival of the fittest," theories of heredity and eugenics, and the germ theory of disease. To be sure, distrust sometimes surfaced when scientific theories conflicted with religious or ethnic values, but the distrust generally held little sway with members of the middle class. As a result, medical and psychological professionals at the turn of the century had vastly more authority to explain behavior than their predecessors had in the insane asylums and training schools. Their opinions and recommendations were sought after, and many of them used this authority in the service of social reform.

The experts who developed the intellectual and institutional framework of child psychiatry did so at first as participants in Progressive-era social movements. Children posed many problems for Progressive reformers. The sons and daughters of immigrants who lived in the cities and who provided the labor for American industrial development seemed to be a particularly troublesome lot. Compulsory-education laws made school attendance mandatory, yet many youths defied the laws, because their labor was needed to help the family (until 1938 the United States had no federal laws prohibiting child labor) or because they preferred the freedom of the streets to the confines of the schoolroom. These same youngsters also filled the dockets of the new juvenile courts; they were unrepentant delinquents who appeared over and over again in the same courtrooms. The children who attended school often had difficulty with the schoolwork; more and more youths seemed to be "slow" or "feebleminded." When Progressive reformers attempted to understand why these problems were occurring and what plans would improve the health and the behavior of city children, they sought the advice of and formed alliances with the experts in both pediatrics and psychology (MacLeod 1998; Jones 1999).

In their textbooks, pediatric specialists began to write about child mental illness. Unlike earlier physicians, these new specialists no longer believed that the child was immune to nervous disorders. L. Emmett Holt, a founder of the American Pediatric Society, explained that the immaturity and rapid growth of the brain during childhood made the child's mind particularly susceptible to stimulation that would have little effect on an adult. He cautioned that the excitement of city life had a particularly detrimental effect on young minds. But Holt was describing nervous temperament rather than mental illness or idiocy. He thought that true insanity (defined in his text as "change in a mind previously sound") was very rare in childhood, and in these severe cases Holt deferred to the authority of a neurologist (quoted in Jones 1999).

Neurologists often specialized in the treatment of nervous symptoms for which there was no apparent physiological cause; they claimed to be particularly adept at treating neurasthenia, a new disease marked by depression and lethargy that often afflicted youths and young adults. The neurologist's practice was not based in an institution (as was the work of the alienists); instead they promoted the "rest cure," a form of sensory-deprivation therapy devised by the Philadelphia physician S. Weir Mitchell (Caplan 1988; Sicherman 1977). The particular neurologist Holt recommended for consultation was Bernard Sachs, whose text, *A Treatise on the Nervous Diseases of Children* (1895), was the most advanced word on the subject from an American physician. Sachs, like Holt, was interested in somatic diseases of the brain, such as meningitis, encephalitis, tumors, and congenital syphilis. He did, however, include a separate chapter on insanity.

In 1894, in an article for the *Boston Medical and Surgical Journal,* Henry M. Hurd, superintendent of the Johns Hopkins Hospital in Baltimore, summarized contemporary expert thinking about mental disorders in childhood. Hurd was particularly sensitive to the symptoms associated with different stages of development. Children from six months to seven years exhibited "convulsive affections, night-terrors, delirium . . . and acute maniacal attacks." Children aged seven to ten showed "comparative immunity," but youths from ten to fifteen could show signs of a "pubescent insanity" marked by "melancholia, hysterical affections, emotional instability, paranoia, and moral perversions" (Hurd 1894). Second, Hurd noted that he had not included in this discussion "morbid impulsions to crime in childhood," including "impulses to kill, to burn, to steal, to commit sexual crimes." To Hurd and his colleagues delinquent behavior did not represent a "genuine" insanity of childhood (Hurd 1894).

By the end of the nineteenth century, few physicians would have dismissed the notion of child mental illness as Benjamin Rush had in 1812. Childhood insanity or nervous disease or neurosis (the terms seemed interchangeable in the 1890s) could be diagnosed more precisely, and the rate of disease seemed to be on the increase. Both pediatricians and neurologists were convinced they were beginning to see more mental disorders among young children and adolescents. Historians have no records to suggest that their contention was true, but we do know that a combination of factors made these physicians believe that insanity was a growing social problem. When physicians said that life in the city was too stimulating for young minds and that educational methods placed unnecessary burdens on immature brains, they were responding to broadly shared anxieties about the changes resulting from industrial development and urban growth. When they talked about "bad heredity," they were often reacting to the anxieties caused by the different cultural values brought to the cities by new groups of immigrants— Russian, Italian, Jewish, Catholic. When they discussed the physiological ailments thought to account for nervous disorders in children, they were sometimes thinking of the poverty and sickness endemic in urban immigrant and working-class communities. There was as yet no significant public awareness equating misbehavior and mental disorder, but physicians had begun to use the apparent rise in nervous disorders among children to draw attention to social and economic problems that also vexed reformers. Actual numbers were less important than the social criticism implicit in diagnoses of child mental illness.

Physicians were not the only professional group to develop a new interest in the child's mind. Psychologists also made the child a subject of scientific investigation, as they began to build a professional identity separate from philosophy and education (Cravens 1993). G. Stanley Hall, of Clark University in Worcester, Massachusetts, was one psychologist whose research into the contents of children's minds helped to legitimate the scientific study of the child and the field of child development. Hall called his program scientific "child study." Its pedagogical and child-rearing implications drew together groups of middle-class mothers into child-study clubs to examine the new psychological expertise. Hall's methods and findings encouraged these mothers to examine and record the growth of their own children, and raised their awareness of both normal and abnormal mental attributes. Hall is perhaps best known, however, for his two-volume study *Adolescence* (1904). This publication focused professional and popular attention on what Hall saw as the inherent instability of the teen years. Though Hall did not create "adolescence," his work helped a broad spectrum of American professionals and reformers see the years between ten and twenty as an emotionally turbulent period of development that required special handling to ensure a safe transition from childhood to adulthood (Smuts 1995; Ross 1972).

Hall's techniques for studying the child's mind (teacher surveys and maternal diaries) fell from fashion by the 1920s. Instead, psychologists became experts in interpreting and labeling intelligence levels. Lightner Witmer of the University of Pennsylvania applied his understanding of mental aptitude to school children through the Psychological Clinic, which he established in 1896. There he used both medical and psychological examinations to help teachers decide where to place students who were performing poorly. Did they belong in institutions, as Kerlin and others argued, because their mental abilities were limited and not likely to change? Witmer found that many of the students he tested suffered from medical problems or from problems in their home lives—his first case merely needed glasses. Witmer's examinations preceded by a decade the development of intelligence testing (O'Donnell 1979).

The "IQ test" was developed in France by Simon Binet and migrated to the United States in 1909. In that year Henry H. Goddard used it to test students at the Vineland, New Jersey, Training School for Backward and Feeble-Minded Children. In 1916 Lewis Terman, a California psychologist, redesigned it for general use with American school children. Terman presented the individual child's score on what was now called the "Stanford-Binet Intelligence Test" as an "intelligence quotient," a number thought at the time to be a foolproof, scientific way to compare mental ability and sort children into education categories. Though it was not a specific test for mental illness, psychologists thought the intelligence test could help them diagnose the causes of problem behavior. On the one hand, a low IQ could explain a youth's failure to do well in school and frequent truancy; the school program was not suited to the aptitude of a feebleminded student. On the other hand, a high IQ could also explain failure and truancy, because a "gifted child" might not find the school program challenging. Using the IQ test, Goddard created a ranking scheme for children with mental retardation, with "imbeciles" being the least trainable, then "idiots," and "morons" the most educable. Terman went on to study the "gifted child" and to disprove a commonly held belief that smart students were emotionally unstable (Jones 1999; Zenderland 1998).

One factor explaining the popularity of intelligence testing in the early twentieth century was the desire of educators to separate students by ability and create "special classes" for slow learners. Although ostensibly grouped by ability, these classes were often used to eliminate troublemakers from regular classrooms and also to cope with large numbers of immigrant children whose grasp of the English language was often minimal. Another explanation for the popularity was the belief that feeblemindedness was something to be feared and that the feebleminded were a "menace" to society. Superintendents of training schools argued that all too many of their young charges would never be able to return to the community as productive citizens. By the late nineteenth century, hereditarian views raised the specter of social pollution. Eugenicists argued that the feebleminded, left to their own devices, would beget future generations of feebleminded and degrade the American population. Finally, many at this time believed that the feebleminded were responsible for much of the juvenile delinquency and adult criminality that seemed to now plague urban areas. This was particularly true of what psychologists termed the "high grade" feebleminded, frequently called "morons." Intelligence testing offered Progressive reformers a way to sort out and institutionalize threats to the social order (Trent 1994).

In short, by the early twentieth century, several groups of scientific and medical experts had become interested in the health of the child's mind, and they were joined in this interest by groups of social reformers. "Mental disorder" continued to suggest a lack of intelligence rather than a lack of sanity, and psychologists had devised technology that could diagnose feeblemindedsss and also distinguish its degrees of severity. This is not to say that faith in the objectivity of IQ tests was unchallenged or that everyone thought people with mental retardation were a public "menace." Particularly during the 1930s, developments in Nazi Germany led some Americans to question the hereditarian ideas that framed use of intelligence quotients and sparked fear of the feebleminded. It was not until after World War II, however, that the idea of "menace" was put to rest and that families were no longer routinely advised to institutionalize sons or daughters born with mental retardation.

It may seem odd that as yet in this history of child mental illness so little of the story has involved psychiatry, the field that at present defines the parameters of child mental health. Indeed, at the turn of the twentieth century, interest in the child's mind, sound and unsound, seemed to be everywhere *except* among the psychiatrists. During these years, however, major changes were taking place in the field of psychiatry, and out of these changes emerged professional interest in the mental health of the child. Four developments in particular command attention. First, psychiatrists began to redirect their work from purely custodial treatment of the insane to the prevention of insanity. Second, reformers interested in juvenile delinquency sought solutions from psychiatry and supported the creation of child guidance clinics to study and treat troublesome youths. Third, two new theories of behavior—behaviorism and psychoanalysis—gave psychiatrists new ways to understand the child's mind and new ideas about intervention. Fourth, psychiatrists began to create specialized residential institutions for youths suffering from specific mental disorders and excluding those with mental retardation.

The first two developments are intimately connected. As asylums came to be viewed primarily as custodial institutions for the hopelessly insane, alienists looked for ways to avoid the need for institutionalization by preventing chronic mental illness. In this search the alienists were driven in part by medical considerations; they viewed mental illness as a cumulative development, the end point of a continuum of symptoms and degrees of disability. The reformist climate of the early twentieth century also encouraged the turn to prevention. Reform-minded alienists recommended healthy personal habits and eugenically sound marriages. They advocated early intervention, while the illness would still respond to treatment. To this end, alienists helped to create new acute care "psychopathic hospitals." As residential units (but not custodial institutions, like the asylums), the psychopathic hospitals served those who could recover with brief intervention, and identified those who would need long-term care. In the psychopathic hospital "early intervention" meant interceding before an acute attack became a chronic problem. Early intervention also meant intervening early, during childhood, to prevent habits or thought processes associated with mental illness. Directors of the psychopathic hospitals noted in their annual reports that children and young people represented a significant percentage of their patients (Lunbeck 1994; Fox 1978).

A more popular form of early intervention was the child guidance clinic, a distinctly new type of mental health facility originally established to work with delinquents referred by the juvenile court. A group of Chicago progressive reformers sponsored the first clinic, which opened in 1909 as the Juvenile Psychopathic Institute. William Healy, the physician they employed to direct the new court-affiliated agency, was one of a group of psychiatrists, psychologists, and social workers who worked during the next thirty years to transform the original idea into a "child guidance movement." By the mid-1930s supporters of child guidance had established hundreds of clinics across the United States, many in large urban areas, some affiliated with state hospitals, others being mobile units. Financial support for the clinics came from state and local governments, from private charitable foundations, and eventually from fees for service (Jones 1999; Horn 1989).

Several features distinguished the new child guidance clinics from the reformatories, training schools, and other institutions built during the nineteenth century for troublesome children. For one thing, the clinics, unlike the asylums, were routinely staffed by "teams" of experts—psychiatrists, psychologists, and social workers. These teams evaluated and treated young people using an interdisciplinary approach that considered medical, psychological, and environmental factors for wrongdoing. Each child, the child guiders argued, was a unique individual, with unique problems caused by a unique combination of elements. This shift was immensely important—child guiders were not talking about the "mind of the child." Rather, they were uncovering many different mental constitutions. Because they looked at children as individuals, they were able to see and distinguish patterns of mental illness unobservable when asylum superintendents talked of "the child." During the years from 1909 to 1940, no one explanation seemed able to explain the acts of all children observed at the clinics. Thus, child guiders were among the first to repudiate the relationship long thought to equate delinquent behavior, feeblemindedness, and insanity. They knew from experience that many of the delinquents they tested were of "normal" intelligence, and they began to look elsewhere for explanations—to the social environment, to family relationships, and to psychological conflicts (Jones 1999).

Child guiders treated children from all classes of society on an outpatient basis. Although initially designed for lower-class youths referred by agents of the juvenile court or the welfare system, the clinics by the 1930s had ceased to be associated only with the Progressive network of social reforms for the poor. Through active and aggressive popularization efforts, child guiders led parents to believe that concern for the psychological health of their children was as important as care for their physical welfare. When these parents (middle-class readers of the child-rearing manuals and parenting magazines for which the child guiders wrote) sought help, the clinics were ready with child guidance evaluation and treatment services (Jones 1999).

The explanations and services of the child guidance movement appealed to families from many social classes because parents of all classes believed they were facing unique problems with their children, especially their adolescents. That puberty was a particularly difficult age was not a new idea; Benjamin Rush, for example, had recognized the instability of the adolescent's mind, as had G. Stanley Hall. During the 1920s and 1930s, however, many parents seemed to find their offspring particularly rebellious—taking up new cultural experiences, trying new styles, spending more time with their peers, and in general pushing families to a state of seething conflict over dates, dress, school, and recreation. Understanding the minds of these rebellious young people became a national obsession in the early twentieth century, and especially during the 1920s when popular psychological explanations of "youth culture" produced a generation of parents ripe for child guidance intervention. Their children were not "insane," yet they often seemed to act insanely, and parents went in search of help. Child guidance offered these parents explanations and intervention strategies (Fass 1977; Jones 1999).

According to the child guiders, behavior problems—everything from truancy to stealing, to just plain rebelliousness—were manifestations of emotional ill health. The child guiders vastly expanded the number of children who could be diagnosed with nervous disorders, and they defined all sorts of previously inconsequential behavior (what the psychiatrist Douglas Thom called "everyday problems of the everyday child") as alarming from a mental health perspective. The problems were preventable by following the guidelines of child-rearing experts, but if the problems appeared, they could be treated at a clinic. To resolve the problems, child guiders encouraged psychotherapy for children and parents, especially mothers (Thom 1927; Jones 1999).

Three groups of professionals (psychologists, psychiatric social workers, and psychiatrists) used the cultural issues addressed by child guidance to enhance their separate professional identities and build their professional authority. These "mental hygienists" (the early-twentieth-century term for mental health experts interested in programs to prevent mental illnesses) set up clinics in public schools and in colleges. They participated in the development of college texts and classes to teach mental health habits to the young. They wrote for parents, and they joined with parent education groups to spread the child guidance gospel. They produced volumes of research studies, edited journals, and published the first American textbook on child psychiatry (Leo Kanner, *Child Psychiatry*, 1935). But to say that child guiders were self-promoters is not to suggest that the problems they evaluated were inconsequential or not real issues for parents or children. Nor is it to suggest that child guiders had nothing new to offer. Indeed, the conceptual framework of child guidance, the ideology that underlay their clinical practice, was a blend of two new ways of thinking about behavior and the mind: behaviorism and psychoanalysis. These two schools of thought have shaped the understanding of child mental illness for much of the past century.

Behaviorism is most often associated with John B. Watson, whose work was instrumental in redirecting psychological research in the 1920s. The ideas were further developed after World War II by stimulus-response researchers, and behavioral analysis continues to shape the experimental and clinical work of a subset of today's psychologists. For Watson, behavior was a product of habit, and he believed that desirable behavior could be taught by careful training and control. The absence of habit training bred nervous disorders, and the person most responsible for the failure to instill good habits was the child's mother. Unlike the nineteenth-century advocates of moral motherhood, who trusted that women were innately nurturing,

Watson firmly believed that mothers were at the root of all emotional and behavioral problems. Behaviorism was a powerful theory that influenced the treatment strategies of many child guiders. During the 1920s and 1930s behaviorists could be found at work with toddlers and elementary school–age children at "habit clinics," new institutional complements to the child guidance clinic's work with adolescents (Watson 1928).

Psychoanalysis as a theory and a treatment strategy owed its origins to Sigmund Freud, whose ideas revolutionized modern understanding of the mind by drawing attention to the power of subconscious thoughts (repressed beneath conscious awareness) to drive behavior and emotions. His theories are very complex and subject to many interpretations, but the child guiders were interested in three in particular. One was the "talking cure," a method of treatment that encouraged patients to describe their thoughts and feelings, in hopes of bringing the unconscious to the surface. At the clinics, the psychiatrists began to listen to what children had to say, a technique they called getting the child's "own story." Freud often talked about sexual repression, or the covering up of feelings about sex, and this was the second element child guiders borrowed from Freud. Through the child's "own story" the clinic psychiatrist tried to elicit a child's guilt about sexual activities, including masturbation, "sex play" with other children, homosexual encounters, or (in the case of girls) "immoral" behavior with boys. (During the 1920s and 1930s child guiders were not looking for evidence of incest or sexual abuse.) Based on their understanding of Freudian theory, child guiders believed that repression of this guilt caused children to have "mental conflicts." In turn, these conflicts were manifested in misbehavior and in neuroses (Freudian for debilitating nervous disorders) until the guilt surfaced and the conflicts were resolved (Hale 1995; Jones 1999; Bennett 1981).

In addition to the child's "own story" and the search for signs of sexual conflicts, the child guiders also absorbed from Freud a belief in the primacy of family dynamics as a cause of emotional and behavioral troubles. The Progressive-era social reformers had considered the economic status of the family to be the source of many behavioral problems. Then too, the eugenicists had found in the family tree an explanation for many social problems, including insanity. The child guiders, however, were more attuned to flawed emotional relationships between parents and children, mothers and fathers, brothers and sisters; the most important of these was the bond between mother and child.

Drawing on the ideas of Watson and Freud, child guiders introduced two new explanations of child misbehavior and mental disorders, models that placed blame squarely on the heads of mothers. The first was "maternal overprotection," or too much attention and involvement, preventing the child from developing an independent personality. The second was "maternal rejection," the behavior of a mother who withheld affection and withdrew from her child. David Levy, the New York City psychiatrist who framed these ideas for American child guiders, believed that overprotection was often a mask for feelings of rejection, and by the 1940s the rejecting mother was the most common cause for concern. Based on this critique of motherhood, child guiders recommended therapy for mothers as well as children, and they often thought that curing a mother's psychopathology would make therapy for a child unnecessary (Jones 1999; Levy 1943). Mother-blaming emanated from both behaviorism and psychoanalysis and owed much to the psychoanalytic studies of children made by Anna Freud and Melanie Klein, the two European disciples of Freud who specialized during the 1920s and 1930s in the emotional problems of young children. It colored psychiatric explanations of nervous disorders, behavior problems, and mental illness for decades. Despite challenges from feminist psychologists and psychiatrists, the bad mother continues to be a powerful figure in modern psychiatric literature and psychological explanations of juvenile misbehavior (Ladd-Taylor and Umansky 1998).

Commonly shared (middle-class, Anglo-Saxon) values about class, race, and gender identities underscored the diagnoses made by the child guiders. They believed, for example, that lower-class children were extroverts and that consequently their emotional problems were manifested as delinquency; they found that middle-class youths, in contrast, tended to be introverts who suffered from emotional disturbances. Gender was another factor that influenced diagnosis. Both boys and girls could suffer from maternal overprotection; however, it was more likely to be characteristic of a mother's relationship with her son. Girls who were "immoral" were often found to be "sexual delinquents," possibly in need of some form of institutionalization; boys who engaged in illicit sexual activities seemed to suffer from sexual conflicts treatable by psychotherapy. Because so many of the clinics were located in urban areas, clients were often sons and daughters of immigrants. Child guiders, like most of their contemporaries, associated some behaviors with certain ethnic groups. The professional literature of the child guidance movement before World War II, however, gave little attention to racial differences. Race would become a more significant issue in child guidance during the 1950s, when civil rights became a more vocal social and political movement (Jones 1999).

In sum, the child guidance movement can be credited with dramatically expanding the range of behaviors and emotions that constituted the mental disorders of childhood. The child guidance psychiatrists, psychologists, and social workers effectively redefined many problems of social development and social environment as medical issues to be dealt with by the individualized psychotherapy. In addition to juvenile delinquency, these problems came to include the psychological traumas of the gifted child and the only child, sibling rivalry, feelings of inferiority and other signs of personality maladjustment, daydreaming, homosexual activities, nail biting, thumb sucking, fear, and jealousy. During World War II, new concerns emerged for child guiders, including the problem of the latchkey child, whose mother was working in one of the war industries. The issues that concerned child guiders, however, should not be confused with the psychopathologies that today constitute extreme mental illness (bipolar disorder, for example, or childhood schizophrenia). When child guiders detected signs of a psychotic disorder, they quite likely referred the case to a psychopathic hospital or to one of the newly established hospitals or asylums for young people.

While some psychiatric professionals were building the child guidance movement, others began to create age-specialized inpatient psychiatric institutions. Residential units for children were often attached to existing mental hospitals for adults—for example, the Franklin School of the Pennsylvania Hospital in Philadelphia and the children's division of the Allentown (Pennsylvania) State Hospital, two of the first state-sponsored psychiatric residential programs for children. The Southard School opened in 1926 at the Menninger Clinic in Topeka, Kansas; representative of new private facilities for children, the school planned to treat and educate youths with personality and behavior disorders. When an epidemic of *encephalitis lethargica* left in its wake children with severe behavior and emotional aftereffects, special hospital units were developed for their care. Bellevue Hospital in New York City added a children's unit in 1921 specifically to handle the casualties of encephalitis. After 1934, with the appointment of Lauretta Bender as director, this unit became one of the most important hospitals for the study of childhood schizophrenia, an illness Bender helped to identify.

The history of specialized children's medical institutions is a relatively unexplored field; these few examples, however, demonstrate a growing professional awareness of the serious psychopathologies of childhood. Child guidance and pediatrics, more than changes in institutional psychiatry, made these specialized units feasible. Both professions highlighted the separate and distinct nature of juvenile disorders and in so doing made it possible for physicians to differentiate among emotional and behavioral symptoms and to construct a taxonomy of juvenile mental disorders. Idiocy was no longer *the* insanity of childhood, as it had appeared to be in the early nineteenth century, and institutions for the feebleminded no longer sufficed to care for all children with mental disorders, no matter what the cause or how severe the problem.

In sum, major changes took place in the half-century from 1890 to 1940. A new age-consciousness emerged in medicine, a new attention to prevention appeared among psychiatrists; a new interest in rehabilitating juvenile delinquents motivated reformers to search psychiatry for the reasons for misbehavior, and a new willingness to create specialized medical institutions for young people led to the establishment of clinics and hospitals to treat the nervous and mental disorders of childhood. There is no doubt that these developments provided benefits to children and parents. Individuals once labeled as idiots were reclassified and aided in more appropriate ways. Public awareness of the emotional needs of children became more pronounced. Medical personnel began to specialize in the field of "child" psychiatry, and psychological services became more widely available. Also, many families found solace at the child guidance clinic. But the consequences of these changes were not all so benign.

As child guiders successfully drew attention to the individual, psychological components of behavior, they also underplayed the role of social and economic factors in aggravating mental disorders and misbehavior. Instead of efforts to question the effects on personality and behavior of racism, poverty, and gender discrimination, child guiders worked to adjust individual personalities to fit established social roles. Motherhood was one of those roles, and mothers found themselves blamed for childhood mental disturbances, whether mild or severe. As mother-blaming became even more pronounced after World War II, mothers found themselves increasingly dependent on child experts to define the skills needed for successful parenting. For young people, the consequences of the child guidance movement could be equally disturbing. With rebellion now categorized as mental imbalance or even illness, a youth might be psychoanalyzed, institutionalized, or even put on drug regimens in order to create family harmony.

THE STORY AFTER 1945

Tracing these effects of child guidance on both mothers and children carries the story of child mental illness forward to the post–World War II decades. One new development was the enhanced presence of the federal government, as a source for research funding and as a financial support for training new mental health professionals. Much of this support was funneled through the new National Institute for Mental Health, created by the National Mental Health Act of 1946. During the 1960s, the federal government also began to provide funds for the establishment of community mental health clinics, in which treatment of children was an important priority. Government policy, therefore, encouraged public awareness of mental health issues and provided psychiatrists with backing needed to make their expertise more widely available. When during the 1970s both state and federal governments enacted policies of "deinstitutionalization," emptying institutions and moving people with mental illness back into the community, children too were affected. The spirit of this policy was evident in educational programs designed to "mainstream" children with mental or physical disabilities—that is, incorporate them into the regular classroom (Grob 1994).

A second development was the discovery of new diseases and the labeling of more behaviors as signs of mental disorders. In the early 1940s psychiatrists identified two new psychopathologies—childhood schizophrenia and infantile autism. While many believed that schizophrenia developed only in adolescence, Leo Kanner reported on pre-adolescent personality traits that could predict the onset of schizophrenia. A child who was surly, peevish, serious-minded, shut-in, taciturn, secretive, careless, flighty, lazy, prone to bear grudges, easygoing, lacking in endurance, or obstinate might be at risk. Kanner suggested that heredity played a role, although he admitted "one does see schizophrenic developments in persons coming from relative stable and well adjusted stock" (Kanner 1935). Other practitioners also began to describe cases of schizophrenia in very young children, and in 1947 Lauretta Bender reported on a clinical study of one hundred schizophrenic children. As Bender put it, "Those who do not believe in childhood schizophrenia [have just] never seen a case" (Bender 1947). The institutional setting (the Bellevue children's ward) enabled Bender to compare the symptoms of many children, and from the comparisons she constructed the parameters of this child psychosis.

"Early infantile autism" was another form of child mental illness identified during the 1940s. A child with autism was one who, from birth, appeared to withdraw from human contact. Although Leo Kanner first described autism in 1943, this severe mental condition was more often associated with the work of Bruno Bettelheim. In *The Empty Fortress* (1967) Bettelheim popularized his efforts to develop a total therapeutic milieu for treating infantile autism. A principal component of Bettelheim's program was removal of the child from its home, and especially from its mother.

The mother-blaming that was evident in the work of the child guiders shaped the psychiatric community's response to these newly identified psychoses. Kanner called her a "refrigerator parent," cold and withholding of affection; Bettelheim agreed that mothers were responsible for autism. Frieda Fromm-Reichmann, an Austrian-born psychoanalyst, attributed childhood schizophrenia to rejecting, restrictive, "schizophrenogenic" mothers. Some researchers and practitioners tried to temper what the psychologist Stella Chess called "mal de mère," or the pathological mother. Lauretta Bender suggested that rather than blame the mother, psychiatrists should recognize that the "mother of the schizophrenic child . . . shows a specific mechanistic process [precisely because of] her efforts to help the child." Chess too believed that the temperament of a child could call forth the style of maternal behavior psychiatrists called pathological. The protesting voices were weak, however, and mothers who lived through this period remember with horror the feelings of guilt these psychiatric interpretations induced (Jones 1999).

Others who worked with children began to pursue a better understanding of the biological component of mental disorders. Even while child guiders were turning to psychoanalytic interpretations, these biological models had never entirely disappeared from the adult psychiatry of mental asylums; after World War II, some child psychiatrists returned to the somatic roots of their profession. Believing that schizophrenia had a biological foundation, Bender attempted to treat her young patients with new psychotropic drug therapies that psychiatrists were prescribing for adults with schizophrenia and other psychoses. Bernard Rimland, in 1964, challenged Kanner's parent-blaming explanation of autism and suggested instead that autism had a biological basis. His work paved the way for an expansion of behaviorist models of treatment. In the field of mental retardation, too, researchers learned that the baby of a woman exposed to German measles could experience developmental delays, and they found that in some cases mental retardation resulted from a specific enzyme deficiency. This shift in attention to the biological bases of mental disorders is also evident in more recently identified illnesses. Attention deficit hyperactivity disorder (ADHD) is a recent addition to the lexicon of child mental disorders; the treatment of choice is often the prescription drug Ritalin.

The reemergence of biological models and the pursuit of drug and behavior therapy is in part related to postwar efforts of child psychiatrists to differentiate their medical specialty from the practice of child guidance and child psychology. Each of the three professions that constituted the original child guidance team began to seek a separate identity after World War II. For the child guidance psychiatrists this meant a turn back to the medical community. Child psychiatrists formed in 1953 a separate professional organization, the American Academy of Child Psychiatry, and followed that move with a drive for formal status as a medical subspecialty licensed by the American Board of Psychiatry and Neurology. As one consequence of this newfound medical professionalism, child psychiatrists began to devote less attention to the prevention and cure of mental diseases and more to the diagnosis and long-term care of young patients.

Greater specialization of practice was yet another element of the professionalization process. Until the second half of the century, "child" psychiatry and "child" guidance referred to all ages of youth. Then, after World War II, this "child" was divided among several new medical subspecialties. The influence of John Bowlby and D. W. Winnicott in England and the work of Margaret Mahler, Margaret Fries, and Margaret Ribble in the United States sparked an interest in "infant psychiatry." At the other end of the age spectrum, as the historian Heather Munro Prescott has shown, adolescent psychiatry developed as a complement to adolescent medicine (which emerged during the 1950s as a subspecialty of pediatrics). The emergence of specialties in the psychiatric disorders of infancy and adolescence depended in part on new research and on specialized clinical practices (Prescott 1998).

The timing of the appearance of these two subspecialties suggests, however, that an equally important factor in psychiatric subspecialization was the Baby Boom and the youth culture it generated. Many new parents with many new infants sought advice, and the psychiatrists responded, just as during the early decades of the century, when Progressives had wanted answers about juvenile delinquency, the psychiatric community had supplied them. The practitioners of child psychiatry are beholden to both their theories and their constituents for the success of their new subspecialty. According to Prescott, it was the demands of the youth culture of the 1950s and 1960s that enabled physicians and psychiatrists to specialize in the health problems of adolescents. The influence of culture on psychiatry was also apparent in the late twentieth century as theories about race, gender, and sexual identity shaped what psychiatrists identified as mental health issues, and how they explained the problems. Feminism, for example, has drawn attention to flaws in the theories of mother-blaming. Race psychology points to the impact of racial stereotyping on mental health. Kenneth Clark's research showing the effects of segregation on the self-perceptions of African American children was instrumental in the Supreme Court's 1954 ruling in *Brown v. Board of Education* that required school districts to desegregate (Prescott 1998; Eyer 1996; Markowitz and Rosner 1996).

The pattern of professional popularization of mental health expertise established by the child guiders during the 1920s and 1930s continued into the postwar period. It would be quite a feat to list all the books published by mental health professionals for parents and for young people during the past fifty years. Psychiatrists and psychologists speak about all aspects of child rearing, and they address issues as diverse as college-student credit-card debt and schoolyard bullying. Ellen Herman calls our fascination with what these professionals have to tell us our "romance with psychology"; Eva Moscowitz declares that "in therapy we trust." Yet for all the consulting that parents do and all the authority they have accorded the mental health professions, parents of children with mental disorders have never been willing to turn over all decision making to the professionals (Moscowitz 2001; Herman 1995).

Parents' resistance can be traced through the organizations parents have established to help each other and lobby for the needs of their children. The Association for Retarded Children (now known as the ARC) was founded in 1947 by a group of parents in New Jersey who wanted to work collectively to overcome the stigma attached to having children who were "mentally deficient" (the 1950s term for mental retardation). What made the ARC unique was the determination of parents to remain in control of the organization. They sought out and evaluated expert advice, but they intended to stay independent of professional leadership. The Autism Society of America was not created until 1965, but the people who established it set as their mission the sharing of information, not the advocacy of a particular theory or philosophy. Finally, NAMI, the National Alliance for the Mentally Ill (founded 1979), is described as a grassroots, self-help, support and advocacy group for families and friends of people with severe mental illnesses. Although not specifically a "child" organization, NAMI maintains a special youth section on its extensive website. More significant are the many local chapters of these organizations that function as support groups for parents coping with the complications of child mental illness and the complexities of the modern mental health system.

A CENTURY OF DECLINING MENTAL HEALTH?

It is not difficult to locate studies from the end of the twentieth century suggesting that 10 to 20 percent of American children were in need of mental health intervention (Costello et al. 1988). When we compare those studies with the reports of Benjamin Rush and other early-nineteenth-century physicians, must we conclude that mental illness among young people has been on the rise in the twentieth century? Most likely, the answer is no. Mental illness, as this history suggests, is a product of its culture. Behavior that at one point in time would express health is at another a sign of disease—compare the mental health of a child who brings a gun to school in 2003 with one who did so in 1803. Emotions and behavior that centuries ago were part of religious experience or everyday life become in a secular, psychologized age evidence of neurological damage or psychological imbalance. What the history of child mental illness tells us is that at the beginning of the twenty-first century we are more aware of the complexity of the child's mind than parents were in 1700, we are more attuned to the emotional needs of children (and to the existence of those needs), and we are more willing to allow mental health professionals to label odd or disruptive behavior as illness. We are also slow, however, to examine the effects of institutional structures and cultural values on our definitions of mental disorders in children. As a consequence, we continue to hold parents responsible for mental illness and withhold from families the support needed to care for a child with mental illness.

WORKS CITED

Bender, Lauretta. 1947. "Childhood Schizophrenia: Clinical Study of One Hundred Schizophrenic Children." *American Journal of Orthopsychiatry* 17: 40–56.

Bennett, James. 1981. *Oral History and Delinquency: The Rhetoric of Criminology.* Chicago: University of Chicago Press.

Bettelheim, Bruno. 1967. *The Empty Fortress: Infantile Autism and the Birth of the Self.* New York: Free Press.

Brumberg, Joan Jacobs. 1988. *Fasting Girls: The Emergence of Anorexia Nervosa as a Modern Disease.* Cambridge, Mass.: Harvard University Press.

Caplan, Eric M. 1988. *Mind Games: American Culture and the Birth of Psychotherapy.* Berkeley: University of California Press.

Costello, Elizabeth M., et al. 1988. "Psychiatric Disorders in Pediatric Primary Care: Prevalence and Risk Factors." *Archives of General Psychiatry* 45: 1107–16.

Cravens, Hamilton. 1993. *Before Head Start: The Iowa Station and America's Children.* Chapel Hill: University of North Carolina Press.

Eyer, Diane E. 1996. *Motherguilt: How Our Culture Blames Mothers for What's Wrong with Society.* New York: Times Books/Random House.

Fass, Paula S. 1977. *The Damned and the Beautiful: American Youth in the 1920s.* New York: Oxford University Press.

Fox, Richard Wrightman. 1978. *So Far Disordered in Mind: Insanity in California, 1870–1930.* Berkeley: University of California Press.

Grob, Gerald N. 1994. *The Mad among Us: A History of the Care of America's Mentally Ill.* Cambridge, Mass.: Harvard University Press.

Hale, Nathan G., Jr. 1995. *The Rise and Crisis of Psychoanalysis in the United States: Freud and the Americans, 1917–1985.* New York: Oxford University Press.

Herman, Ellen. 1995. *The Romance of American Psychology: Political Culture in the Age of Experts.* Berkeley: University of California Press.

Holt, L. Emmett. 1897. *The Diseases of Infancy and Childhood.* New York: D. Appleton.

Horn, Margo. 1989. *Before It's Too Late: The Child Guidance Movement in the United States, 1922–1945.* Philadelphia: Temple University Press.

Hurd, Henry M. 1894. "Some Mental Disorders of Childhood and Youth." *Boston Medical and Surgical Journal* 131: 281–85.

Illick, Joseph E. 2002. *American Childhoods.* Philadelphia: University of Pennsylvania Press.

Jones, Kathleen W. 1999. *Taming the Troublesome Child: American Families, Child Guidance, and the Limits of Psychiatric Authority.* Cambridge, Mass.: Harvard University Press.

Kanner, Leo. 1935. *Child Psychiatry.* Springfield, Ill.: Charles C. Thomas.

———. 1943. "Autistic Disturbances of Affective Contact." *Nervous Child* 2: 217–50.

Kerlin, Isaac. 1879. "Juvenile Insanity." *Transactions of the Medical Society of the State of Pennsylvania* 12: 611–20.

Kett, Joseph F. 1978. "Curing the Disease of Precocity." In *Turning Points: Historical and Sociological Essays on the Family.* Edited by John Demos and Sarane Spence Boocock. Chicago: University of Chicago Press.

King, Wilma. 1995. *Stolen Childhood: Slave Youth in Nineteenth-Century America.* Bloomington: Indiana University Press.

Kushner, Howard I. 1989. *Self-Destruction in the Promised Land: A Psychocultural Biology of American Suicide.* New Brunswick, N.J.: Rutgers University Press.

Ladd-Taylor, Molly, and Lauri Umansky, eds. 1998. *"Bad Mothers": The Politics of Blame in Twentieth-Century America.* New York: New York University Press.

Levy, David M. 1943. *Maternal Over-Protection.* New York: Columbia University Press.

Lunbeck, Elizabeth. 1994. *The Psychiatric Persuasion: Knowledge, Gender, and Power in Modern America.* Princeton, N.J.: Princeton University Press.

MacLeod, David I. 1998. *The Age of the Child: Children in America, 1890–1920.* New York: Twayne.

Markowitz, Gerald E., and David Rosner. 1996. *Children, Race, and Power: Kenneth and Mamie Clark's Northside Center.* Charlottesville: University Press of Virginia.

Mills, Charles K. 1891. "Hysteria." In *Cyclopaedia of the Diseases of Children, Medical and Surgical.* Edited by John M. Keating. Philadelphia: J. B. Lippincott.

Moscowitz, Eva S. 2001. *In Therapy We Trust: America's Obsession with Self-Fulfillment.* Baltimore: Johns Hopkins University Press.

Neuman, R. P. 1975. "Masturbation, Madness, and the Modern Concepts of Childhood and Adolescence." *Journal of Social History* 8: 1–27.

O'Donnell, John M. 1979. "The Clinical Psychology of Lightner Witmer: A Case Study of Institutional Innovations and Intellectual Change." *Journal of the History of the Behavioral Sciences* 15: 3–17.

Pols, Johannes, 1997. "Managing the Mind: The Culture of American Mental Hygiene, 1910–1950." Ph.D. dissertation, University of Pennsylvania.

Prescott, Heather Munro. 1998. *A Doctor of Their Own: The History of Adolescent Medicine.* Cambridge, Mass.: Harvard University Press.

Ross, Dorothy. 1972. *G. Stanley Hall: The Psychologist as Prophet.* Chicago: University of Chicago Press.

Rush, Benjamin. 1981. *Benjamin Rush's Lectures on the Mind.* Edited by Eric T. Carlson et al. Philadelphia: American Philosophical Society.

Schwartz, Marie Jenkins. 2000. *Born in Bondage: Growing Up Enslaved in the Antebellum South.* Cambridge, Mass.: Harvard University Press.

Sicherman, Barbara. 1969. "The Quest for Mental Health in America, 1880–1917." Ph.D. dissertation, Columbia University.

———. 1977. "The Use of a Diagnosis: Doctors, Patients, and Neurasthenia." *Journal of the History of Medicine and Allied Sciences* 32: 33–54.

Smith-Rosenberg, Carol. 1972. "The Hysterical Woman: Sex Roles and Role Conflict in 19th-Century America." *Social Research* 39: 652–78.

Smuts, Alice. 1995. "Science Discovers the Child, 1893–1935: A History of the Early Scientific Study of Children." Ph.D. dissertation, University of Michigan.

Sommerville, C. John. 1982. *The Rise and Fall of Childhood.* Beverly Hills, Calif.: Sage.

Thom, Douglas. 1927. *The Everyday Problems of the Everyday Child.* New York: D. Appleton.

Trent, James W., Jr. 1994. *Inventing the Feeble Mind: A History of Mental Retardation in the United States.* Berkeley: University of California Press.

Tyor, Peter L., and Leland V. Bell. 1984. *Caring for the Retarded in America: A History.* Westport, Conn.: Greenwood Press.

Watson, John B. 1928. *Psychological Care of Infant and Child.* New York: W. W. Norton.

Zenderland, Leila. 1998. *Measuring Minds: Henry Herbert Goddard and the Origins of American Intelligence Testing.* New York: Cambridge University Press.

4 Children's Health: Caregivers and Sites of Care

Janet Golden

The history of children's health care involves both change and continuity. The continuity is obvious—sick children have always been and continue to be cared for at home by family members. The changes are more numerous and reflect shifting patterns of disease and population, the development of medical science, the growing cultural authority of physicians, changes in household size, a shift from an agricultural and artisan economy to one that is urban and industrial, new patterns of public life, and the rise of institutions ranging from public schools to general hospitals.

These historical developments made caregiving an increasingly complex enterprise. After the Civil War, sick children received an increasing proportion of their care from physicians and nurses, and they did so in institutional settings—medical offices, hospitals, school infirmaries, and clinics. Along with this shift in caregiving came a new understanding that healing sick children and keeping them well was a public matter as well as a private, family responsibility. Charitable organizations as well as local, state, and eventually the federal government played expanding roles in assessing children's health needs and providing services. But while family responsibility for defining and managing disease diminished, worries about the health of children and caregiving remained a substantive part of family life.

CHILDREN'S HEALTH CARE IN THE SEVENTEENTH AND EIGHTEENTH CENTURIES

In the seventeenth century, immigrants from Europe and slaves from Africa arrived in the New World, bringing with them both diseases and beliefs about their courses, cure, and prevention. Old and new settlers experienced epidemics of smallpox and measles and coped with endemic illnesses that regularly afflicted individuals, such as cholera infantum (a deadly gastrointestinal ailment of the very young) and respiratory problems (such as pneumonia and tuberculosis), which were common in older children as well as adults. Other childhood illness and accidental injuries, most notably burns that resulted from crawling, playing, and working near open fires in the home, also took a heavy toll.

Women assumed most of the responsibility for caring for sick members of the household. Doctoring was a domestic chore involving the preparation of herbal medicines and other treatments, and ministering to sick family members day and night. Family receipt books as well as diaries and letters tell of the remedies women concocted and applied. New Englander Anna Cromwell recorded in her diary that she prepared a bowl of "sack posset" (a mixture of eggs, wine, and milk warmed slowly over the coals) for her daughter, who was suffering from "flux with fever" (Tannenbaum 2002). Had her daughter taken a turn for the worse, becoming gravely ill and in need of more care, Cromwell might have turned to local healers, perhaps a neighboring woman, known as a "doctoress," who had experience diagnosing and treating major illnesses, or a physician, who had learned his craft through apprenticeship. The kinds of medicine practiced by doctors, neighborhood healers, and mothers were similar, based on ideas of putting the body in balance.

Advice about caring for sick children could be found in many publications, reflecting the fact that illness was a matter of widespread concern. Newspapers and almanacs contained advice freely plagiarized from medical books. In 1749, the *Gazette* of Charleston, South Carolina, published installments of William Cadogan's *An Essay upon Nursing and the Management of Children,* which had been published in England the previous year (Waring 1964). Families often owned domestic medical books that provided instructions for the treatment of various illnesses, including common childhood ailments. The most popular, William Buchan's *Domestic Medicine,* first published in Edinburgh in 1769, appeared in the United States in 1771, and went through 142 printings over the next century (Rosenberg 1992). Buchan's recommended treatment for a common childhood problem, worms, was a mixture of rhubarb, jalap, and a small amount of calomel taken as a purgative; other purgative mixtures are also described (Buchan 1772/1885). Eventually American physicians began writing domestic guidebooks that, they promised, were attuned to local conditions. Physician John Gunn of Tennessee published a popular domestic medical guidebook in 1830 written for "families in the Western and Southern States"; it continued to be printed until 1920 (Rosenberg 1992). For worms, Gunn prescribed various purgatives including calomel, worm-seed oil, Carolina Pink root and Spirits of Turpentine (Gunn 1830/1986). With domestic medical books to consult and the advice, knowledge, and help of relatives and neighbors, families had little reason to rely on doctors. Typical was one woman did so only four times— to deliver three babies and to vaccinate the family for smallpox. On all other occasions she relied on "Dr. Gunn" for ailments ranging "from hiccoughs to tapeworms" (Abel 2000).

By the late eighteenth century, physicians were appearing more frequently at the bedsides of sick children. The growth of medical apprenticeships increased the number of practitioners, while the formation of elite medical societies increased their status. Yet female healers remained a vital force in the community, especially in rural areas, and they accounted for much of the doctoring that children received. When an outbreak of scarlet fever erupted in the frontier New England town of Hallowell (in what was then Massachusetts and is now Maine), midwife Martha Ballard attended to many in the community, treating children and adults with herbal remedies she prepared herself from plants grown in her garden (Ulrich 1990).

In the South, climate, economy, geography, and culture combined to create different patterns of health and health care than were common in the North. In addition, the South was home to the vast majority of the nation's slaves. Slave owners wanted to protect their investments and keep slave children healthy, but they also exploited them as workers from an early age. Slave children suffered enormously from the brutal effects of servitude. Living in extreme poverty, eating a meager, sometimes nutritionally incomplete diet, facing the demands of punishing physical labor and enduring whippings and beatings, young slaves suffered terribly from the endemic diseases of the region, such as malaria, as well as from outbreaks of epidemic diseases.

Like white southerners, African American children living in the South received most of their care from family members. Some slave women applied home remedies based on available plants and called for assistance from community healers when expert care was needed. In South Carolina, which had an environment similar to that of West Africa, local plants were commonly used as remedies; children with worms, for example, received medicines made from gypsum weed (Joyner 1984). In other cases, sick slave children received care from white physicians, particularly on large plantations, where wealthy slave owners contracted with physicians to provide services to their workers. But most often, the work of doctoring was carried on by older slave women who knew how to prepare and apply medications and were called to tend to the sick during outbreaks of disease. In addition to treating those who fell ill, the women prepared herbal medications designed to keep children healthy (Fett 2002). In some cases, enslaved women also provided health care to their owners, serving as nursery maids and midwives (Savitt 1978).

CHILDREN'S HEALTH CARE IN THE NINETEENTH CENTURY

Two critical changes occurred in the doctoring of children in the nineteenth century. First, the kind of medicine doctors practiced changed, as medical theories of illness evolved and as regular physicians faced increased competition from other healers. Second, the sites of medical practice changed. In urban areas especially, hospitals become the primary sites for surgical and acute care, while dispensaries provided ambulatory care and medications to those who could not afford a private physician. While advances in medical theory and practice and the creation of new medical institutions enhanced the cultural authority of medicine, neither development displaced family members from the bedsides of sick children, nor did they eliminate popular reliance on traditional home remedies, patent medicines, popular advice manuals, or other healers.

As in earlier centuries, sick children continued to receive herbal remedies concocted at home or produced by local practitioners. James Still, a self-taught African American doctor, developed a thriving practice in southern New Jersey in the mid-nineteenth century after curing several children of scrofula (tuberculosis of the lymph glands in the neck), typhus, and other serious conditions with medicines he produced (Still 1973). In other cases, families relied on patent medicines to cure their sick children. Manufacturers sold them through druggists and via traveling salesmen, who lured customers with medicine shows combining entertainment with testimonials for their tonics, cure-alls, and remedies for specific complaints. Among the most popular children's medicines were soothing syrups laced with opiates, alcohol, or both, which were designed to quiet crying, colicky babies and ease the pains of teething. Other patent remedies claimed (falsely) to cure constipation and far more serious (and sometimes incurable) diseases such as tuberculosis and diabetes. Another type of commercial product, artificial infant formula, also entered the marketplace in the late nineteenth century. This was sold to women who did not want to hire wet nurses, could not breast-feed their own babies, and did not want to use cow's milk, which is not well suited to babies (Apple 1987).

Advertisements for the new infant foods and for patent medicines appeared with growing frequency in women's magazines, which also contained articles about how to treat common childhood ailments. Mothers also learned how to treat their children's bouts of sickness by consulting home medical guides and general housekeeping books. At midcentury, Catharine Beecher's *Treatise on the Domestic Economy* (1841) was a prominent source of practical advice on infant care and child health. By the end of the century, books written by doctors were more likely to be consulted, among them the best seller by pediatrician L. Emmett Holt, *The Care and Feeding of Children,* which was first published in 1894 and went through numerous editions (Jones 1999). The popularity of this book and of others written by doctors was a sign of the growing regard in which medicine was held.

In the nineteenth century, family members and neighbors sometimes performed tasks that by the twentieth century would be considered the responsibility of professionals. They diagnosed diseases and supplied medicines for their treatment, as well as offering meals and nursing care. In the 1890s Nannie Stillwell Jackson, the wife of a small Arkansas farmer, helped a neighbor nurse three children through pneumonia; when one died, she helped prepare the child for burial (Abel 2000). In a few reported cases, family members even performed surgical procedures. One man, who as a child had nearly severed three fingertips, recalled that it was his mother who sewed them back on (Abel 2000). Yet there were situations, often as a last resort, after home remedies failed, in which families called a doctor, who came to the bedside.

Why were doctors a last resort in some cases? In the opening decades of the nineteenth century, as in the previous century, physicians practiced what has come to be called "heroic" medicine, which relied on tough regimens designed to restore health. Doctors theorized that disease caused the body to be overstimulated and in order to restore the patient to a natural state of health recommended treatments that aggressively depleted excess energy. Examples of depletion included extensive bloodletting and the use of drugs to empty the bowels and stomach. Even children were given these harsh remedies. A child with croup might have blood drawn until she fainted, and then have leeches applied to the trachea and a large blister raised on her chest (Cone 1979). Before submitting their children to such treatments, which often failed to provide relief, families may have thought it best to try gentler remedies. In other situations, after seeing the harsh medical regimes fail, families may have decided that in the future they would doctor on their own. One Iowa woman, after watching her daughter succumb to diphtheria following vigorous medical intervention, vowed to care for her children on her own and successfully nursed three of them through bouts of scarlet fever (Abel 2000).

The extreme measures proposed by what were then called "regular" or "orthodox" physicians helped increase the popularity of those who practiced alternative forms of healing that relied on different and often gentler remedies. These alternative practitioners, deemed "irregulars" or "sectarians," included a number of different types of healers. There were "Thomsonians," who applied the theories of Samuel Thomson, a self-taught doctor who rejected the bleeding and drugs favored by orthodox physicians and developed a system of cure based on emetics and purgatives. Rather than calling a doctor when a family member became ill, followers of Thomson were to apply the therapies described in the treatment system he sold directly to consumers. Another group of practitioners was labeled "eclectics." Like Thomsonians, they favored the use of botanical (plant-based) therapies, as did the water-cure advocates, whose system of healing and maintaining bodily well-being depended for the most part on consumption of and baths in fresh, cold water. Instead of treating a child with scarlet fever with harsh drugs and bleeding, a water-cure practitioner might prescribe a wet sheet wrap (Cayliff 1987). Dietary cures coupled with health regimens also found a niche in the medical marketplace. Sylvester Graham, for example, advocated personal hygiene, exercise, fresh air, and a diet marked by whole-grain foods and vegetables.

The most powerful alternative to regular medicine was the system of homeopathy, imported into the United States from Germany before mid-century. The homeopathic system of treatment involved prescribing extremely diluted doses of drugs, which were given as a means of stimulating the body's own healing power. The mild treatments were especially welcomed by parents, who turned to homeopathic "domestic kits" with vials of tiny pills and books telling when to use them (Murphy 1991). One homeopathic doctor, J. Compton Burnett, reported curing "delicate, backward, puny and stunted children" through the prescription of homeopathic remedies (Burnett 1896). Homeopathic doctors had their own medical schools, hospitals, and medical societies, which helped make them appear to be educated professionals rather than sectarians and made them particularly competitive with "orthodox" physicians among middle-class patients.

Facing challenges from alternative practitioners in an unregulated medical marketplace in the mid-nineteenth century, regular physicians gradually abandoned their heroic, depletive treatments in favor of more limited interventions. They turned instead to therapies designed to stimulate the body, such as tonics and drugs made of quinine and alcohol. More important, regular physicians organized themselves and established standards for education and licensure, moving from apprenticeship to a system of formal training. Early medical schools were for the most part proprietary institutions run by doctors seeking to make a profit through teaching, but a few schools were linked to universities and offered a more scientific and scholarly education. Physicians also organized to protect their interests. They formed the American Medical Association, in part to differentiate themselves from the sectarians, and they began to push for state licensing laws for doctors—a goal they would not achieve until the late nineteenth century.

During this era, medical understanding of the disease process increased, although physicians still lacked the ability to cure most ailments. The use of quinine for malaria was one example of where physicians had something to offer patients, but their efforts to use it to cure other conditions causing fever were not effective. Later in the nineteenth century the medical arsenal included more effective treatments for pain, such as morphine, but again doctors often lacked the ability to understand and remedy the condition responsible for the pain.

In addition to confronting what are known today as infectious diseases and to caring for people with chronic and life-threatening illness of all types, nineteenth-century physicians and patients confronted new problems of public health in the nation's growing cities. In the antebellum years, periodic cholera epidemics swept through major cities. Public officials organized sanitary measures to combat the disease, removing filth, horse manure, and dead animals from public streets, although they failed to confront the problems of overflowing privies and the lack of sanitary water systems. After the Civil War, with the rapid growth of cities, the rise of major industries, massive increases in the numbers of Americans who were first- and second-generation immigrants, and the growth of crowded working-class neighborhoods, other public health measures were applied. Sewer systems were built, efforts were made to clean up the water supply, and laws were passed allowing the sick to be quarantined and requiring some immigrants to undergo health inspections before being permitted entry.

Homes and educational facilities for the blind, deaf, crippled, and what were then termed "feebleminded" children were also constructed in the nineteenth century. In 1817, the Connecticut Asylum for the Education and Instruction of Deaf and Dumb Persons opened in Hartford, Connecticut. After the Civil War, schools began teaching the Braille system to blind children. Traditional shelters for the poor, such as almshouses and workhouses, added infirmaries and hospitals and cared for the children of the poor who were forced to seek refuge behind their walls.

Urbanization created new problems and enabled (or necessitated) their solution. Municipal and state boards of health, established to oversee efforts to halt epidemic diseases, later turned their attention to such endemic problems as the high rate of infant mortality (Meckel 1990). While philanthropic groups worked to create "milk stations," which distributed clean milk in poor communities, public officials passed laws regulating the milk supply and would eventually mandate pasteurization. Visiting nurses working for municipal agencies and private groups taught poor urban mothers how to feed their babies, and they established classes in settlement houses where they demonstrated nursery and home hygiene to neighborhood residents.

Public agencies and private groups also erected institutions to house and care for sick and needy children. While not all of them provided medical care, most congregate care facilities were forced to do so because diseases spread quickly among children living in close quarters. Foundling homes and infant asylums took in abandoned babies, many of whom needed medical care from the outset and others of whom soon required it because of infections that spread rapidly from crib to crib. The problem of infection proved so difficult that it led to schemes for placing babies in foster homes and to their exclusion from other health and welfare facilities. Older children living in other congregate institutions also confronted deadly infectious diseases. The boarding schools created for Native American children in the late 1870s to inculcate "American values, language and religion" often succeeded in nurturing diseases, among them tuberculosis and trachoma, a contagious disease of the eyes (Child 1993).

Most of the poor urban children who needed medical attention in the nineteenth century received it from freestanding dispensaries that provided medical exams and medications. When children needed surgery and long-term care outside the home, they entered hospitals. Patients on the wards would include adolescent boys injured on the job and poor children with broken bones and other orthopedic problems. Going to the hospital posed a substantial risk; infections spread easily from patient to patient. In a fundamental sense, hospital care involved an exchange: poor children and adults served as teaching material for physicians, who learned their craft by serving as attending physicians on the wards; in return, patients received free care, living for weeks or even months in a hospital ward.

With changes in medical theory and practice, the development of the germ theory, improvements in hospital sanitation, and the use of antiseptics and latter asepsis (which prevented infection of the surgical site), hospitals came to be places of cure. In the late nineteenth century, scientists discovered evidence that organisms invisible to the eye were the cause of many illnesses in adults and children. The new science of bacteriology transformed practices in the home and the hospital. In place of hygienic measures aimed at removing filth, efforts were made to kill germs. Surgery, once fraught with risk because of the dangerous infections that arose at the site of the incision and spread throughout the body, became less dangerous when antiseptic chemicals were used to disinfect the operating room and the incision site. Later efforts to prevent the presence of bacteria made surgery even safer—instruments were sterilized, physicians wore gloves, and only sterilized dressings were applied to the body. Care on the wards was also transformed by these new measures to control infection. As a result, beginning in the early twentieth century hospitals began to attract patients who would previously been cared for in their homes—the middle class and well-to-do.

Trained nurses, who provided bedside care and maintained sanitation, proved critical to the work of modern hospitals. The care of patients had once been the work of institution residents who had recovered from their illnesses (especially in charity and almshouse hospitals) and of individuals of few skills who were simply hired to perform tasks for patients confined to bed. But as medical and surgical care grew increasingly sophisticated, the recovery of patients increasingly required the assistance of staff with knowledge, training, and skill. Hospitals began to recruit and train women to undertake this work and as a way of maintaining a supply of skilled but inexpensive workers. Student nurses learned on the job and cared for hospital patients. Graduates typically became private duty nurses, employed in the homes of families who could afford them.

When hospitals became curative institutions, more were erected by private groups, often to serve particular religious, ethnic, and racial communities. For example, in urban centers with large groups of Catholic immigrants, Catholic hospitals were built to serve the community and to provide a place where priests could provide comfort and, if necessary, last rites. Jewish immigrants also erected facilities for their own kind. Similarly, African Americans opened hospitals where they could receive care (in regions that practiced segregation) and not face the second-class treatment they often found in segregated hospitals. Hospitals not only segregated patients by race; they treated the well-to-do in private rooms while confining charity patients to large wards.

Patients were also segregated by age. Sick children received care in wards or buildings set aside for them, rather than mixing with the general patient population. They also entered hospitals erected for their use. The first children's hospital opened in Philadelphia in 1855, ministering to sixty-seven inpatients and 306 outpatients its first year. It soon grew from a twelve- to a twenty-bed facility. Other children's hospitals opened in large cities, mainly in the East. Most were very small and provided significant amounts of outpatient care in their clinics and dispensaries. The Children's Hospital of Washington, D.C., founded in 1870, had six beds; the Albany Children's Hospital, which opened in 1875, had two; and the Detroit Children's Hospital, founded in 1877, had twelve.

While general hospitals expanded rapidly in the late nineteenth and early twentieth centuries, children's hospitals remained few in number. By 1909 there were only about twenty-five in the entire country, as compared to 4,359 general hospitals (Radbill 1955; Rosenberg 1987). Their most significant contribution may have been in helping to promote the idea that children needed a special kind of medical attention and nursing care. The managers of general hospitals acknowledged this by separating children from adult patients. Chicago's Michael Reese Hospital and Cook County General Hospital both constructed separate buildings for children (Radbill 1955). In Cleveland, the general hospital shifted from a children's ward to a separate cottage for children (Halpern 1988).

Many children's hospitals were built and run by female philanthropists, who brought to their charitable work a distinct mission. In addition to caring for sick children, they believed it was their duty to inculcate in their patients middle-class rules of health and hygiene. It was thought that when the children left the hospital, they would take what they had learned and teach it to their families. This kind of "moral training," as it was called by contemporaries, led hospital leaders to keep children away from their parents during their illnesses (Vogel 1980). The St. Louis Children's Hospital permitted children to receive visitors only once a week, for an hour, and similar restrictions were in place in Boston's Children's Hospital (Hunt 1980; Vogel 1980).

The hours doctors spent diagnosing sick youngsters in dispensaries, combating outbreaks of diarrhea on the wards of foundling homes, and making the rounds in children's hospitals or on the children's wards in general hospitals helped create the specialty of pediatrics. Physicians learned about the kinds of illnesses particular to the young, how the course of illness might differ in young patients from its course among adults, the practical issues of trying to diagnose patients who found it hard (or in the case of infants, impossible) to articulate their symptoms, and the special needs of children for support and encouragement. Abraham Jacobi, deemed the father of pediatrics, was an attending physician at the Nursery and Child's Hospital in New York City in the 1860s and later taught in clinics specializing in the diseases of children. Other early specialists also had careers working in children's hospitals and institutions, and would help to create organizations of like-minded practitioners (Halpern 1988).

The rise of scientific medicine in which physicians based their diagnoses and treatments on discoveries arising from clinical and experimental research, improvements in infection control and surgery arising from germ theory, and the development of new treatments for childhood ailments led parents to place greater faith in physicians. Among the most important and dramatic developments in pediatric medicine was the development of diphtheria antitoxin for the treatment of this deadly disease of childhood. Diphtheria antitoxin, followed by the creation of toxin-antitoxin to immunize children against this ailment, was one of the most prominent examples of how medicine applied the science of bacteriology to make childhood a safer time (Hammonds 1999). As medicine improved, families increasingly turned to doctors rather than friends, neighbors, or relatives for advice about keeping children well.

The work of teaching urban, immigrant families about preventing disease and maintaining the health of their children increasingly fell to public health and visiting nurses. Visiting nurses helped cared for sick children in their homes and taught families how to manage contagious illnesses, such as tuberculosis. They also gave instructions in the prevention of illness, providing advice about how to prevent the contamination of food, milk, and water and teaching mothers and other caregivers modern techniques of infant and child care. While public health nurses brought science to the bedside, school nurses brought scientific medicine to the classroom. They examined children for communicable diseases and physical problems, communicated with parents about how to care for ailing youngsters, and provided routine medical treatments under the supervision of physicians (Kalisch and Kalisch 1978).

Despite improvements in medical education and medical science linked to the germ theory of disease, and despite the development of children's hospitals, the challenge of caring for sick children remained arduous, and much of the work was performed by family members in the home. Physicians might be called to the case, but the burden of care fell on the family. Moreover, while scientific medicine provided new imperatives for family members, it offered few useful remedies. Poor families might follow the advice of dispensary physicians and visiting nurses and still lose a child to a common infectious illness. Middle-class families might screen their windows—to keep out the flies, known as "germs with wings"—turn the rooms of sick children into "home hospitals" that were carefully disinfected, and follow all the latest rules of hygiene, and still lose a child to a deadly disease (Tomes 1998).

MEDICINE AND CHILD HEALTH IN THE TWENTIETH CENTURY

The changes in medicine begun in the late nineteenth century accelerated in pace and expanded in scope during the twentieth century. In recounting changes in health practices in homes, institutions, and communities, it is necessary to examine the shifts thematically before noting the critical events occurring in each decade. The most important change in the provision of child health in the twentieth century was that the diagnosis, treatment, and management of very sick children was placed firmly in the domain of medicine; families were expected to consult doctors rather than friends, relatives, or domestic medical manuals, as had been the case earlier. At the beginning of the twentieth century it was likely to be a general practitioner who called at the home of the sick child; by the end of the century it would most likely be a pediatrician, seen in an office visit or, in the case of an emergency, at the hospital.

Another critical change was in the site of care. At the beginning of the century, a well-off child diagnosed with a serious illness would most likely be cared for at home with the assistance of a private duty nurse, while poor sick children might receive care from visiting nurses sent by municipal agencies or charitable groups. By the end of the century, rich and poor sick children alike would be treated in hospitals, where they would be overseen by nurses employed by the hospitals. Hospital care became the norm because families perceived that in the modern hospital their children would have access to round-the-clock, highly skilled medical and nursing care and to the latest technologies and therapies. Chronic care was a different matter. In many cases, it remained the responsibility of family members, who were instructed by physicians in the management of children's illnesses.

Advances in medical science and technology propelled the cultural authority of pediatrics and made pediatricians increasingly able to provide preventive and curative care. Births moved from home to hospital over the course of the twentieth century, and care of newborns became increasingly sophisticated. Technologies such as incubators helped preserve the lives of premature infants and helped to make care of the neonate (an infant less than four weeks old) a critical part of pediatric practice (Baker 1996). As pediatricians gained a foothold through their work in children's clinics and hospitals, they used their expertise, particularly in the area of infant feeding, to become trusted family advisors to the upper and middle classes.

Improvements in surgery, including asepsis and anesthesia, also benefited children, who were now able to enter the hospital for common operations (such as removal of tonsils and adenoids), for emergency operations (such as appendectomies) and for treatment of physical deformities, such as crooked bones and spinal problems. Old scourges such as tuberculosis and diphtheria began to be conquered with new medications and preventive measures following the development of germ theory and the research that followed. Other critical developments included the discovery of insulin in 1921. Insulin treatment for diabetes transformed a fatal illness into a chronic condition, albeit one with serious associated problems requiring careful management and monitoring. The development of antibiotics after World War II provided effective treatments for many previously fatal infections, while the development of vaccines meant that many once-common childhood ailments could be vanquished with a few injections.

During the twentieth century, the education of doctors included more training in pediatrics; growing numbers of pediatric specialists cared for sick children and oversaw the health of those who were well. The development of pediatrics as a specialty began in children's hospitals and infant asylums, and the knowledge doctors gained in these places led them to create specialty pediatrics journals in which they published their findings and communicated with others serving young patients. In 1880 the American Medical Association established a Section on Diseases of Children, acknowledging that this had become a separate area of practice; by 1933 it would be renamed the Section on Pediatrics. On the eve of World War I only 879 doctors identified themselves as pediatricians; twenty years later their numbers had grown to 3,889 and the field was expanding at twice the overall growth rate of other medical specialties (Halpern 1988). Pediatrics not only attracted more practitioners but became a regular part of the medical school curriculum, and pediatrics departments developed in all the medical schools. This helped to spawn more research. In 1941, research-oriented pediatricians organized the American Pediatric Society, in which they could share the results of their investigations and communicate with others who had mutual interests.

It is difficult to untangle the critical transformations in caregiving and sites of care that took place over the twentieth century. They were linked by both the expansion of medical science and by the growing cultural authority of those who applied this science to the care of the young. Additionally, ongoing social changes supported and shaped these developments, among them increasing government support for medical and public health services, the movement of Americans from rural communities and small towns into cities and then into suburbs, the arrival of millions of immigrants from Southern and Eastern Europe, and the internal migration of African Americans out of the South and into the large cities of the North.

During the first two decades of the twentieth century increasing attention began to be paid to the children of the poor. Municipal health departments along with private voluntary organizations investigated the health needs of infants and children, offering an array of supportive services. The American Association for the Study and Prevention of Infant Mortality—begun in 1909 to, as its name suggested, investigate and publicize the problems of infant mortality—became the American Child Hygiene Association in 1918, by which time many states and cities had established public agencies to promote child health. In New York City, S. Josephine Baker, a physician in charge of the Bureau of Child Hygiene, arranged for school nurses to spend the summer months visiting impoverished families of newborn babies in order to teach them proper hygiene and infant care.

Efforts to assist poor and immigrant families were not always successful. During a polio outbreak in New York City in 1916, immigrant families hid their children from the authorities, while others rejected calls to expose their young ones to fresh air, believing that it was dangerous (Rogers 1992). In some cases the problem came from the attitude of medical professionals who viewed immigrant diets and habits as dangerous or simply "un-American" and who failed to understand the fiscal restraints on these families. For example, a book on immigrant health published in 1921 criticized Jewish children for eating too many pickles and highly spiced foods as well as for enjoying too few vegetables and not enough milk, while Italian children were criticized for taking tea or coffee with bread for breakfast (Davis 1993). Little attention was paid to the poverty that frequently dictated limits on family food purchases.

Attempts to remove children from their homes also met with mixed success. Tuberculosis brought close scrutiny from public authorities, who sometimes tried to remove children from homes in which it was present. In some instances, the children were sent to "preventoriums" designed to provide healthy diets and sunshine in an effort to improve their health. Weight gain was considered a sign of improving health; one institution boasted that the fifty-three children who stayed during the 1915 summer season gained from two to ten pounds during their stay (River Crest 1915). More commonly, rather than taking children from their homes, public health workers tried to enlist children and mothers in campaigns designed to eradicate the disease through improved hygiene and diet (Feldberg 1995).

By the eve of the Great Depression, increasing numbers of children were receiving medical care in children's hospitals, general hospitals, hospital-based clinics, and in special convalescent facilities. Clinics provided outpatient services for those who could not afford to see a private physician and sometimes specialized in particular diagnoses, such as epilepsy or diabetes. Specialty hospitals also provided care to children. The Children's Orthopedic Hospital in Seattle, for example, performed surgery on crippled children and provided additional therapies, such as massage, for those stricken with polio.

Other reforms in the first half of the twentieth century emphasized disease prevention as well as treatment for the sick. In Philadelphia, the Children's Hospital sponsored a Department for the Prevention of Disease; it included a dental and oral hygiene clinic, a prenatal clinic, and a diphtheria prevention clinic, among others. While the clinics were open to all children, many of the special health classes organized for neighborhood youths were segregated by race, reflecting a larger picture of racial separation and discrimination (Golden 1996). In rural areas, disease prevention and child health were promoted in part by Better Baby contests and health exhibits at state fairs (Curry 1999; Stern 2002). Beginning in 1921, the Sheppard-Towner Act (discussed in detail in chapter 6) increased the number of rural clinics providing maternal, infant, and child care and health instruction in underserved communities.

Later, during the Great Depression, public health nurses were employed in federal programs such as the Civil Works Administration and the Works Progress Administration, where they engaged in child health projects ranging from immunization campaigns to expanded programs of school health nursing. While public health nurses in cities visited immigrant tenements, in rural areas public health nurses reached out to children and families by horseback—as was the case with the Kentucky Frontier Nursing Service— as well as by automobile.

The need for further government support for child health programs was made apparent in wartime. During World War I and again in World War II, nearly 50 percent of the young men called to military service were rejected because of poor physical condition (King 1993). Despite all the new methods for diagnosing, treating, and even preventing disease that marked the twentieth century as a time of progress in medical science, factors of poverty, poor housing, nutritional deficits, and overwork often undermined the health of children and made them vulnerable to illness or stunted their development.

The conquest of many infectious diseases after World War II led to the closure of some institutions, while advances in scientific knowledge led to the opening of others. Tuberculosis preventoria closed as rates of infection declined and as the disease became treatable with the advent of new drugs in the 1940s and 1950s (Connolly 2002). Similarly, as the numbers of children left severely handicapped by rheumatic fever that damaged their hearts and made them "cardiac cripples" declined, convalescent beds and homes for them were emptied (English 1999). With advances in understanding and later treating what became known as blood diseases, wards and clinics arose to care for African American children (and adults) suffering from the excruciating pains and debility of sickle-cell anemia (Wailoo 2001).

Thanks to the development of new vaccines, antibiotics, and other chemotherapeutics in the postwar era, many diseases were prevented and life-threatening illnesses vanquished. Meningococcal meningitis, a deadly infection, responded to sulfonamide drugs and then to penicillin, lowering the fatality rate from this disease from 40 percent to less than 5 percent (Cone 1979, 215). There were advances in understanding and later in treating sickle-cell anemia and childhood leukemia (Wailoo 1997).

One of the most dramatic breakthroughs of all came with creation of the Salk vaccine for polio, followed by the subsequent development of the Sabin vaccine. Periodic polio epidemics had left many youngsters dead or crippled. Known as infantile paralysis, it struck most often those who lived in clean, middle-class homes (because most poor children had become infected and immune at an early age). After being stricken himself, Franklin D. Roosevelt helped to establish the National Foundation for Infantile Paralysis, which began the March of Dimes campaign to raise money for research. The development of polio vaccines proved to be not only a scientific triumph in its conquest of a deadly ailment but also an important contribution to the development of virology, helping to push medicine beyond the bacteriological era.

While in the late nineteenth century the idea of being a specialist in the care of children seemed absurd to many, by the late twentieth century many pediatricians were themselves subspecialists, limiting their practices to certain age groups—such as the neonatologists, who cared for newborns, or the adolescent medicine practitioners, who worked with teenagers (Prescott 1998). In other cases, physicians specialized in certain categories of disease, such as pediatric neurology or pediatric endocrinology. General pediatrics had become, increasingly, an office-based medical practice, with a focus on well-child care and preventive medicine. Children had regular checkups with doctors who treated the common ailments of childhood and paid growing attention to newly discovered behavioral problems found in children and adolescents (Halpern 1988).

As the interest in childhood behavioral difficulties suggests, medical understanding of childhood mental illness advanced over the course of the twentieth century. Growing recognition of children's mental health concerns, from schizophrenia to learning disabilities, prompted new efforts to train professionals to recognize children's needs and to provide counseling, support, and medication appropriate to their age as well as their diagnoses. It also resulted in the development of new sites of care, including child guidance clinics and school psychologists' offices. Other new sites of care included community health centers, which began to open in the 1960s to provide primary care to residents of medically underserved communities.

Today, despite the enormous changes in medicine and society over the course of the twentieth century that improved the life chances of sick children and put doctors and hospitals at the forefront of diagnosis and treatment, several elements of caregiving remain unchanged. First, seeing a doctor and obtaining needed preventive and curative services continues to be governed to a significant degree by a family's ability to pay for care. Many who could not afford a doctor in the first half of the twentieth century obtained charity care from hospitals and clinics. In the second half of the twentieth century, and at present, government payment schemes such as Medicaid and later the State Children's Health Insurance Program aided children whose families lacked private insurance. However, access to government programs is uneven and limited, and enrollment is limited to those with extremely low incomes; some poor families might make too much money to be eligible but have no means of paying for care on their own. All too often their children receive medical treatment only when they become seriously ill or injured and go to a hospital emergency room. A second continuity is that families continue to assume a large burden of care for children with chronic conditions, helping infants, children, and adolescents with asthma, diabetes, physically handicapping conditions, mental illness, birth defects, or developmental delays cope with the medical, social, and physical tasks of daily life (Abel 2000). Families are also faced with supporting children with critical illnesses, such as childhood cancers, and new ailments such as HIV/AIDS, helping them through hospitalization and long-term treatments. Finally, and most profoundly, illness remains a continuing part of life for all children, whether they suffer from short-term minor ailments or more serious diseases. While many more individuals survive infancy and childhood than has ever been the case in human history, pain, illness, suffering, and death still threaten children and the families that care for them.

WORKS CITED

Abel, Emily K. 2000. *Hearts of Wisdom: American Women Caring for Kin, 1850–1940*. Cambridge, Mass.: Harvard University Press.

Apple, Rima D. 1987. *Mothers and Medicine: A Social History of Infant Feeding, 1890–1950*. Madison: University of Wisconsin Press.

Baker, Jeffrey B. 1996. *The Machine in the Nursery: Incubator Technology and the Origins of Newborn Intensive Care*. Baltimore: Johns Hopkins University Press.

Buchan, William. 1772/1985. *Domestic Medicine: Or, A Treatise on the Prevention and Cure of Diseases by Regimen and Simple Medicines*. New York: Garland.

Burnett, J. Compton. 1896. *Delicate, Backward, Puny, and Stunted Children: Their Developmental Defects and Moral Peculiarities Considered as Ailments Amenable to Treatment by Medicines*. Philadelphia: Boericke and Tafel.

Cayliff, Susan E. 1987. *Wash and Be Healed: The Water Cure Movement and Women's Health*. Philadelphia: Temple University Press.

Child, Brenda. 1993. "Homesickness, Illness, and Death: Native-American Girls in Government Boarding Schools." In *Wings of Gauze: Women of Color and the Ex-*

perience of Health and Illness. Edited by Barbara Bair and Susan E. Cayliff, 168–79. Detroit: Wayne State University Press.

Cone, Thomas E., Jr. 1979. *History of American Pediatrics.* Boston: Little, Brown.

Connolly, Cynthia A. 2002. "Nurses: The Early Twentieth Century Tuberculosis Preventorium Movement's 'Connecting Link.'" *Nursing History Review* 10: 127–57.

Curry, Lynn. 1999. *Modern Mothers in the Heartland: Gender, Health, and Progress in Illinois, 1900–1930.* Columbus: Ohio State University Press.

Davis, Eric Leiff. 1993. "The Era of the Common Child: Egalitarian Death in Antebellum America." *Mid-America* 75: 135–63.

English, Peter C. 1999. *Rheumatic Fever in America and Britain: A Biological, Epidemiological, and Medical History.* New Brunswick, N.J.: Rutgers University Press.

Feldberg, Georgina D. 1995. *Disease and Class: Tuberculosis and the Shaping of Modern North American Society.* New Brunswick, N.J.: Rutgers University Press.

Fett, Sharla M. 2002. *Working Cures: Health, Health and Power on Southern Slave Plantations.* Chapel Hill: University of North Carolina Press.

Golden, Janet. 1991. *A Social History of Wet Nursing in America: From Breast to Bottle.* Cambridge: Cambridge University Press.

———. 1996. "The Iconography of Child Public Health: Between Medicine and Reform." *Caduceus* 12: 55–72.

———, ed. 1989. *Infant Asylums and Children's Hospitals: Medical Dilemmas and Developments, 1850–1920: An Anthology of Sources.* New York: Garland.

Grant, Julia. 1998. *Raising Baby by the Book: The Education of American Mothers.* New Haven, Conn.: Yale University Press.

Gunn, John C. 1830/1986. *Gunn's Domestic Medicine.* Knoxville: University of Tennessee Press.

Halpern, Sydney A. 1988. *American Pediatrics: The Social Dynamics of Professionalism, 1880–1980.* Berkeley: University of California Press.

Hammonds, Evelynn Maxine. 1999. *Childhood's Deadly Scourge: The Campaign to Control Diphtheria in New York City, 1880–1930.* Baltimore: Johns Hopkins University Press.

Hunt, Marion. 1980. "Women and Child Saving: St. Louis Children's Hospital, 1879–1979." *Missouri Historical Society Bulletin* 36: 65–79.

Hutchins, Vince L. 1997. "A History of Child Health and Pediatrics in the United States." In *Health Care for Children: What's Right, What's Wrong, What's Next.* Edited by Ruth E. K. Stein, 79–106. New York: United Hospital Fund of New York.

Jones, Kathleen W. 1983. "Sentiment and Science: The Late Nineteenth Century Pediatrician as Mother's Advisor." *Journal of Social History* 17: 79–96.

———. 1999. *Taming the Troublesome Child: American Families, Child Guidance, and the Limits of Psychiatric Authority.* Cambridge: Harvard University Press.

Joyner, Charles. 1984. *Down by the Riverside: A South Carolina Slave Community.* Urbana: University of Illinois Press.

Kalisch, Philip A., and Beatrice J. Kalisch. 1978. *The Advance of American Nursing.* Boston: Little, Brown.

King, Charles R. 1993. *Children's Health in America: A History.* New York: Twayne.

Meckel, Richard A. 1990. *Save the Babies: American Public Health Reform and the Prevention of Infant Mortality, 1850–1929.* Baltimore: Johns Hopkins University Press.

Murphy, Lamar Riley. 1991. *Enter the Physician: The Transformation of Domestic Medicine, 1760–1860.* Tuscaloosa: University of Alabama Press.

Prescott, Heather Munro. 1998. *A Doctor of Their Own: The History of Adolescent Medicine.* Cambridge, Mass.: Harvard University Press.

Quiroga, Virginia Anne Metaxas. 1989. *Poor Mothers and Babies: A Social History of Childbirth and Child Care Hospitals in Nineteenth-Century New York City.* New York: Garland.

Radbill, Samuel X. 1955. "A History of Children's Hospitals." *American Journal of Diseases of Children* 90: 411–16.

River Crest, Phoenixville, Pa. 1915. *Second Report, Preventorium of the Kensington Dispensary Collection,* College of Physicians of Philadelphia, Pennsylvania.

Rogers, Naomi. 1992. *Dirt and Disease: Polio before FDR.* New Brunswick, N.J.: Rutgers University Press.

Rosenberg, Charles E. 1987. *The Care of Strangers: The Rise of America's Hospital System.* New York: Basic Books.

———. 1992. *Explaining Epidemics and Other Studies in the History of Medicine.* New York: Cambridge University Press.

Savitt, Todd L. 1978. *Medicine and Slavery; The Diseases and Health Care of Blacks in Antebellum Virginia.* Urbana: University of Illinois Press.

Stern, Alexandra Minna. 2002. "Better Babies Contests at the Indiana State Fair: Child Health, Scientific Motherhood, and Eugenics in the Midwest, 1920–35." In *Formative Years: Children's Health in the United States, 1880–2000.* Edited by Alexandra Minna Stern and Howard Markel, 121–52. Ann Arbor: University of Michigan Press.

Still, James. 1887/1973. *Early Recollections and Life of Dr. James Still, 1812–1885.* New Brunswick, N.J.: Rutgers University Press.

Tannenbaum, Rebecca J. 2002. *The Healer's Calling: Women and Medicine in Early New England.* Ithaca, N.Y.: Cornell University Press.

Tomes, Nancy. 1998. *The Gospel of Germs: Men, Women, and the Microbe in American Life.* Cambridge, Mass.: Harvard University Press.

Ulrich, Laurel Thatcher. 1990. *A Midwife's Tale: The Life of Martha Ballard Based on Her Diary, 1785–1812.* New York: Alfred A. Knopf.

Vogel, Morris J. 1980. *The Invention of the Modern Hospital, Boston, 1870–1930.* Chicago: University of Chicago Press.

Wailoo, Keith. 1997. *Drawing Blood: Technology and Disease Identity in Twentieth-Century America.* Baltimore: Johns Hopkins University Press.

———. 2001. *Dying in the City of the Blues: Sickle Cell Anemia and the Politics of Race and Health.* Chapel Hill: University of North Carolina Press.

Waring, Joseph Ioor. 1964. *A History of Medicine in South Carolina, 1670–1825.* Columbia: South Carolina Medical Association.

5 Teaching Children about Health

Elizabeth Toon

Today a multitude of sources offer American children lessons about health, disease, and the body. On the Cartoon Network and other television stations with child audiences, fast-moving advertisements created by the Centers for Disease Control (CDC) urge young viewers to get physically active by choosing their "verb." Kid-friendly websites and software packages introduce Internet-savvy preteens to the basics of human anatomy. Milk-mustache advertisements in magazines and on billboards offer teens photographs of their favorite athletes and celebrities endorsing dairy products, while MTV offers guest spots on *Total Request Live* as a prize for teens who enter a drawing by taking a "Milk Rules" pledge. Meanwhile, complementing these glitzy, glossy approaches to kids' health education is the formal instruction delivered by schools. Just as they have for over 150 years, American classrooms and gymnasiums teach children about the body's structure, functioning, and care.

Why, how, and what have American children been taught about health? How have schools and other institutions interacted to help children understand their bodies, care for themselves, and respond to the health needs of others? This chapter answers those questions by providing a synthetic historical overview of health teaching aimed at children, particularly that delivered by schools, from the early nineteenth century through the end of the twentieth. Bringing together studies written by historians of medicine, education, and childhood, it outlines major trends in the rationales for, methods of, and content of health instruction for American children. For example, the methods educators have used to teach children about health have changed considerably, just as the knowledge educators set out to teach has changed. Nevertheless, adults with quite varied backgrounds and concerns—educators, physicians, social reformers, moral authorities, public health workers, and parents—have all assumed that health instruction for children could solve pervasive national problems, from the "Americanization" of immigrants to high rates of teen pregnancy. By the mid-nineteenth century, schools had become the primary institutions entrusted with health instruction, and they are therefore the central focus of this chapter. But because the efforts of groups and movements outside the classroom have also had an important influence on what children have learned about their bodies and their health, their work in educating American children about health is also discussed.

Of course, we must remember that asking what experts, communities, teachers, and curricula *set out to teach* children about health does not necessarily tell us exactly what those children *learned or thought* about health. Historians of medicine, education, and childhood have all drawn on diverse source material to try to comprehend what experts wanted, what communities expected, what teachers taught, and what students learned. These sources, like all primary historical sources, have their strengths and weaknesses. Legislative debates and newspaper editorials, for instance, help us see what priorities earlier generations set for schools. Principals' evaluations and teachers' reports suggest how school personnel approached the everyday work of classroom instruction. Textbooks, films, and other materials created for school use reveal the constellation of ideas and practices that experts considered essential and appropriate for children to know. Architectural plans introduce us to the classroom environment, while photographs offer glimpses of the daily activities and interactions that constituted "health education." If we do as the historians cited in this chapter do and take these sources as a group, we will see that these sources give us multiple, overlapping portraits of what health education might have been like for the children who experienced it as well as the adults who promoted it.

"THE HOUSE I LIVE IN": ANTEBELLUM CHILDREN LEARN ABOUT ANATOMY, PHYSIOLOGY, AND HYGIENE

In the colonial era, children learned about health much as adults did. By observing parents, relatives, and community members, children acquired such practical knowledge as what foods to eat and how to care for the sick; young adults with a particular aptitude for healing might apprentice with or receive special instruction from a midwife or even a physician. Sermons, especially those published by well-known and learned ministers, provided another source of guidance for those who wished to lead healthy lives—and those who could not read or who had such works read aloud to them. Like sermons, the domestic medical guides available to colonists mixed medical and moral advice, as health and religious authorities saw little distinction between health teaching and moral injunction. For those who instructed early Americans about the body and its care, avoiding disease and leading a healthy life was a spiritual duty, and immoral or intemperate conduct often led to illness.

It was in the nineteenth century, when the public school movement made education available to more American children and when health advice books flooded a rapidly expanding publishing market, that health instruction specifically intended for children appeared. In the 1830s, educational and social reformers in the North set out to create a system of locally supported schools open to all children; as historians of education and medicine have pointed out, one of these reformers' central demands was that schools be simultaneously healthful places and places that taught health (Meckel 2002; Duffy 1979). Massachusetts educator Horace Mann was among the most vocal on this cause, urging in an influential 1843 report that hygiene and physiology be a subject "of the first rank" in the elementary curriculum. Advocates of the public school hoped to form the American character, to create citizens capable of considering others' interests as well as their own. Such character, Mann insisted, could be built only on a foundation of physical and moral health (Means 1962; Mann 1843). By the middle of the nineteenth century, then, and with the encouragement of leading reformers and educators, some schools had begun to include some hygiene and physiology teaching in their curricula—although it would never become a subject of the first rank as Mann had envisioned.

In nineteenth-century schools, schoolbooks would serve as the anchor for this teaching. After all, as medical and educational authorities recognized, few schoolteachers had the detailed knowledge necessary for instructing children in these subjects, especially anatomy and physiology. But the physicians and health reformers who wrote health primers also realized that the potential readership for such books was quite broad and that in places where children did not learn about hygiene, anatomy, and physiology in schools, parents might wish to provide such instruction themselves. Thus many antebellum children's health books were consciously multifunctional, like Jane Taylor's 1858 *Wouldst Thou Know Thyself, or The Outlines of Human Physiology*, were described as being "designed for the use of families and schools" (Rosenberg 1995; Murphy 1991). In other words, home and school both served as sites for teaching children about health, and both drew on the same sorts of expert knowledge to do so.

What kinds of lessons did children's health books, and the parents and schools employing them, offer antebellum children? Some of these texts, like their enormously popular cousins intended for adult readers, focused on general hygienic commandments. Bernard Faust's *Catechism of Health*, the pioneer of this genre, taught the laws of health using a question-and-answer format. Other texts—again, like those for adults—mixed home-nursing and disease-prevention information with instructions for physical exercise and suggestions about health conduct. But most antebellum health texts for children used anatomy and physiology to teach hygiene. In other words, the authors of these primers described, in relatively simple terms, the body's physical structure and explained how it worked, expecting that once children understood the human body they would appreciate the need to care for their own bodies. For instance, the hugely popular and frequently republished *The House I Live In,* by educational and health reformer William Alcott, declared that the human body was like a house. The ingenious construction of this house, Alcott explained, was evidence of the majesty of its Creator, and the majesty and complexity of such a wondrous gift required that the inhabitant of this house care for and maintain it in keeping with His laws (Rosenberg 1995; Murphy 1991). Such arguments, which echoed those offered by proponents of natural theology, would persist throughout the nineteenth century and after. This message was also reinforced by the "nature-study" movement, a popular form of science teaching that (like health instruction) emerged in the antebellum period and grew throughout the nineteenth century. Directed by books and teachers, nature-study pupils explored the natural world around them. This world, these students learned, provided ample evidence of the Creator, and they could infer knowledge about how humans should live by witnessing how God's laws governed the lives of plants and animals (Keeney 1992).

Although educational reformers and health authorities had hoped that instruction in anatomy, physiology, and hygiene would make for innovative learning and productive knowledge, the historical evidence suggests that health teaching in schools for the most part resembled that in other subjects. The usual mode of instruction in the nineteenth-century school was memorization and recitation, and students were drilled in anatomy and physiology as they were in geography and grammar. But there are some indications of what we today would term "active" learning in physiology and hygiene instruction (Rosenberg 1995). Textbooks and published curricula, for instance, urged teachers and children to obtain animal material, such as bones or organs, for classroom study and dissection. This was relatively easily done, as most Americans lived in farming communities or at least in close proximity to a butcher. (Children who helped rear and tend animals and who observed butchering and cooking at home had already absorbed some of this knowledge.) Exposure to animal bodies, whether by watching a teacher dissect or a parent prepare meat for sale or consumption, taught the rich detail of anatomical structure in ways that even the fine illustrations of textbooks could not.

Another form of active learning about health that antebellum children experienced came in the form of physical education. Many nineteenth-century German immigrants to the United States brought with them an enthusiasm for gymnastics and physical training, as systematized by the German Alfred Jahn, and in many cities they established *Turnvereine,* or gymnastic societies. Other health reformers also promoted exercise, arguing that calisthenics would make healthier American men, women, and children. Catharine Beecher, a health advocate who had published popular advice on "domestic economy," also devoted her attention to health advice, publishing a guide (*Physiology and Calisthenics*, 1856) that linked the quest for knowledge of the body to specific physical exercises that would maintain health. In the 1860s, temperance advocate Dio Lewis offered a system he called "New Gymnastics," which he claimed was (unlike the strenuous exercises of the *Turnvereine*) suitable for the bodies of health seekers of all types, including children and young women. Lewis's Normal Institute for Physical Education trained young men and women in his system and sent them out to teach others the principles of physical education (Verbrugge 1988; Whorton 1982). By the 1860s, some common schools were encouraging gymnastics and calisthenics for their young pupils, and many colleges had created courses in these forms of physical education (Park 1989; Hackensmith 1966). Thus, like their elders, antebellum children learned that physical exercise was essential if they hoped to know themselves and live healthy, vigorous, truly American lives.

TEMPERANCE PHYSIOLOGY, SCHOOL HYGIENE, AND PHYSICAL FITNESS: EDUCATING CHILDREN IN HEALTH FROM THE CIVIL WAR TO THE GREAT WAR

Nevertheless, despite the best efforts of antebellum educators, physicians, health reformers, and moral authorities, health teaching had only a shaky foothold in American schools (and that primarily in schools in the Northeast) before the Civil War. That would change after the war, when the Women's Christian Temperance Union (WCTU) began an extensive campaign that made the classroom a major battleground in its war against alcohol use. The WCTU's leaders argued that morality and science alike dictated temperance—the avoidance of alcohol, tobacco, and narcotics. In the 1880s and 1890s, former chemistry and physiology teacher Mary Hanchett Hunt headed the WCTU's Scientific Temperance Institute (STI), which created teaching materials that used scientific evidence to claim that alcohol was physiologically dangerous. WCTU members attended local school board meetings and state legislative hearings to demand temperance teaching in schools, and STI representatives consulted with legislators and state education officials to convince them to mandate that the temperance message appear in the curriculum (Zimmerman 1999).

As historians of education have shown, the WCTU and its STI were remarkably successful in their campaign for what was later called "temperance physiology." By the 1890s, WCTU lobbyists had convinced all state legislatures to require schools to provide hygiene and physiology instruction that addressed the temperance issue. Many state laws even mandated that the textbooks adopted for hygiene and physiology instruction include a specified amount of content (a certain number or proportion of each textbook's pages) focused on the evils of alcohol, tobacco, and narcotics. Meanwhile, Hunt's STI endorsed physiology textbooks written by others that met the temperance standards set out in state textbook-adoption laws.[1] Hunt and her allies sought to convince children—and through them, the nation—that temperance was a cause rooted in scientific truth and that not just morality but reason and experiment compelled abstinence (Zimmerman 1999) On that front, the WCTU faced strong opposition, as some noted medical and biological scientists disputed the information put forth by "temperance physiology" texts as fact (Pauly 2000; Zimmerman 1999). The WCTU also faced opposition from some communities, where political leaders argued that the local people who paid for schools and sent their children there should retain control over what those children learned. National educational leaders, meanwhile, argued that charting the content and course of children's education was a matter for pedagogical experts—most of whom were male—rather than crusading women (Zimmerman 1999). Nevertheless, the WCTU's STI succeeded where several generation of educators and reformers failed, establishing a secure place for health teaching in the American school.

The school itself, meanwhile, was changing considerably. New laws mandated that all children attend school for at least a certain number of years, producing a large and, given the increases in immigration at the end of the century, more diverse population of students. Some reformers insisted that local control of schools had devolved into corruption and that schools and school systems should be placed under the control of a new group of expert (and thus presumably incorruptible) administrators. These professional educators hoped to create more "efficient" schools, schools where trained teachers used pedagogically up-to-date modes of instruction, and where precise schedules and specialized spaces for study and play accompanied an increasingly differentiated curriculum. These changes took hold more quickly and thoroughly in urban and suburban sections of the Northeast and Midwest. There, in new buildings and under regimented schedules, children learned in graded classrooms, increasingly under the direction of teachers trained in teaching by "normal schools" and themselves guided by pedagogical experts and professional journals. In the nation's many rural areas, however, such changes took longer—sometimes much longer—to take effect. Children of several age groups and learning levels often still occupied the same classrooms, and teachers—albeit often quite committed to their work and innovative in their approaches to teaching—had less formal training and fewer resources at their command. In the rural South, agricultural labor needs still took priority over schools in many communities, meaning that many children were absent for substantial portions of the school year despite compulsory-education laws. Nevertheless, the influence of school reform was felt even in rural areas, as a new category of professional literature emerged to guide rural teachers and school board members, and as state educational officials increased their watch—and control—over rural schools and districts (Tyack and Hansot 1990; Cremin 1988; Cuban 1993; Link 1992).

What did this transformation in the experience of schooling mean for children's health, and for what they learned about health? A vocal group of reformers and physicians felt that American education had had quite dire consequences for children's health and urged that the "hygiene of instruction" be taken into account as schools were reorganized and new buildings constructed. According to many well-known physicians, the small print in textbooks and poor lighting of most classrooms produced myopia; long hours in stale and "vitiated" air induced fatigue; and "overstudy" fed the mind at the expense of the body (Meckel 2002). By the early twentieth century, many of the physicians and reformers interested in public health work had decided that the school was an ideal anchor for broader health-improvement programs. So while turn-of-the-century school buildings were inspected for faults and conditions that could induce illness, the school children within these buildings themselves became the targets of medical inspection, as physicians and nurses at the health department's behest examined pupils for contagious diseases like trachoma, ringworm, and impetigo. A physician employed by the New York City Health Department to work in child hygiene, S. Josephine Baker, later remembered the "solemn procession" of pupils past the physician and nurse:

> Each child stopp[ed] for a moment, opening his mouth hideously wide and pulling down his lower eyelids with his fingers. For our purposes it gave the doctor an opportunity of looking at the child's hands . . . , his teeth, throat and eyes all at the same time. For the children's purpose it was a beautiful opportunity for making a face at teacher unscathed and they made the most of it. (Baker 1939/1980, 78)

One important legacy of school medical inspection was the school nurse. In the 1910s, health departments and educational authorities employed nurses to rotate among a small number of schools or even serve full-time at a single large school. These nurses surveyed the student body for health problems and tried to keep contagious illnesses to a minimum, all while offering general health advice to school children and their parents (Buhler-Wilkerson 1989; Baker 1939/1980; Vollmer 1968).

But schools, while increasingly a collective locus for health instruction and public health services, were hardly the only institutions teaching late-nineteenth- and early-twentieth-century children about health. A veritable multitude of organizations complemented school lessons about disease, health, and the body, mostly by creating programs and activities intended to help children experience good health. The YMCA, for instance, was originally founded to give young men in the cities a moral haven, safe from the myriad temptations of urban life. The Y's gymnasia and later its pools were intended to offer young working men physically—and thus morally—health-ful outlets for their energies. From the 1910s on, Scouting offered Ameri-can boys in their early teens exposure to the outdoor life, as well as physical training programs said to keep them vigorous and pure; likewise, the Girl Scouts made exercise, outdoor adventure, and hygiene instruction part of their program for better girlhood (Green 1986; Miller 2001). Finally, influ-enced by theories about the physical and psychological development of the child and adolescent, turn-of-the-century educators, medical authorities, and advocates of "physical training" sought to encourage forms of recreation that would ensure the mental, moral, and bodily vigor of American youth. Pro-ponents of playgrounds urged cities and towns to create spaces specifically dedicated to children's recreation, shielded from the crowding and danger of the streets (soon made even more dangerous by the automobile). Schools themselves began to incorporate exercise and athletics—just a more ad-vanced form of play, their advocates argued—into school life. Physical train-ing would make the student's body a sort of object lesson in health, by counteracting the physiological and mental dangers caused by extensive time spent on study and "brain-work" (Park 1989).

The apparent physiological and educational benefits of physical training made it part of larger discussions about the future of womanhood and man-hood in an era when gender conventions and ideologies were undergoing substantial change. In the 1870s and 1880s, one argument made by oppo-nents of higher education for women was that too much learning put the female body's reproductive health—and thus, the nation's future—in peril. Proponents of women's education responded by supporting physical edu-cation for young women and girls enrolled in colleges and schools, so par-ents could rest assured that their daughters, the nation's future mothers, would develop body and mind simultaneously, and neither at the expense of the other (Verbrugge 1988). Meanwhile, their male counterparts urged competitive athletics as a mentally and physically healthful element of young men's high school and college lives. Within a few decades, some of these educational authorities began to reevaluate the healthfulness of inter-collegiate athletics, worried that such competition bred overexcitement and nervous strain rather than mental and physical balance. Most, however, saw collegiate athletics as a continuing force for healthy manhood, even as they admitted that intercollegiate contests had become the province of a relative few, especially skilled athletes rather than a system for promoting the health of all students (Park 1989).

FROM "LEARNING THE BONES" TO "THE RULES OF THE GAME": THE "NEW" HEALTH EDUCATION, 1915–1950

Even as they reveled in the many new extracurricular venues for teach-ing American children about health, early-twentieth-century educators, social reformers, and health authorities grew disenchanted with the situation of health instruction in schools. To these 1910s advocates of a new approach to teaching health, the "temperance physiologies" mandated by the WCTU were indicative of an old-fashioned pedagogy, one that emphasized memorization and morbid detail at the expense of any real knowledge of health. The only things that "learning the bones" instilled in children, these educators argued, was boredom and—even decades later—"painful memories" (Conrad and Meister 1939). Thomas D. Wood's *Health and Education,* published by the National Society for the Study of Education in 1910, further underscored the apparent failure of American physiology and hygiene instruction as well as the poor condition of pupils and schools.

This situation seemed especially problematic in the light of the recent growth of biomedical knowledge. In the late nineteenth century, the germ theory of disease provided physicians and public health workers with a new understanding of why people got sick and what could be done about it. Advocates of a "new public health" sought to teach everyday men, women, and children how to live their lives according to a "gospel of germs," thus giving the public the tools to defend itself against disease (Tomes 1998). Research findings in nutritional science, meanwhile, offered new ideas about what and how much people should eat, and scientists and health workers agreed that disseminating this knowledge would improve personal and public health (Levenstein 1988).

Meanwhile, by the 1910s new public and private organizations had made children's health a nationally visible issue. The Children's Bureau, an organization within the U.S. Department of Labor, had created an extensive program of education and health advice for the nation's mothers, with the aim of improving women's and children's health. Reformers and medical professionals concerned with high rates of infant mortality soon broadened their focus to consider the health of children of all ages (Klaus 1993; Meckel 1990; Ladd-Taylor 1986). Likewise, the National Tuberculosis Association—the nation's largest and best known voluntary health agency—made children's health a particular interest, as its leaders argued that improving children's diet and health habits would increase their resistance to disease (Tomes 1998; Teller 1988).

Nationalist considerations further augmented this concern with child health in the early twentieth century. First, fearful of the apparent "foreignness" of the waves of immigrants to the United States in the late nineteenth and early twentieth centuries, reformers created "Americanization" programs intended to modify the ideas and behaviors of the millions of Southern, Eastern, and Central Europeans entering the country. Hygiene instruction was an especially pivotal part of efforts to teach immigrants to live more "American" lives, since many reformers and health workers blamed the high rates of communicable disease among immigrants on old-country habits and ignorance of sanitation (Hoy 1995; Kraut 1994). Some of the reformers and health workers who wrote about the conditions of poor rural southerners, white and black, similarly attributed disease to ignorance, either at the individual or community level (Link 1992).

Because compulsory education laws now mandated children's attendance at school, schools were potentially very powerful agents of Americanization. Health authorities followed through on this potential, seeing hygiene instruction and medical inspections as means for improving the health of urban immigrant or poor rural children, who would then—ideally, at least—carry the lessons learned home to teach their own parents. This reliance on teaching children and expecting children to teach their parents was most noticeable in the 1910s development of "little mothers' clubs." In these after-school groups, nurses taught girls how to care for infants according to hygienic rules. Not only would such instruction prepare these girls for future motherhood, health workers argued, it would improve the health of younger siblings, since the care of small children often settled on their adolescent sisters. But the little mothers' clubs also made their girl members into emissaries of the health department, carrying home expert knowledge about feeding regimens, well-baby clinics, and proper play to their mothers.

The experience of the Great War further solidified public and political interest in child health, spurring growing interest among authorities in improving school health instruction. Americans learned that some one-third of those called up for military service were unhealthy or riddled with physical defects, many of which could have been prevented or corrected in childhood (Hutchinson 1997). Reformers and health workers used this data to amplify an argument they had begun to make in the decade before, that national security and prosperity required a greater investment in the health of America's children. These proponents of a new approach to teaching health to children offered the war as proof of the need for innovation:

> We won the war, but when the smoke of battle had cleared away, we realized, as never before, the pathetic weakness of our citizens. . . . A large proportion of these physical defects might have been corrected or prevented if the schools had been doing their part to train children to conserve and improve their health. (Andress 1925, v)

Finally, early-twentieth-century changes in pedagogical theory led educators to call for changes in the modes of instruction used in the school, changes that would make health education an increasingly important part of the school's mission. In the two decades before the Great War, the child-study movement had already convinced many educators that young children were best understood as creatures governed by emotion rather than reason (Kliebard 1995). The child's natural tendencies should be allowed to flourish, child-study advocates maintained, and her innocence should not be perverted by the "morbid" facts and "horrible examples" said to be common to hygiene teaching, particularly of the "temperance physiology" variety. The educators who gained prominence after the Great War disagreed with elements of the child-study approach, but they agreed wholeheartedly that hygiene and physiology instruction was anything but appropriate or effective. These advocates of educational reform, inspired in part by John Dewey and calling their movement "progressive education," held that teaching, regardless of subject matter, should be done in an environment that downplayed boundaries between subjects, that built learning around the child's life and interests, and that encouraged intellectual development and the acquisition of knowledge through problem-based activity and cooperative action (Kliebard 1995; Zilversmit 1993). Leading progressive theorists urged teachers to allow children's questions and interests to shape the lesson plan and to make everyday life, not abstract subject matter, the center of learning. Health instruction, these theorists maintained, was an especially suitable venue for this approach. In the progressive education schema, health was not a subject—it was

> an objective, just as the development of civic ideals is an objective. Health motives and practices should permeate the whole school life and work. Methods of teaching health, of illustrating health, and of living health cannot be torn out or set apart from the child's life, but should be woven into its very fabric. (U.S. Department of the Interior, Bureau of Education 1923, 5)

To differentiate it further from the supposed stale and pedagogically bereft hygiene instruction of old, proponents of the new approach to teaching children about their bodies even coined a new term for their endeavor—"health education." "Hygiene" instruction suggested a teacher drilling students in the factual subject areas of anatomy, physiology, and hygiene, but "health education," reformers agreed, conveyed a vision of children learning through exploration and experience to develop attitudes and practices conducive to health.

The "new" health education gained considerable support from voluntary health groups that had created programs for children that schools could in turn adopt. For instance, the National Tuberculosis Association's Modern Health Crusade (popular in the late 1910s) allowed children to climb the ranks from "page" to "knight banneret" by performing a list of health habits regularly; the Child Health Organization supplied its own "Rules of the Game" to schools as a template for health behavior. Both organizations, as well as the Junior Red Cross, supplied plays, games, and other curricular materials to teachers who sought to make classroom health instruction more playful and thus (they thought) more likely to gain children's interest (Tomes 1998; Teller 1988; Hutchinson 1997).

This emphasis on playful learning of rules for health conduct similarly pervaded health textbooks of the 1920s and 1930s. Color illustrations and fanciful tales of health "royalty" in distant lands (the "King of the Land of

Good Health," for instance) became standard tropes for readers aimed at the youngest students, while textbooks intended for children in the middle grades offered stories about children who—presumably like the books' readers—struggled with but eventually learned the rules of healthy living. Only in the upper grades or in high school texts would students encounter the detailed discussions of bodily structure and function that had been common in nineteenth-century hygiene and physiology texts. Instead, the elementary school child who experienced the "new" school health education was expected to learn through activities: making posters, acting in plays, singing songs, and keeping personal health notebooks or diaries. Her older siblings, meanwhile, would experience a slightly different form of "active" learning. As historians of biology have shown, an important trend in the early to mid-twentieth century advanced biology education was the emphasis on civic relevance and involvement, and this was the case for advanced health education as well (Pauly 2000; Engles 1991). Thus, students reading texts like George William Hunter's *A Civic Biology* (1914) would learn how biological knowledge could play a substantial role in modern life, whether by influencing national policies regarding eugenics or by inspiring local public health statutes on garbage and other nuisances; likewise, upper-level students who encountered J. Mace Andress's and I. H. Goldberger's *The Health School on Wheels* (1933) would follow a fictional class traveling by bus around the city of Brightville, learning the myriad ways in which health knowledge supported civic progress. In other words, while younger students were expected to make good personal health choices every day by following a prescribed list of health habits, older students were expected to use health knowledge to make good public health choices, as citizens and consumers.

Health textbooks and curricula in this era sought to put health education on a more "scientific" basis in other ways. In the 1910s and 1920s, well-baby clinics had made regular weighing and measuring of infants a central feature of efforts to monitor and assess child health (Brosco 2002; Meckel 1990). Health officials and educators, convinced that tracking child growth by monitoring gains in height and weight would help them find children with physical defects, poor health habits, or inadequate diets, instituted regular programs for assessing growth in the elementary classroom. Competitions within and between classrooms and schools urged children up "the Hill of Health" (a child-friendly depiction of the normal growth curve) or to attain the milestones that would make her a "five-point" child. This ritual of measuring weight and height and being concerned with their relations to a "healthy" norm would be one of the most lasting innovations of the early-twentieth-century classroom, as it formed a regular part of school health and physical education through the 1950s and, in many schools, through 1970s and after (Prescott 2002).

Even as they transformed classroom materials and practices, advocates of the new school health education also sought to transform school buildings, making them healthful places. While nineteenth-century reformers had been concerned with stale air, tiny typefaces, poor lighting, and unhygienic seating, their twentieth-century heirs hoped to apply bacteriological and environmental insights in the schoolhouse. For instance, well-to-do urban and suburban schools introduced hygienic water fountains to make it possible for children to do as their health texts said and "bite the bubble." In less fiscally flush districts, paper cups allowed students to follow hygienic dictates when they drank water at school. Health workers and nutrition advocates also pushed school systems to ensure that eating lunch was both healthy and pleasant by making the lunchroom a comfortable, clean space that provided good food, including safe and ample quantities of milk. (Students themselves were frequently urged by their textbooks and by curricular units to get involved in this transformation of the lunchroom.) School hygiene authorities, supported by the private Cleanliness Institute (an educational arm of the nation's soap manufacturers' association), sought to make the most basic hygiene rule of the microbiological age—wash your hands—possible in American schools. This was no easy feat, as it required schools to institute bathroom facilities that included hot running water, an ample supply of soap, sinks at appropriate heights, and paper towels, and to fund janitorial support that would keep these spaces clean (Tomes 1998; Hoy 1995; Vinikas 1992; Vollmer 1968).

The Cleanliness Institute's support for hand-washing facilities in schools was but one of many efforts by outside commercial organizations to get involved in health education. Starting in the 1920s, soap manufacturers, paper products marketers, and food companies all began to supply classroom materials and lesson plans that would augment the health textbook and provide the harried or untrained teacher with new classroom activities. But these commercial concerns' involvement in the classroom paled in comparison to that of the Metropolitan Life Insurance Company and the National Dairy Council. The Metropolitan's leaders, advised by school health and public health experts, considered an investment in the nation's health classrooms to be a civic duty that would also produce good public relations for the firm in the United States and Canada. Perhaps the most prominent of its programs was the *Health Heroes* pamphlets, a series of short biographies of Louis Pasteur, Florence Nightingale, and other famous scientists and health workers. Millions of these colorfully illustrated booklets were distributed to schools and teachers; reading, writing, and watching filmstrips about accomplishments of the "health heroes" became a standard part of health education for a great many American children of this era (Toon 1998). A group with a far more direct interest in the health habits of school children was the National Dairy Council (NDC), formed in the 1910s to promote the use of milk and with it the interests of dairy farmers and producers. The NDC joined with the U.S. Department of Agriculture to promote "milk for health" campaigns in American schools, and educators employed by the NDC wrote curricular materials encouraging ample milk consumption as part of a healthy lifestyle; portions of these materials would find their way into the interwar health curriculum through textbooks and other classroom materials (DuPuis 2002).

A final innovation in the early- to middle-twentieth-century school health curriculum was the formal introduction of sex education, albeit usually for older students and usually in very carefully phrased language (Moran 2000). Historians of the sex education movement have shown how, despite fervent support from leading biologists and some health workers, sex education met up with strong opposition in many school systems, sometimes from religious groups, sometimes from parents, and sometimes from civic leaders. Often information about sexual attitudes, development, and behavior was subsumed in a general discourse on the need for "control" as part of a healthy life. Just as children would learn that avoiding alcohol, tobacco, and narcotics was a matter of will and self-control, they would learn—albeit elliptically— that control of the body in other situations was imperative for social and economic success.

HEALTH AND WELL-BEING IN THE POSTWAR AMERICAN SCHOOL

By the 1950s, school health education in the United States had assumed the basic format that it retains today. In the early grades, health teaching is integrated into the general curriculum, although young students frequently read books or participate in activities specifically related to health. In the middle grades, daily or weekly periods may be set aside for health instruction; in the upper grades and in high school, health classes are often partnered with or alternate with physical education, safety and driver's education, and home economics. Since the 1950s, teachers of these upper level courses have been expected to have had official training in health instruction, and their work is frequently monitored by specialists in health education who serve local school districts and state school systems (Sliepcevich 1964).

Likewise, the subject matter of health education has gelled, as the essential outlook developed in the early and middle twentieth century has come to dominate textbooks, lesson plans, and activities. Postwar children learned (and continue to learn) that personal health is essential to social and economic success, that personal health results from daily choices, and that attaining health is mostly a matter of applying scientific knowledge to daily living. In keeping with the most up-to-date pedagogical theory and health education research, this message has been presented simply and often playfully in the lower grades, through colorful storybooks that talk about washing, eating, playing, and interacting. In the middle and upper grades, textbooks and classroom activities offer students a combination of scientific knowledge about the body and recommendations about social interaction.

Physical, social, and mental health are interrelated and inextricable, postwar children were and are told, and the person who hopes for success of any kind requires them all.

Yet health education in the postwar era continued to be responsive to larger policy needs and social concerns. For instance, fears about (as historian Robert Griswold has termed it) the "flabby American" motivated Cold War support for enhanced physical education programs, just as national fretting about American children's knowledge of math and science fostered the National Defense Education Act in the late 1950s. This support took visible form in the President's Council on Physical Fitness, introduced by the Eisenhower administration and supported and expanded by the Kennedy administration (Griswold 1998). Soon students in physical education classes throughout the nation were expected to take regular tests of strength, flexibility, and agility that—ideally—would spur them to seek and treasure physical fitness, benefiting both themselves and their country.

Postwar health educators also sought to enhance the social development of American children, by emphasizing mental hygiene and social adjustment. Units in textbooks, for instance, tried to teach high school students to adjust to the new social interactions they would encounter as young adults and to understand how family life influenced the development of individual personality. Mental health education in the postwar era tended to blend with its close cousin, "family life education," which included discussions of sexuality, reproduction, and adulthood (Moran 2000). A new educational technology, the film, was central to mental health and family life education. Films offered basic information about the body's reproductive physiology, sometimes in frank and plain language. Nevertheless, these films (and the textbooks they accompanied) maintained that it was vitally necessary for viewers to manage their sexual desires if they hoped to achieve healthy mental adjustment and social identity; they underscored these lessons by dramatizing the twin dangers of early sexual activity—physical disease and social embarrassment—for their viewers (Smith 1999). While many films shown in health classrooms were made by companies that specialized in educational films, some were the products of companies that hoped to promote their own products to a generation of consumers. The "menstrual education" film, for instance, became a coming-of-age ritual for American girls after World War II. Frequently made by companies that wished to market their "feminine hygiene products," these films portrayed menstruation as a personal and social milestone for the growing girl—but, as historians have noted, a marker of feminine adulthood ushered in by a new set of consumer behaviors (Brumberg 1997; Kennard 1989). Whether these films discussed the social and health benefits of good grooming or the management of physical transformation in the social milieu, these films often appear to our twenty-first-century eyes to be humorous and even dangerous mixes of gender stereotypes and conformist expectations, ripe for parody. We should remember, though, that the postwar health and educational authorities who encouraged and created these films saw them as a progressive educational strategy, one that emphasized social health as well as physical health and that could facilitate open discussion of children's and adolescents' concerns.

From the 1960s on, worries about adolescents' use of alcohol and drugs have propelled efforts to educate students about the dangers of substance abuse. In driving education classes, films like *The Last Prom* (1972) graphically illustrated the results of driving under the influence of alcohol. Biology and health classes, meanwhile, stressed the physical consequences of drug use for the brain and the body. By the middle 1980s, several organizations had revitalized the anti-drug crusade and sought to coordinate messages about drug use both inside and outside schools. In 1981, a Massachusetts high school student founded SADD (Students Against Driving Drunk), and chapters of SADD soon became fixtures at American high schools. SADD proceeded on a peer education model, working as an extracurricular group to sponsor alcohol-free alternatives to after-prom activities. A central feature of the SADD campaign was (and is) the "Contract for Life," where teens promise to call parents for help if intoxicated, and parents promise to give such help without immediate recriminations. By the late 1990s, SADD had decided to broaden its mandate and bring its peer and promise-focused approach to other teen concerns, and its acronym now stands for Students Against Destructive Decisions.

Other anti-drug initiatives that found their way into American classrooms and homes have sought to reach children at younger and younger ages, as their organizers argue that education about the dangers of drugs needs to take place before children have the opportunity to use drugs. In the 1980s, First Lady Nancy Reagan worked with anti-drug organizations to urge even elementary and middle-school children to "Just Say No." She even appeared on a 1983 episode of the popular sitcom *Diff'rent Strokes* to discuss the dangers of drug use. An approach used since the 1980s has been that of the organization DARE—its officers (local police officers trained by and using the group's curricula) visit schoolrooms to talk with young students about the dangers of drug use and about strategies for refusing drugs and alcohol. Unlike the peer-oriented approaches used by SADD and some classroom curricula, DARE seeks to change student behavior through authoritative guidance—albeit from an authority figure who is made friendly and accessible in the classroom. That authority is backed up by other school efforts to control drug use, such as drug testing for student athletes and others engaged in extracurricular activities.

CONCLUSION

Now, at the beginning of the twenty-first century, health education is expected to address a variety of social and political concerns, creating what critics sometimes argue is a not entirely coherent selection of important topics rather than a curriculum organized to develop a balanced interest in and knowledge of physical, social, and mental health. Myriad concerns and questions fall under the rubric of health education and populate the texts and curricula that teachers use in American classrooms: the individual as physical, mental, and social entity who is adapted and adapting to her environment; the body's physical structure and function, from the molecular to the organ system levels; social adjustment and sexuality; the physical and social dangers of alcohol, tobacco, illegal drugs, and firearms; consumer rights and responsibilities; and health careers. Of course, the health curricula tries to integrate the newest biomedical knowledge, with increasing discussions about how individual genetic makeup is related to health and disease, and about neuroscientific insights into behavioral health.

But contemporary initiatives to change children's health behavior share important continuities with past strategies, approaches, and assumptions. Consider, for instance, recent campaigns for physical exercise. Since the 1980s and especially since the middle 1990s, public health officials and physicians have expressed great concern about rapidly growing rates of obesity in the American population, particularly among children and teenagers. These concerns have motivated national attempts to teach children about the benefits of exercise, the dangers of a sedentary lifestyle, and the importance of healthy food choices. In the 1980s, the bodybuilder turned action movie star Arnold Schwarzenegger served as national representative for the President's Council on Physical Fitness, and set out to revitalize a media-savvy generation's interest in exercise, health, and strength. In the 1990s and early 2000s, Schwarzenegger continued to advocate fitness programs for youth through personal appearances and his website, and now, as governor of California, will likely continue such advocacy. Meanwhile, official public health agencies enlist the mass media in campaigns for physical activity—such as the Centers for Disease Control's "verb" campaign mentioned at the beginning of this essay. These campaigns, their supporters hope, can undergird "official" health education provided in the classroom and the gymnasium, and simultaneously counteract the advertising for junk food, fast food, and sedentary recreation, such as video games, offered on the same television channels. Some activists and experts have connected the health woes of American youth to the influence of outside commercial groups in the school and the classroom. Leading nutrition scientists, for example, criticize the use of industry-sponsored (and thus, they argue, presumably biased) materials about food and nutrition in the health curriculum (Nestle 2002). These scientists, together with political critics of the "commercialization" of American schools, also worry that the presence of junk-food vending machines, fast food in the school cafeteria, and exclusive contracts with soft-drink companies all undermine the lessons health classes are meant to teach (Klein 2000; U.S. General Accounting Office 2000). Who will ultimately determine what children eat—or at least how and what children *learn* about what they should eat? Is this an issue for national policy makers, local school boards, health education experts, or individual families to decide?

The same questions arise with regard to school-based sexuality education, as vocal proponents of alternative approaches battle to change what American children think and do regarding sex, each group claiming that it should rightfully control what children learn about sex, sexuality, and health. In the 1980s, amid the AIDS epidemic and increases in teenage pregnancy, policy makers, educators, health authorities, and parents agreed that American school children needed education about sex. What form that education should take, however, was a contentious topic (Moran 2000). In some school districts, an approach known as "comprehensive" sex education reigns—teachers and sex education curriculum specialists try to offer positive messages about sexuality alongside relatively complete information on contraceptives, disease prevention, and management of peer pressure around sexual behavior. Perhaps the most famous icon of comprehensive sex education is the condom-on-the-banana demonstration, intended to make students knowledgeable about and comfortable with condom use—and satirized in the Drew Barrymore back-to-high-school film *Never Been Kissed* (1999). The great majority of schools, however, provide "abstinence only" or "abstinence plus" sex education. Abstinence-only curricula teach that abstinence until marriage is the only certain way for children and young adults to avoid disease, pregnancy, and social and emotional maladjustment due to early sexual activity; abstinence-plus curricula present abstinence until marriage as by far the safest sexual option but also provide some information on contraceptives and disease prevention methods for the sexually active teen. Abstinence-only programs have been adopted by a substantial number of school districts—as many as one in four, according to one mid-1990s estimate (Cooper 1994, 34). *Sex Respect*, developed by Catholic schoolteacher Coleen Kelly Mast, is perhaps the best known and most widely adopted of the abstinence-only curricula. The controversy over which form of sex education is best at preventing disease and teen pregnancy continues to rage in the national media and in the political arena, as diverse groups each claim responsibility for shepherding children towards healthy social, psychological, and sexual lives. As during the previous two centuries of efforts to teach children to manage their bodies, sex education curricula are and will continue to be the product of intense negotiation among state, professional, educational, religious, and private interest groups. Perhaps what we learn from the history of American children's health education, and what we should remember as we study current practices, is that in their efforts to teach children about health, American adults have articulated with particular clarity their hopes and fears for the nation's future.

NOTE

1. The WCTU's *Hygiene for Young People: Adapted to Intermediate Classes and Common Schools* (New York: A.S. Barnes and Company, 1885), is available online, along with other volumes from the John Nietz Old Textbook Collection made available by the University of Pittsburgh's Digital Research Library (digital.library.pitt.edu/nietz/index.html).

WORKS CITED

Andress, J. Mace. 1925. *Health Education in Rural Schools.* Rev. ed. Boston: Houghton Mifflin.

Baker, S. Josephine. 1939/1980. *Fighting for Life.* New York: Macmillan; Huntington, N.Y.: Robert E. Krieger.

Brosco, Jeffrey P. 2002. "Weight Charts and Well Child Care: When the Pediatrician became the Expert in Child Health." In *Formative Years: Children's Health in the United States, 1880–2000.* Edited by Alexandra Minna Stern and Howard Markel, 91–120. Ann Arbor: University of Michigan Press.

Brumberg, Joan Jacobs. 1997. *The Body Project: An Intimate History of American Girls.* New York: Random House.

Buhler-Wilkerson, Karen. 1989. *False Dawn: The Rise and Decline of Public Health Nursing, 1900–1930.* New York: Garland.

Conrad, Howard L., and Joseph F. Meister. 1939. *Teaching Procedures in Health Education.* Philadelphia: W. B. Saunders.

Cooper, Marc. 1994. "Chastity 101." *Village Voice,* June 7.

Cremin, Lawrence A. 1988. *American Education: The Metropolitan Experience, 1876–1980.* New York: Harper & Row.

Cuban, Larry. 1993. *How Teachers Taught: Constancy and Change in American Classrooms, 1880–1990.* 2nd ed. New York: Teachers College Press.

Duffy, John. 1979. "School Buildings and the Health of American School Children in the Nineteenth Century." In *Healing and History: Essays for George Rosen.* Edited by Charles E. Rosenberg, 161–78. New York: Science History.

DuPuis, E. Melanie. 2002. *Nature's Perfect Food: How Milk Became America's Drink.* New York: New York University Press.

Engles, Eric W. 1991. "Biology Education in the Public High Schools of the United States from the Progressive Era to the Second World War: A Discursive History." Ph.D. dissertation, University of California at Santa Cruz.

Green, Harvey. 1986. *Fit for America: Health, Fitness, Sport, and American Society.* New York: Pantheon.

Griswold, Robert L. 1998. "The 'Flabby American,' the Body, and the Cold War." In *A Shared Experience: Men, Women, and the History of Gender.* Edited by Laura McCall and Donald Yacovone, 323–48. New York: New York University Press.

Hackensmith, C. W. 1966. *History of Physical Education.* New York: Harper & Row.

Hoy, Suellen. 1995. *Chasing Dirt: The American Pursuit of Cleanliness.* New York: Oxford University Press.

Hunter, George William. 1914. *A Civic Biology: Presented in Problems.* New York: American Book.

Hutchinson, John F. 1997. "The Junior Red Cross Goes to Healthland." *American Journal of Public Health* 87 (1997): 1816–23.

Keeney, Elizabeth. 1992. *The Botanizers: Amateur Scientists in Nineteenth-Century America.* Chapel Hill: University of North Carolina Press.

Kennard, Margot E. 1989. "The Corporation in the Classroom: The Struggles over Meanings of Menstrual Education in Sponsored Films, 1947–1983." Ph.D. dissertation, University of Wisconsin–Madison.

Klaus, Alisa. 1993. *Every Child a Lion: The Origins of Maternal and Infant Health Policy in the United States and France, 1890–1920.* Ithaca, N.Y.: Cornell University Press.

Klein, Naomi. 2000. *No Logo: No Space, No Choice, No Jobs.* Toronto, Canada: Alfred A. Knopf.

Kliebard, Herbert M. 1995. *The Struggle for the American Curriculum, 1893–1958.* 2nd ed. New York: Routledge.

Kraut, Alan M. 1994. *Silent Travelers: Germs, Genes, and the "Immigrant Menace."* Baltimore: Johns Hopkins University Press.

Ladd-Taylor, Molly. 1986. *Raising a Baby the Government Way: Mothers' Letters to the Children's Bureau, 1915–1932.* New Brunswick, N.J.: Rutgers University Press.

Levenstein, Harvey A. 1988. *Revolution at the Table: The Transformation of the American Diet.* New York and Oxford: Oxford University Press.

Link, William A. 1992. *The Paradox of Southern Progressivism, 1880–1930.* Chapel Hill: University of North Carolina Press.

Mann, Horace. 1843. "Sixth Annual Report of the Secretary of the Board of Education." *Sixth Annual Report of the Board of Education Together with the Sixth Annual Report of the Secretary of the Board.* Boston: Dutton and Wentworth.

Means, Richard K. 1962. *A History of Health Education in the United States.* Philadelphia: Lea and Febiger.

Meckel, Richard A. 1990. *Save the Babies: American Public Health Reform and the Prevention of Infant Mortality, 1850–1929.* Baltimore: Johns Hopkins University Press.

———. 2002. "Going to School, Getting Sick: The Social and Medical Construction of School Diseases in the Late Nineteenth Century." In *Formative Years: Children's Health in the United States, 1880–2000.* Edited by Alexandra Minna Stern and Howard Markel, 185–207. Ann Arbor: University of Michigan Press.

Miller, Susan A. 2001. "Girls in Nature/the Nature of Girls: Transforming Female Adolescence at Summer Camp, 1900–1939." Ph.D. dissertation, University of Pennsylvania.

Moran, Jeffrey P. 2000. *Teaching Sex: The Shaping of Adolescence in the 20th Century.* Cambridge, Mass.: Harvard University Press.

Muncy, Robyn. 1991. *Creating a Female Dominion in Reform.* New York: Oxford University Press.

Murphy, Lamar Riley. 1991. *Enter the Physician: The Transformation of Domestic Medicine.* Tuscaloosa: University of Alabama Press.

Nestle, Marion. 2002. *Food Politics: How the Food Industry Influences Nutrition and Health.* Berkeley: University of California Press.

Park, Roberta J. 1989. "Healthy, Moral, and Strong: Educational Views of Exercise and Athletics in Nineteenth-Century America." In *Fitness in American Culture: Images of Health, Sport, and the Body, 1830–1940.* Edited by Kathryn Grover, 123–

68. Amherst: University of Massachusetts Press; Rochester: Margaret Wood-bury Strong Museum.

Pauly, Philip J. 2000. *Biologists and the Promise of American Life: From Meriwether Lewis to Alfred Kinsey.* Princeton, N.J.: Princeton University Press.

Prescott, Heather Munro. 2002. "'I Was a Teenage Dwarf': The Social Construction of 'Normal' Adolescent Growth and Development in the United States." In *Formative Years: Children's Health in the United States, 1880–2000.* Edited by Alexandra Minna Stern and Howard Markel, 153–84. Ann Arbor: University of Michigan Press.

Rosenberg, Charles E. 1995. "Catechisms of Health: The Body in the Prebellum Classroom." *Bulletin of the History of Medicine* 69: 175–97.

Sliepcevich, Elena M. 1964. *School Health Education Study, 1961–1963: Summary Report of a Nationwide Study of Health Instruction in the Public Schools.* New York City: Samuel Bronfman Foundation; Washington, D.C.: School Health Education Study.

Smith, Ken. 1999. *Mental Hygiene: Classroom Films, 1945–1970.* New York: Blast Books.

Teller, Michael E. 1988. *The Tuberculosis Movement: A Public Campaign in the Progressive Era.* New York: Greenwood.

Tomes, Nancy. 1998. *The Gospel of Germs: Men, Women, and the Microbe in American Life.* Cambridge, Mass.: Harvard University Press.

Toon, Elizabeth. 1998. "Managing the Conduct of the Individual Life: Public Health Education and American Public Health, 1910–1940." Ph.D. dissertation, University of Pennsylvania.

Tyack, David, and Elisabeth Hansot. 1990. *Learning Together: A History of Coeducation in American Schools.* New Haven, Conn.: Yale University Press; New York: Russell Sage Foundation.

U.S. Department of the Interior, Bureau of Education. 1923. "Health for School Children: Report of the Advisory Committee on Health Education of the National Child Health Council." *School Health Studies,* no. 1. Washington, D.C.: U.S. Government Printing Office.

U.S. General Accounting Office. 2000. *Commercial Activities in Schools: Report to Congressional Requesters.* Washington, D.C.: U.S. Government Printing Office.

Verbrugge, Martha H. 1988. *Able-Bodied Womanhood: Personal Health and Social Change in Nineteenth-Century Boston.* New York and Oxford: Oxford University Press.

Vinikas, Vincent. 1992. *Soft Soap, Hard Sell: American Hygiene in an Age of Advertisement.* Ames: Iowa State University Press.

Vollmer, Marguerite. 1968. "Sally Lucas Jean: Her Contribution to Health Education." Ed.D. dissertation, Columbia University.

Whorton, James C. 1982. *Crusaders for Fitness: The History of American Health Reformers.* Princeton, N.J.: Princeton University Press.

Wood, Thomas Denison. 1910. *Health and Education: Ninth Yearbook of the National Society for the Study of Education.* Part 1. Bloomington, Ill.: Public School Publishing.

Zilversmit, Arthur. 1993. *Changing Schools: Progressive Education Theory and Practice, 1930–1960.* Chicago: University of Chicago Press.

Zimmerman, Jonathan. 1999. *Distilling Democracy: Alcohol Education in America's Public Schools, 1880–1925.* Lawrence: University of Kansas Press.

6 The Federal Government and Child Health

Kriste Lindenmeyer

Stories of parents mourning the deaths of children are found in every family's history. In many parts of the world childhood remains a very dangerous time of life. This was true in the United States for most of American history. Nonetheless, by the mid-nineteenth century, new medical advances had shown that high infant and child mortality rates were not inevitable facts of life. Private charities stepped in to help with medical care for pregnant mothers, pure-milk stations, and child health clinics, but there was no comprehensive federal effort to save children's lives. Responding to progressive reformers' calls to "conserve" the nation's children, Congress established the U.S. Children's Bureau in 1912. The bureau was directed to "investigate and report . . . upon all matters pertaining to the welfare of children and child life among all classes of our people" (37 *Statutes at Large*, 79). This mandate made the Children's Bureau the first national agency in the world to focus solely on the interests of a nation's youngest citizens. President William Howard Taft named Julia Lathrop the new agency's first chief (Muncy 1991; Lindenmeyer 1997). Lathrop was the daughter of Illinois Republican congressman William Lathrop and a Rockford Seminary (later renamed Rockford College) graduate, Sarah Adeline Potter Lathrop. Like her mother and a growing number of middle-class females of the post–Civil War generation, Julia Lathrop attended college and chose a career over marriage. She went to Rockford Seminary for a year and then Vassar College, where she graduated in 1880. Lathrop returned to Illinois after graduation and worked for ten years as a secretary in her father's law office. In 1890 she moved to Chicago's Hull House settlement and began a social work career. Lathrop remained at Hull House until her appointment as chief of the Children's Bureau in 1912 (James et al. 1971).

Lathrop was excited but also overwhelmed by her appointment. Congress had authorized a broad mandate, embracing a wide range of issues that touched children's lives. After consulting with supporters, Lathrop decided to direct the bureau's earliest work toward discovering how and why babies died. Protecting life and maintaining good health seemed be the first rights of childhood. The choice was important. Americans were concerned but naïve about how to improve child health and save lives. The early work of the Children's Bureau established a blueprint for implementing federal child health policies throughout the twentieth century and beyond (Muncy 1991).

THE STATE STEPS IN: SAVING BABIES IN THE LATE NINETEENTH AND EARLY TWENTIETH CENTURIES

During the Gilded Age and Progressive era, rising immigration rates and longer average life expectancy combined to swell the U.S. population, from 31.4 million in 1860 to 105.7 million in 1920 (Census Bureau 1976). In addition, a shift from farm to factory within the country spurred dramatic social and economic changes. One result was a new national emphasis on childhood as a special time of life, separate from the responsibilities of adulthood. A more abundant food supply, improved diet, and advances in medical treatment helped an increasing percentage of children survive or avoid the dangers of childhood diseases. As early death diminished, a growing number of couples, especially those in the expanding urban middle class, chose to have fewer offspring and focus more attention on their children's psychological and physical needs. Public education expanded and became a more important means for raising socioeconomic status. In general, young people spent more time in school than their parents had. The value of children was no longer rooted in the labor they could provide on the family farm. Instead, it shifted toward sentimentality and the long-term opportunities a well-educated child could provide for raising a family's socioeconomic status (sons through employment, daughters through marriage) (Zelizer 1985; Illick 2002). The move to a more urban America seemed to suggest a bright future for children.

Nonetheless, not everything about the shift was progress. Overcrowded cities infested with crime, disease, and violence highlighted the harmful effects of rapid and unregulated urbanization. By 1900, calls for "progressive reform" were springing from the nation's cities, and government regulation promoting "order" became a political trend permeating American life (Wiebe 1967). For example, social-purity campaigns advocated the passage of laws to stop the sale and manufacture of alcohol, eliminate prostitution, and outlaw gambling. Club women called for "municipal housekeeping" to clean up political and economic corruption in the nation's cities. Women's suffrage activists maintained that granting women the right to vote would curb the aggressive nature of men by creating a more moral and equitable

America (Muncy 1991). Conservationists demanded regulation of the nation's limited natural resources (Hays 1959/1999). Physicians standardized medical education while defining a larger role for government in promoting good public sanitation (Starr 1982). To many Progressives, the negative consequences of unregulated urbanization, poverty, hunger, disease, and despair seemed to hit children the hardest (Bremner 1956; Wiebe 1967).

Protecting children became one of the most popular aspects of the late nineteenth and early twentieth centuries' widening reform agenda. Muckraking journalist Jacob Riis argued in his 1890 condemnation of New York City's tenement districts, *How the Other Half Lives,* that "the problem of the children [was enough] to make one stand aghast." He maintained that "nothing is now better understood than that in the rescue of children is the key to the problem of city poverty" (Riis 1890/1957). Infant mortality rates became the standard for measuring children's general welfare. Nevertheless, there was no reliable data on the topic. To the surprise of many, experts argued that unlike its effect on life expectancy among adults, modernization actually lessened an infant's chances of survival. In Massachusetts, where state statistics had been kept since 1851, urbanization paralleled rising infant mortality rates. From 1851 to 1854 131.1 babies in Massachusetts died for every thousand live births. From 1895 to 1899 the rate was almost 17 percent higher, with 153.2 infants per thousand live births dying before reaching one year of age. Extrapolated to a national rate, this meant that approximately 15–20 percent of all infants born in the United States from 1860 to 1900 died before reaching their first birthdays. In other words, one in every five babies died in the world's most democratic and industrial country, a rate higher than that of almost any other modern nation (Meckel 1990; Lindenmeyer 1997).

Professional medical societies had begun to focus on the problem of high infant mortality during the 1880s. The American Medical Association (or AMA, created in 1847) established a pediatric section in 1880 to focus exclusively on infant deaths and children's overall health. Nine years later the pediatric section became the autonomous American Pediatric Society (APS), a vocal advocate for reforms directed at helping children. The APS noted that infant mortality rates were especially high during the warm summer months, when thousands of babies died from "summer diarrhea," an intestinal infection caused by drinking contaminated milk. Milk for babies and children had been a concern for health officials since the 1830s. Municipal health officials recognized the nutritional problems associated with feeding "swill milk" to babies. Swill milk was nutrient poor because it came from cows fed on brewery slops (an inexpensive by-product of brewing beer). Health officials hoped that the expansion of railroads would make high-quality cow's milk more readily available to urban families. By the 1880s, however, it had become clear that many commercial dairies producing the ostensibly higher-quality milk failed to follow good sanitation practices. Although scientific knowledge about the advantages of pasteurization was well known, milk was often prepared for distribution at temperatures too low to destroy unhealthy bacteria. Contaminated storage containers and unreliable refrigeration methods added to the problem. But above all, even if safe to drink, most commercial cow's milk was too expensive for many urban working-class parents. In response, late-nineteenth-century municipal health officials, private physicians, and charities combined to establish "milk funds" that distributed safe and affordable milk for babies and children. Milk fund programs often expanded to include physician-controlled health clinics. The success of these efforts showed that clean milk and preventive medicine could save children's lives, but these private charities did not reach everyone who needed them (Meckel 1990).

The federal and state governments were slow to act, despite evidence showing the need for a broad-based program to improve children's health. Some states established health departments, but their services were limited by small budgets. At the federal level, the U.S. Public Health Service (PHS) failed to develop programs directed at preventing infant mortality or improving children's health. As child welfare activist Florence Kelley complained to her close friend Lillian D. Wald in 1903, "If lobsters or young salmon become scarce or are in danger of perishing, the United States Fish Commission takes active steps in the matter. But infant mortality continues excessive, from generation to generation. . . . [Y]et not one organ of the national government is interested" (Bradbury 1956).

ESTABLISHING THE U.S. CHILDREN'S BUREAU

Kelley and Wald were important activists in the national child welfare movement. Kelley wrote a book, *Some Ethical Gains through Legislation* (1905/ 1969), in which she proposed the establishment of a federal children's bureau. Wald was a public health nurse and founder of New York's Henry Street settlement. Her work included a public nursing program designed to lower infant mortality and improve child health. Kelley and Wald enlisted support for the idea of a federal children's bureau from the National Child Labor Committee (incorporated in 1906), APS physicians, public health officials, social workers, and women's clubs. The times were ripe for child welfare–reform ideas. Such efforts are never immediately enacted at the federal level; nonetheless, in 1909, after enthusiastic lobbying from a variety of sources, President Theodore Roosevelt sponsored the first White House Conference on Children. Meeting participants endorsed the idea of a Children's Bureau. After three more years of lobbying, Congress passed and President Taft signed legislation establishing the U.S. Children's Bureau in the Department of Commerce and Labor (the Department of Labor was created as a separate agency the next year, and the Children's Bureau fell under its jurisdiction). Taft named Julia Lathrop as the new agency's head in recognition of the important role women had played in lobbying for the bureau's establishment (Muncy 1991; Lindenmeyer 1997).

Lathrop quickly set to work, although she realized the new agency's effectiveness was limited by a small budget of only $25,640. In addition, there were critics who argued that the Children's Bureau overreached federal authority. Others felt that the new agency duplicated responsibilities already given to the PHS. Lathrop cleverly concluded that helping to reduce the nation's abominable infant mortality rate should be the agency's first priority. Baby-kissing politicians found it almost impossible to criticize plans designed to save babies' lives, and PHS officials, influenced by physicians associated with the APS, supported the Children's Bureau's program.

The Children's Bureau used data to embarrass Americans into action. Lathrop's staff estimated that an infant mortality rate of 131 deaths per thousand live births placed the United States behind New Zealand (83), Norway (94), Ireland (99), Sweden (104), Australia (108), Bulgaria (120), and Scotland (123). "The mere business of being a baby in the United States," Lathrop noted in the agency's first annual report, "must be classified as an extra-hazardous occupation." Data from the U.S. Census Bureau confirmed that adults seventy-five to eighty-four years old had a better chance of surviving to their next birthdays than did newborns. Making matters worse, argued Lathrop, children who "weathered the storms of the first year" grew up "in a battered, weakened, and crippled condition." Using language familiar to Progressive conservationists and efficiency advocates, the U.S. Children's Bureau denounced the nation's high rates of infant mortality and child morbidity as an immoral waste of national resources (Muncy 1991; Lindenmeyer 1997).

Lathrop argued for two major strategies to combat the problem: federally mandated birth certificates and detailed "scientific" studies to understand how and why babies died. Death certificates were already mandated by law. Matching death certificates with mandatory birth registration would help health officials to identify trends where preventive care might save children's lives. In addition, birth certificates would help to identify newborns, so that local health departments could send visiting nurses to instruct new mothers in the most modern techniques of well-baby care. Visiting nurses could also administer silver nitrate to the eyes of newborns, a preventive technique used to kill gonorrheal infections contracted by babies during delivery from infected mothers. Gonorrheal infection was the most common, and preventable, form of blindness in children.

Lathrop's second strategy focused on "scientific investigation." With a small staff of only fifteen it was impossible for the Children's Bureau to undertake a national infant mortality study. Instead, on January 15, 1913, four Children's Bureau "special field agents" arrived in Johnstown, Pennsylvania, a "typical" urban community, to conduct a scientific study of infant births and deaths. The work took 349 days and established the model for later child health investigations. The four bureau field agents assisted by volunteers from local women's clubs interviewed the mothers of 1,551 of the 1,931 babies born in Johnstown during 1911 (they were unable to locate 361 of the children or their mothers).

The Johnstown study was the first comprehensive examination of infant mortality conducted in the United States. Its results pointed to specific problems and their possible solutions. The fact that Children's Bureau's staff comprised trained social workers but no physicians led the agency to avoid medical questions. Investigators inquired about social conditions such as "income, ethnicity, the mother's maternal history and age, parentage, and environmental conditions" that might put babies at risk. In order to encourage full cooperation among Johnstown mothers, interviewers also avoided questions about venereal disease and alcoholism; such topics were deemed "personally humiliating."

The study's results underscored the important relationship between social conditions, access to medical care, and babies' deaths. Johnstown's infant mortality rate of 134 deaths per thousand live births was close to the estimated national average. Children of native-born mothers survived at a much higher rate (104.3 deaths per thousand) than those of foreign-born mothers (171.3). Other important factors included whether the mother was literate, her age, length of recovery, outside employment, marital status, and reproductive history. Uneducated women tended to live in the poorest households and in the most unsanitary conditions. Recent immigrants and poorly educated mothers were the most likely to report working long hours at low wages, a history of multiple pregnancies, and the deaths of other children. One mother, age thirty, told of "11 pregnancies in 12 years; all live born; [but] 5 died [within their] first year." Babies whose fathers' earned the lowest wages were more than twice as likely to die as those in the most prosperous households. Infants whose fathers earned less than $625 per year died at a rate of 213.5 per thousand, but babies with father's incomes of over $900 died at rates of 96.8, less than half that of the poorer families. Children born to women without husbands, no matter what their household income, had infant mortality rates twice that of married mothers (281.3 and 103.7, respectively). The social stigma directed at unmarried mothers clearly contributed to this circumstance. But poverty and its associated conditions, including inadequate access to medical care, were the most important factors threatening babies' lives (Duke 1915; Lindenmeyer 1997).

The study's conclusions placed the major responsibility for saving babies on mothers and their communities. To help, the Children's Bureau published instructional pamphlets directed at mothers and urged state and local authorities to improve public sanitation. Bureau publications like *Prenatal Care* and *Infant Care* offered practical advice to women, but some recommendations were impractical. The bureau encouraged pregnant women to seek

medical care from private physicians, eat a balanced diet, engage in moderate exercise, get plenty of rest, breast-feed, and hire a nurse for two or
three days after delivery. Obviously, many poor women could not afford all
of these recommendations without assistance. The Children's Bureau also
advised couples to have only as many children as the father's income alone
would allow, in order that the wife could be a full-time mother, able "to conserve her strength for her family"(West 1914/1915). This attention to the
mother's health and income status as significant for a baby's survival was progressive for the time. But the agency never described how to avoid having
unwanted children by endorsing the use of birth control. It also failed to
call for government-funded maternal benefits, a program being established
at the time in many European countries. Instead, the Children's Bureau simply recommended higher wages for fathers so that mothers could stay out
of the wage-labor force, and paid even this limited attention to the redistri-
bution of wealth for only a brief time. Despite its lack of aggressive calls for
social and economic change, as well as its failure to endorse birth control,
women welcomed Children's Bureau advice, coming at a time when there
were few other sources of reliable information about pregnancy, childbirth,
or protecting children's health.

The bureau's popular publications and Lathrop's continued reliance on
an army of female volunteers was a clever strategy that fostered growing
popular support for the Children's Bureau. In response, Congress granted
the bureau larger appropriations, although the amounts remained small in
comparison to other constituent-based federal agencies. As the United States
entered World War I, President Woodrow Wilson gave the Children's Bureau
an additional $150,000 from a special wartime defense fund to implement
the Children's Year program. The effort was designed at least to maintain,
if not improve, the conditions for American children despite entrance into
the Great War. Through Children's Year the bureau distributed more than
6,500,000 weighing-and-measuring cards to public health officials. The cards
were used at diagnostic clinics to record the height and weight of children
six years of age and under. The cards could then help identify children with
rickets (deformed bones caused by a lack of vitamin D), tuberculosis (an air-
borne contagion), and other treatable medical problems. Consistent with
the bureau policies, ill children were referred to private physicians for medical care.

Though a useful endeavor, the Children's Year program had some down-
sides. It implemented standards that did not always fit the needs of individual
children. Even more important, the Children's Year program's emphasis on
physician-administered medical care ignored the inability of many low-
income parents to pay for such services. This aspect also overlooked the
negative social conditions of poverty that the agency had recognized earlier
in its Johnstown study. Apparently Lathrop had learned from experience that
even children's issues could cause controversy. Since the agency's early

attention to infant mortality had proved so popular, beginning in late 1915 she had added calls for child-labor reform to the Children's Bureau's agenda. But this topic faced difficult fights in Congress, the press, and in the courts. By 1918 Lathrop had refocused the Children's Bureau's attention on infant mortality, well-baby care, and the promotion of physician-administered medicine. Besides, it seemed that effort was working. By 1920 infant mortality rates had fallen from the bureau's 1913 estimate of 131 per thousand live births to 85.8. Saving babies' lives through the education of mothers and promotion of physician administered care seemed to face little political opposition and produce measurable results (Meckel 1990; Muncy 1991; Lindenmeyer 1997).

THE SHEPPARD-TOWNER MATERNITY AND INFANCY ACT

Encouraged by the success and popularity of the agency's early work, Lathrop and her supporters envisioned a permanent federal program focused on saving the lives of babies and improving the overall health of America's children. This vision relied on federal funding matched by the states, the standardization of medical care and of referrals to private physicians for care, public sanitation standards enforced by state health departments, and the education of mothers about the importance of prenatal care and preventive medicine for children.

Ratification of women's suffrage through the Nineteenth Amendment in 1920 led many politicians to favor proposals that they believed appealed to women voters. The Children's Bureau's call for a permanent maternal and child health program fit this category. Passage of the Sheppard-Towner Maternity and Infancy Act signaled this new, albeit short-lived, political atmosphere. It was sponsored by Senator Morris Sheppard (D-Texas) and Representative Horace Mann Towner (R-Iowa); President Warren G. Harding signed the act into law on November 23, 1921. This pioneering legislation provided an annual federal appropriation of $1,240,000 for a national education and diagnostic program designed to reduce infant and maternal mortality, with the added benefit of improving children's overall health. Congress gave the U.S. Children's Bureau authority to administer the law. Each state could apply for an outright grant of five thousand, with an additional five thousand available to state legislatures that approved matching funds (Lemons 1973; Muncy 1991; Lindenmeyer 1997).

Lathrop envisioned the program as only a first step in promoting good health care for the nation's children. Confident that the 1921 passage of Sheppard-Towner showed that government policy was moving in the right direction, Lathrop announced her retirement. She chose a successor who, she believed, would continue her agenda. Grace Abbott had just the right credentials. She had worked at Hull House from 1912 to 1917 and had a master's degree in political science from the University of Chicago. During late 1918 and early 1919 she had traveled with Lathrop to Europe to invite representatives from allied nations to Washington's second White House Conference on Children. When Abbott became chief, she made Sheppard-Towner the Children's Bureau's first priority. From 1922 to 1929 Sheppard-Towner funds supported a total of 183,252 health conferences for mothers and babies. It also helped finance the establishment of 2,978 permanent diagnostic clinics and paid for 19,723 classes for mothers, midwives, teachers, and adolescent girls. Diagnostic clinics were often held in local schools, making health exams available to a wide range of American children. The Children's Bureau also distributed 21,030,489 pieces of instructional literature. State annual reports revealed that from 1925 to 1929 approximately four million infants and preschool children and seven hundred thousand women benefited from some part of the Sheppard-Towner program. Women's groups, state public health officials, and the general public praised Sheppard-Towner as one of the most successful government efforts in U.S. history. During its existence, only three states—Connecticut, Illinois, and Massachusetts—refused Sheppard-Towner funds (Meckel 1990; Patel and Rushefsky, 1931; Muncy 1991; Lindenmeyer 1997).

Despite Sheppard-Towner's popularity and its at least limited focus on education and diagnosis, the political atmosphere in Washington changed during the 1920s in three important ways that eventually spelled the death of the program. First, it had become clear by the mid-1920s that women were not voting at the same proportions as men and that they were not voting as a bloc for "women's issues." As a result, male politicians no longer felt obligated to support programs identified as "women's issues." Second, a renewed wave of anti-Catholicism rose during the 1920s, sending shivers through the American Roman Catholic Church. In this atmosphere the church feared that any government-sponsored health efforts directed at mothers and children might encourage the use of birth control (against Catholic theology) or interfere with the operation of parochial schools. Third, the American Medical Association (AMA) labeled Sheppard-Towner "socialized medicine" and called for its termination, or at least its transfer to the AMA-controlled Public Health Service. Despite the fact that the Children's Bureau had named a physician to its staff in 1915 (Grace Meigs, MD), the AMA criticized the agency as a group of "lay women" with no medical training. This criticism also ignored the facts that many AMA member physicians were employed in diagnostic clinics funded by Sheppard-Towner and that the clinics sent mothers and children to private physicians for medical care. The AMA criticisms rested on prejudice against women physicians, female social workers, and fears that the United States would nationalize its health care system as other Western nations had. In this political atmosphere, Congress allowed Sheppard-Towner to expire in 1929 (Lemons 1973; Meckel 1990; Muncy 1991; Lindenmeyer 1997).

Was the Sheppard-Towner Maternity and Infancy Act a success? In 1921 the U.S. infant mortality rate was 75.6 per thousand live births. By 1929 the rate had fallen to 67.9, although the maternal mortality rate did not markedly change (68.2 versus 69.5). While it is not clear how much credit the Children's Bureau can take for the positive changes, it is clear that the Sheppard-Towner program's emphasis on the promotion of good medical care for mothers and babies encouraged greater public awareness and higher state expenditures for such efforts. For the U.S. Children's Bureau the program was what historian Richard Meckel has called in his 1990 book *Save the Babies: American Public Health Reform and the Prevention of Infant Mortality, 1850–1929* "a defeat in victory" (Meckel 1990).

THE GREAT DEPRESSION AND CHILD HEALTH

Herbert Hoover's election to the presidency in 1928 gave the U.S. Children's Bureau and its supporters hope for a renewed federal child health effort. Hoover's past suggested that he would support combined federal, state, and private sector roles in protecting children's health. He had earned credentials as a humanitarian by serving as head of the Commission for Relief in Belgium following World War I and as president of the American Child Health Association in 1921. Republican campaign literature called Hoover "the greatest of humanitarians . . . [and a] benefactor of children." Edith Abbott, a prominent child welfare activist and sister of the Children's Bureau's chief, Grace Abbott, could "hardly believe that anything as good as Herbert Hoover in the White House can come to pass. . . . It is like rubbing the lamp." Former Children's Bureau chief Julia Lathrop agreed: "He is [by] far the greatest man in the Republican ranks & one of the ablest men on the planet" (Lindenmeyer 1997).

But not long after the election, female reformers like Grace Abbott came to a very different conclusion about Hoover. Abbott's new attitude reflected the growing divisions in the federal government over child health issues. Hoover's choice of Ray Lyman Wilbur, MD, as Secretary of Interior signaled the change. Wilbur was a close friend and confident to Hoover. A former president of the AMA, Wilbur believed that *all* federal health efforts should be consolidated under the authority of the PHS. He had the support of many physicians, especially those associated with the AMA, and policy strategists who rejected the Children's Bureau's claim that a single agency could best meet the diverse needs of children. During the 1930 White House Conference on Children, Wilbur and Abbott engaged in a vicious philosophical turf war over children's health responsibilities. Abbott and her supporters successfully resisted Wilbur's move to relocate all health efforts for children in the PHS, but the very public debate weakened the Children's Bureau claim over children's health (Starr 1982; Muncy 1991; Lindenmeyer 1997).

Although the Great Depression was worsening during his presidency, Hoover refused to endorse a program of direct government aid for children and their families. Abbott and her supporters considered this another betrayal of children by the administration. Hoover feared that giving direct government aid to families would make individuals forever dependent on government handouts, and thereby weaken the very character of Americans. He also argued that putting the government in debt would only worsen the depression. Instead of governmental assistance, the president called for "voluntarism." In a December 9, 1931, address to Congress, Hoover ignored data collected by his own staff showing a rise in malnutrition and suffering among Americans. Instead he stated figures from the PHS showing "an actual decrease of sickness and infant and general mortality below normal years." The president contended that the PHS data offered no "greater proof . . . that our people have been protected from hunger and cold." Even as the depression worsened, Hoover's misguided optimism continued. It is true that the nation's infant mortality rate was reduced to 57.6 in 1932, but, as the Children's Bureau and the APS noted, it took time for the negative consequences of unemployment and malnutrition to manifest in infant mortality statistics. In other words, dying babies and poor child health would be increasingly common as the nation's unemployment rate rose to 25 percent (Lindenmeyer 1997).

In February 1932, Senator Robert M. La Follette (R-Wisc.) provided Congress with a Children's Bureau report examining the effects of the poor economy on children's overall well-being. Among a myriad of problems, malnutrition was a serious health issue and one that had "increased over the past year." The National Organization for Public Health Nursing maintained that requests for public health care services had risen at the same time communities faced shrinking resources. "Although demands on public-health nurses had increased enormously during the past two years, 41 percent of the agencies suffered reduction, 33 percent are operating on the same budgets, [and only] 25 percent have had increases" (Bremner 1971; Lindenmeyer 1997). Such circumstances contributed to Franklin Delano Roosevelt's overwhelming victory over Hoover in the election of 1932.

FDR's election opened a floodgate of new programs to help Americans struggling during the Great Depression. Roosevelt's secretary of labor, Frances Perkins, the first woman to hold a cabinet-level position, called a Child Health Recovery Conference in Washington, D.C., in October 1933. First Lady Eleanor Roosevelt attended the meeting, along with representatives from a wide variety of federal agencies (including the Children's Bureau) and 140 officials from state departments of public health, private health organizations, medical societies, and relief agencies. Conference proposals focused on limiting the effects of malnutrition and inadequate health care. The resulting Child Health Recovery Program (CHRP) was a joint effort of the recently created Federal Emergency Relief Administration (FERA) and the Children's Bureau. The CHRP provided emergency food and medical care to the nation's neediest children. In each state the Children's Bureau hired five physician consultants, and the Civil Works Administration paid the salaries of up to two hundred full and part-time public health nurses. Commercial food suppliers worked with private physicians, nutritionists, and home economics teachers to distribute food to needy children and their families. The CHRP did not live up to expectations, but Grace Abbott maintained that its most important results showed "the urgent need [for a] more extensive and permanent program for maternal and child health" (Abbott 1941; Lindenmeyer 1997).

President Roosevelt agreed that the federal government should do more. He appointed advisors to a Committee on Economic Security (CES) to draw up a proposal for a broadly defined national social insurance plan similar to those already established in Germany and Great Britain. Early discussions included health insurance. The topic of national health insurance had first been proposed during the William Howard Taft administration in 1913. The issue had again surfaced in the context of the debate over Sheppard-Towner. Looking at this history and the strong resistance to national health insurance from the AMA and private insurers, the CES choose to drop the idea from its proposal, fearing that opposition from the AMA might threaten passage of the entire social security program. The committee's suspicions may have been right. The Social Security Act, without a national health insurance plan, was signed into law on August 14, 1935. This significant act contained programs never before seen at the federal level, including unemployment insurance, an old-age pension plan for retired workers, and a mother's pension program called Aid to Dependent Children (later renamed Aid to Families with Dependent Children) for families without male breadwinners. Despite the absence of national health insurance, the Social Security Act also included two health care programs for poor mothers and children. Title V offered $5,280,000 annually to states: to help improve existing and new maternal and infant health care programs, establish special services for "crippled" children, and expand existing child health programs. State health departments used Title V funds to provide a wide variety of services for needy children and mothers: prenatal and child health clinics, medical examinations for school-age children, dental health services, and salaries for public health nurses (Bradbury 1962).

The Great Depression made life very difficult for most children and their families, but advances in medical science helped to counter some of the health problems associated with poverty. Congress established the National Institutes of Health (NIH) in 1930, thereby encouraging research in the cause, prevention, and cure of disease. Sulfa drugs, penicillin, and immunization prevented many deaths, especially among children. The number of hospitals increased, and doctors welcomed patients insured through expanded third-party, employer-based insurance programs such as Blue Cross and Blue Shield. Title V centered new public attention on preventive health care for expecting mothers, newborns, and school-age children. Beginning in 1937 the Children's Bureau recommended a major expansion of Title V.

Senator Robert F. Wagner introduced a bill in Congress the next year build-
ing on the Children's Bureau's recommendations and calling for a National
Health program. As might be expected, the AMA opposed the new bill. The
1939 Social Security Act's revisions did not include an expanded role for
Title V's maternal and child health provisions (Patel and Rushefsky 1999;
Lindenmeyer 1997).

WORLD WAR II'S LEGACY ON CHILD HEALTH POLICY

The threat of war, however, caused Congress to revisit the issue. By late
1940, the commanding officer at Fort Lewis in Washington State was com-
plaining that he had a major morale problem on his hands. As the army expanded its ranks, the Fort Lewis hospital was unable to handle the growing
number of requests for prenatal, delivery, postdelivery, and child medical
care for soldiers' wives and newborns. Denied service at the post hospital,
most servicemen and their wives could not afford private medical care. Private charities, already stretched during the Great Depression, could not fill
the need. The Fort Lewis commander turned to the Children's Bureau for
help, asking for an exception to use Title V funds for soldiers' wives and
children. In August 1941, the Children's Bureau agreed. After U.S. entrance
into the Second World War that December, veterans groups and the American Red Cross called on Congress to expand the Title V program beyond
Fort Lewis as a measure to improve military morale throughout the services.
The resulting Emergency Maternal and Infant Care program (EMIC), in
effect from 1943 to 1949, provided $130,500,000 for the medical care of the
wives and children of men enlisted in the military's four lowest pay grades.
Although EMIC cannot be given all the credit, it is noteworthy that the national infant mortality rate fell from 45.3 in 1943 to 31.3 in 1949. The program paid for the medical care of one of every seven babies born in the
United States (Sinai and Anderson 1948). The Children's Bureau and its
supporters hoped that EMIC was the start of a permanent and expanded
national health care program for all American mothers and children; the
majority in Congress, however, viewed it only as an emergency wartime
measure and ended EMIC on August 30, 1949. President Harry Truman tried
to introduce a new national health insurance program as part of his Fair Deal
agenda after the war, but that effort faced the same opposition from AMA
and private insurance companies as had past proposals.

Nonetheless, Title V's original program for poor mothers and babies remained, though not in a format devised by the Children's Bureau. In 1946,
as part of a postwar government reorganization, all federal child health efforts were consolidated in the Public Health Service. Children's Bureau supporters denounced the change as a "dismemberment" of the bureau and its
mandate to care for the needs of the "whole child" (Lindenmeyer 1997).
Their protests fell on deaf ears, but the agency's model of combining federal

and private health care resources under the Social Security Act remained the foundation for federal child health policy throughout the twentieth century. This was a path very different from that undertaken by the nation's wartime ally Great Britain. In 1943 the British adopted a comprehensive "from cradle to grave" social insurance plan and established the National Health Service (Starr 1982; Patel and Rushefsky 1999).

Although the United States chose a path other than establishing a national health insurance system, in the postwar years a growing percentage of Americans expected good heath care and had a better understanding of what constituted good health care. The millions of Americans who had served in the military during World War II had observed the benefits of good medical care firsthand. Such public support for access to good health care influenced Congress to fund an expansion of hospital construction through the 1946 Hill-Burton Act. Although the law's benefits were often denied to blacks and other Americans, by the 1950s high-quality hospitals became standard throughout America. The AMA supported the Hill-Burton Act and welcomed the convenience of new hospitals and efforts to make private medical insurance an expected employment benefit. By 1958, almost two-thirds of Americans had some form of medical insurance for hospitalization, and 55 percent of babies born that year were covered by private insurance (Starr 1982; Patel and Rushefsky 1999). As private medical insurance expanded, calls for national health insurance declined. In addition, the Children's Bureau, which had served as the major advocate for child health reforms prior to World War II, was now a diminished agency, located in the Department of Health, Education, and Welfare with no responsibilities for administering child health programs. The PHS, on the other hand, gained authority and influence but retained its minimal interest in protecting child health. The result was a further reduced role for the federal government in child health at the same time that the nation's birthrate rose to the twentieth century's highest levels. At the same time there was a leveling-off of the nation's infant mortality rate. The 1950 rate of 29.2 placed the United States sixth among comparable industrialized nations. The 1960 rate of 26.0 ranked eleventh. The small rate of improvement reflected the inequities of postwar American life. As medical historian Paul Starr explains in his 1982 book *The Social Transformation of Medicine*, "Gleaming palaces of modern science, replete with the most advanced specialty services, now stood next to neighborhoods that had been medically abandoned, that had no doctors for everyday needs, and where the most elementary public health and preventive care was frequently unavailable" (Starr 1982).

The postwar years also marked a change in federal interest in medical research. The NIH grew from a small agency funded with $180,000 in 1938 to a $400 million powerhouse in 1960. In 1950 Congress established the National Science Foundation and authorized the PHS's surgeon general to initiate medical research institutes at his discretion (Starr 1982; Patel and Rushefsky 1999). Private foundations such as the National Foundation for Infantile Paralysis (established in 1937) cooperated with and benefited from federal efforts to expand medical research, although not all funding came from government resources. A case in point is the campaign against polio. Polio was not usually a fatal disease for children, but it was the leading cause of paralysis and other crippling conditions among youngsters of all socioeconomic groups during the late 1940s and early '50s. In addition, polio's increasing frequency, unpredictability, and legacy of suffering made it among the era's most frightening threats to children's health. The National Foundation for Infantile Paralysis's annual March of Dimes campaigns raised more money than any other private medical effort. In 1954 Jonas Salk, MD, enlisted millions of families in polio vaccine trials. On April 12, 1955, the results were announced— the vaccine worked. Americans celebrated, and Congress expanded medical research budgets. Medical research seemed to be the most effective pathway to ensuring the public's health, including that of children (Paul 1971; Starr 1982).

LIBERALIZING ACCESS TO HEALTH CARE

Along with the election of John F. Kennedy came another shift in public attitudes toward health. Medical research continued to draw support, but it also became increasingly clear that many American children did not have access to even the most basic medical care. On October 24, 1963, Congress passed the Maternal and Child Health and Mental Retardation Planning Amendments to the Social Security Act. This important legislation expanded funding for Title V and added grants for mentally handicapped children. The PHS further boosted the effort by establishing a National Institute of Child Health and Human Development within the NIH. Research revealed that despite such efforts, children from low-income families were unable to gain access to the health care system. The Kennedy administration responded by expanding Title V funds for prenatal, delivery, postpartum, and infant care to high-risk rural and urban areas lacking hospitals. This effort was the initial step in the 1965 Medicaid Act, providing federal matching funds to allow states to supply private medical care for needy Americans. The Special Supplement Food Program for Women and Infants (WIC), launched in 1968, provided milk, cereal, and other foodstuffs as an extension of federal assistance to needy mothers and young children (Starr 1982; Patel and Rushefsky 1999).

A NEW POLICY OF CONTAINMENT

As part of President Lyndon Baines Johnson's War on Poverty, programs like Medicaid and WIC offered a promise of better health care for America's children. However, by the early 1970s a looming energy crisis and a declining economy mired in "stagflation" limited funding and progress. In 1975, nearly two-thirds of all needy families were receiving Medicaid benefits, but by 1983 the proportion had dropped to less than 46 percent. Medical costs were rising, and efforts to reduce the nation's infant mortality rates seemed stalled (Starr 1982; Patel and Rushefsky 1999).

One response drew attention to the growing number of adolescents having children outside of marriage. The 1978 Adolescent Health, Services, and Pregnancy Prevention Act increased federal funds for pregnant teens. Although the previous two decades had registered the century's highest teen pregnancy rates, most of those young mothers had chosen to marry. The rising number of unmarried young mothers during the 1970s gained attention from policy makers as a social and health concern for both the mothers and children. It was true that teen mothers were more likely to give birth to underweight and premature babies. They were also most likely to live in poverty. Nonetheless, it was not clear that marriage would solve these problems. Therefore, the federal effort focused on stopping unintended pregnancies among teens. By the 1980s, the measure took on a moral tone, led by First Lady Nancy Reagan—the "Just Say No" campaign. The result, argues Maris A. Vinovskis in his 1988 book *An Epidemic of Adolescent Pregnancy,* has been limited (Vinovskis 1988). Poverty, not behavior, remained the greatest threat to children's health.

Since the 1980s, nonprofit child welfare advocacy groups like the Children's Defense Fund have noted that minors are the most likely cohort in the U.S. population to live in poverty and suffer from preventable disease. Dramatically rising hospital costs during the 1970s and 1980s made matters worse. President Bill Clinton's attempts to devise new health care proposals highlighted uninsured children as an issue that threatened the nation. In 1993 nearly ten million children had no health insurance. After several years of debate, Congress enacted the State Children's Health Insurance Program (CHIP, Title XXI of the Social Security Act) in 1997. The program was designed to target uninsured children in families not eligible for Medicaid under previous standards. Congress appropriated from three to five billion dollars annually as block grants to states for the next ten years for the program (capped at forty billion dollars total). The program's first two years drew in over two million children, However, CHIP began to run into problems in several states as budgets tightened, health care costs rose, some physicians and hospitals refused to participate, and outreach programs floundered. States gained extensive federal funding, enabling them to extend health insurance coverage to children from families as high as 200 percent above the poverty line. But states also had to raise money to implement the program. After three years of operation, $1.9 billion of $4.2 billion allocated for the program from the federal government remained unspent, and the majority of eligible children were not enrolled in CHIP. In 2000, the federal government admitted that CHIP had not reached its goal to cut the number of uninsured children in half. States responded with some ambivalence. They wanted federal money for children's health care through Medicaid, but they did not implement programs to reach this goal. Results have gotten better since the end of 2000, but other problems are arising. Since the program was implemented in 1997, there have been reductions in the number of uninsured children from low-income families, particularly those at 100 to 200 percent of the federal poverty level. On the other hand, over 25 percent of all children in families with incomes below 100 percent of the federal poverty level remain uninsured, and things do not appear to be getting better for this group (Patel and Rushefsky 1999; Dubay, Hill, and Kenney 2002).

Other concerns involve the rising costs of health care. Some critics complain that CHIP added to the rising overall expenditure for Medicaid. Medicaid spending for children rose from $9.1 billion in 1990 to $17.5 billion in 1996. But this is a small percentage of the overall rise in Medicaid costs. Expenditures for the elderly and disabled encompassed approximately 72 percent of Medicaid's annual budget. There also fears that by 2007 as many as eighteen states will need more funding than is available through the federal program (Patel and Rushefsky 1999; Dubay, Hill, and Kenney 2002). This is an especially daunting problem because in 2003 a majority of states face some of the highest budget deficits since the Great Depression.

Entering the twenty-first century, the U.S. infant mortality rate of 7.2 is a dramatic improvement from the Children's Bureau's early estimates of 131 per thousand live births. Children's overall health is greatly improved as public sanitation has standardized and vaccination has become the norm. However, inequities remain, and child health issues are deeply embedded in many of the same social and political concerns that faced child welfare advocates throughout the twentieth century. For example, lead poisoning from flaking paint has been known to be a serious threat to children's health for decades. Nonetheless, a lack of social and political will has contributed to the fact that lead paint continues to be a threat to children. Efforts to limit tobacco use among young people have faced similar ambiguities. Overall, skyrocketing health care costs and inequitable access to high-quality health care remain the primary problems hindering federal programs designed to secure children's health and "conserve" this important national resource. The American model of combining private and state-funded health care for children is an ongoing experiment.

WORKS CITED

Abbott, Grace. 1941. *From Relief to Social Security*. Chicago: University of Chicago Press.

Bradbury, Dorothy E. 1956. *Four Decades of Action for Children: A Short History of the Children's Bureau, 1903–1946*. U.S. Children's Bureau Publication no. 358. Washington, D.C.: U.S. Government Printing Office.

———. 1962. *Five Decades of Action for Children.* U.S. Children's Bureau Publication no. 358. Washington, D.C.: U.S. Government Printing Office.

Bremner, Robert H. 1956. *From the Depths: The Discovery of Poverty in the United States.* New York: New York University Press.

———. 1971. *Children and Youth in America: A Documentary History.* 3 vols. Cambridge, Mass.: Harvard University Press.

Dubay, Lisa, Ian Hill, and Genevieve Kenney. 2002, October 1. "Five Things Everyone Should Know about SCHIP." Urban Institute. Available at www.urban.org/Template.cfm?Section=ByAuthor&NavMenuID = 63&template=/TaggedContent/ViewPublication.cfm&PublicationID=7958.

Duke, Emma. 1915. *Infant Mortality: Results of a Field Study in Johnstown, Pa., Based on Births in One Calendar Year.* U.S. Children's Bureau Publication no. 9. Washington, D.C.: U.S. Government Printing Office.

Hays, Samuel P. 1959/1999. *Conservation and the Gospel of Efficiency.* Pittsburgh: University of Pittsburgh Press.

Illick, Joseph E. 2002. *American Childhoods.* Philadelphia: University of Pennsylvania Press.

James, Edward T., Janet Wilson James, and Paul S. Boyer, eds. 1971. *Notable American Women, 1607–1950: A Biographical Dictionary*, vol. 2. Cambridge, Mass.: Belknap Press of Harvard University.

Kelley, Florence. 1905/1969. *Some Ethical Gains through Legislation.* New York: Macmillan; New York: Arno Press.

Lemons, J. Stanley. 1973. *The Woman Citizen: Social Feminism in the 1920s.* Urbana: University of Illinois Press.

Lindenmeyer, Kriste. 1997. *"A Right to Childhood": The U.S. Children's Bureau and Child Welfare, 1912–1946.* Urbana: University of Illinois Press.

Meckel, Richard A. 1990. *Save the Babies: American Public Health Reform and the Prevention of Infant Mortality, 1850–1929.* Baltimore: Johns Hopkins University Press.

Muncy, Robyn. 1991. *Creating a Female Dominion in American Reform, 1890–1935.* New York: Oxford University Press.

Patel, Kant, and Mark E. Rushefsky. 1931. *Promotion of the Welfare and Hygiene of Maternity and Infancy, the Administration of the Act of Congress of November 23, 1921: Fiscal Year Ended June 30, 1927.* U.S. Children's Bureau Publication no. 203. Washington, D.C.: U.S. Government Printing Office.

———. 1999. *Health Care Politics and Policy in America.* 2nd ed. New York: M. E. Sharpe.

Paul, John R. 1971. *A History of Poliomyelitis.* New Haven, Conn.: Yale University Press.

Riis, Jacob. 1890/1957. *How the Other Half Lives: Studies among the Tenements of New York.* New York: Hill and Wang.

Sinai, Nathan, and Odin W. Anderson. 1948. *EMIC: A Study of Administrative Experience.* Bureau of Public Health and Economics, Research Series 3. Ann Arbor: University of Michigan School of Public Health.

Starr, Paul. 1982. *The Social Transformation of Medicine.* New York: Basic Books.

Tiffin, Susan. 1982. *In Whose Best Interest? Child Welfare Reform in the Progressive Era.* Westport, Conn.: Greenwood Press.

U.S. Bureau of the Census. 1976. *Historical Statistics of the United States, Colonial Times to 1970.* Bicentennial ed., Part 1. Washington, D.C.: U.S. Government Printing Office.

United States Statutes At Large. 1913. Vol. 79. Washington, D.C.: U.S. Government Printing Office.

Vinovskis, Maris. 1988. *An "Epidemic" of Adolescent Pregnancy?: Some Historical and Policy Considerations.* New York: Oxford University Press.

West, Mrs. Max "Mary." 1914/1915. *Infant Care.* U.S. Children's Bureau Publication no. 8. Washington, D.C: U.S. Government Printing Office.

———. 1914. *Prenatal Care.* U.S. Children's Bureau Publication no. 4. Washington, D.C.: U.S. Government Printing Office.

Wiebe, Robert. 1967. *The Search for Order, 1877–1920.* New York: Hill and Wang.

Zelizer, Viviana A. 1985. *Pricing the Priceless Child: The Changing Social Value of Children.* New York: Basic Books.

II Documents

7 Recounting Health and Illness

The following sources include excerpts from diaries, letters, fiction and oral histories which recount children's bouts with illness or remedies for childhood ailments. The spellings in the letters has been left unchanged.

1. Elizabeth Sandwith Drinker, *The Diary of Elizabeth Drinker,* ed. Elaine Forman Crane (Boston: Northeastern University Press, 1991), vol. 2. Elizabeth Drinker, a wealthy Quaker from Philadelphia, kept a daily diary for nearly fifty years, from 1787 until 1807. Her writings are a rich source for understanding eighteenth-century life in America's big city. In the following excerpt she records the illness and death of her grandson James Drinker, as well as the health of others.

November 1, 1801
   MS. Gone to meeting—JS. Up stairs—Js. Smiths Nurse came to inform us that little Js. Drinker was very ill of the Hives, that J and E—Smith were going directly to North Bank expecting to find the dear little boy dead—Hannah went from hence last second day, whe[n] it seems she found the Child unwell—WD. Wrote a receipt for the hives and sent it,—Elizath. Skyrin went with her father to dine at Saml Rhoades—she says her Aunt and Children are well—John spent this evening up stairs with Nancy.—I sent Peter to know how they were at J Downings, Sandwith is broke out with a rash, and has 2 pustles of small pox come out—

November 2
   WD. Went this evening to Js. Smiths to enquire if they had heard from N. Bank—they have not, wether the dear Child is deseased or better, we must

remain in suspence 'till tomorrow—sent Peter to enquire how Sandth. Downing is, Sally told him there was no more signs of small pox than Yesterday, that the Doctor says he is in a good way.

November 3

HD. MS. Gone to meeting received a letter from my Son Henry with the account of the death of his little Son James, who departed on first day last about one o'clock, near twenty months old—his disorder was, or had been, the Hives, which does not last so long as a week in a general way, we have not yet heard the perticulars. . . . James Drinker was a very fine Child, of a strong constitution, amiable temper, and fine Countenance.—there is consolation in the thought that he is out of all pain, in this world and hat to which he is gone—yet it is very trying to part with a dear child, just beginning to know and love you.

November 5

Jams. Smith was here this evening we were talking of our dear little deseased grandson, he was scarcely ever known to cry, or make any complaint, he was the same during his illness:—Our Son Henry sleept none for 3 Nights, attended him diligently: and he died in his Arms.—My Son feels much as a father—

November 6

N.W. Peter went to know how Sandwith Downing is, Sally told him that he had 20 pustles, and is bravely, what a favour!—dear little James Drinker had had the small pox—little Esther was 3 years old the day her brother died the first of this month.

November 7

Jacob Downing and his Son Henry were here afternoon, they have not been to see us for some time past on little Mary's account for fear of brining the small pox.

2. Anne Sinkler Whaley LeClercq, ed. *Between North and South: The Letters of Emily Wharton Sinkler, 1842–1865* (Columbia: University of South Carolina Press, 2001). In the following excerpt from a letter to her father Emily Wharton Sinkler, a young married woman of nineteen who had moved to her husband's plantation home in South Carolina, writes about her bout of whooping cough.

February 6th 1843

I have something to tell you which I think will surprise you. What do you think of my having the regular whooping cough? I did not intend to have said anything about it until it was all over but it is so much better now and I am afraid you might hear an exaggerated account of it that I thought it best to tell you myself. One of the servants had been up the country this fall where the whooping cough was raging and returned about two weeks after I got here. He had a cough but insisted upon it that he had never whooped. I shook hands with him and he was constantly about and next thing was his brothers all got it and then it spread all over the Plantation. As soon as they had any suspicion they kept them all away from the house and I was not in the least afraid of catching it. Before Christmas I got a little cough and cold which I thought nothing of until four weeks ago when I began to whoop.

It is now just four weeks since I first began and the worst is now decidedly over. I am delighted that I have had it for it has not been violent though I never had an idea what a distressing thing it was. Brother Seaman was up here about two weeks ago when it had nearly reached the height and said there was nothing to be done for it but time. He says now that it is on the decline and will not last many weeks longer. He gave me a little bottle of paregoric, squills, nitre etc. which I took one night but I did not sleep any the better for it so I left it off. About a week ago he sent me from town another bottle a mixture of ether, belladonna and opium, a most horrid tasting thing but it did not do me any good. I really have suffered a great deal. For ten days I was not able to leave my room and now I cannot taste or smell anything. I am just beginning to sleep at night but I used to have at least twelve fits in the night and every time I coughed be obliged to stand up in bed to get my breath. To show you how much better I am I only had three fits last night and three before breakfast. I have not been able to eat anything but liquids ever since I began and indeed I don't see much use in taking anything for the first fit I have after eating anything I cough every thing up without the slightest hesitation. That has been symptom with all the Negroes on the Plantation. I am afraid I have been rather tediously minute but I thought Mamma would like to hear.

3. The letters excerpted below come from the Alexander Graham Bell Papers at the Library of Congress, which can be accessed online at memory.loc.gov/ammem/bellhtml/bellhome.html. Alexander Graham Bell, known as the inventor of the telephone, received several letters from his wife regarding the health of their daughter Elsie, who suffered from diphtheria at the age of fourteen, during the time the family was traveling in Italy. Elsie recovered from her bout of illness and lived to the age of eighty-six; she had seven children.

From Mrs. Alexander Graham Bell to Mrs. Alexander Melville Bell

Florence, March 12, 1892

You will have heard ere this reaches you of Elsie's diphtheria. The poor child has had more than her share of illness these last two years. I did hope that she had got through and was going to devote herself to getting thoroughly well and strong, and I cannot imagine where she can have taken the infection. . . . She has had the disease in its mildest form I think, or has been very skillfully treated, for she has had absolutely no fever, and until today has suffered very little inconvenience. Now however, I suppose that she is getting better and the disease breaking up she feels worse and is having a much harder time . . . [text broken up] . . . and the poor child doesn't get much at best as she has to be roused every three hours to have her throat sprayed. Tonight she is more quiet, but not being so comfortable I am afraid the may not do much better.

From Mrs. Alexander Graham Bell to Dr. Alexander Graham Bell

Florence, March 22, 1892

I think Elsie's letter will reassure you as no words of mine could. A child who can play hide and seek in this way can't be very ill or very weak! The diphtheria is all over now I think, the doctor has made only one visit today, and says she need not be waked tonight. She does not seem to have lost strength at all, and I can't see why we cannot sail April 16th, but the doctor won't give an opinion, and as I cannot wait indefinitely I am going to inquire about the steamer from Genoa April 20. . . . You see as it turns out, I haven't needed Mr. McCurdy, but I might have and with such a dangerous and treacherous illness as diphtheria beginning, I could not let him go out of reach.

From Mrs. Alexander Graham Bell to Dr. Alexander Graham Bell

March 25 [no year given, probably 1892]

Elsie is getting on, slowly. The doctor says she is better every day, but I do not think she feels quite well each day. The confinement is beginning to tell on her, but I only wonder that it has not done so before. The throat the doctor says is pretty well today, but the diphtheria still lingers in the nose where it is hardest to reach. She complains today of difficulty of breathing but the doctor seems to attach no importance to this. I think it rather strange that he confines himself so entirely to the throat and makes no examination of the bowels, urine or heart, both of which must surely be more or less affected, or at least in danger of being affected as he says that there is danger of such complications after diphtheria. Elsie is sitting up in bed all the time, she never seems to need to lie down and her strength seems very well maintained.

Letter from Mrs. Alexander Graham Bell to Dr. Alexander Graham Bell

March 30, 1892

Elsie had a slight relapse the very day I cabled you, she was convalescent, not a bad one at all, but it made me very nervous. Elsie felt quite ill that night for the first time since her illness and she seemed feverish and said her throat hurt, so altogether things looked disagreeable. Next day she was better again, and she has been gaining since, but very very slowly. The doctor said the trouble probably was because the diphtheria had gone into the nose where it was extremely difficult to dislodge it, and that it spread thence to the throat again. Elsie uses a tremendous number of handkerchiefs, and the chief approach to real discomfort lies in the feeling of stoppage of the nose. But she has absolutely no real discomfort or if she has she is most wonderfully heroic in concealing all appearance of it. She was to have got up Wednesday, now I hope she may get up that time next week, but she has not expressed the least regret at her lengthened stay abed, she has never said she wished to get up to see the parlor or to go out, she has not lost strength in the least as I know to my own cost when she grips my hand so that the rings cut, and as I see when she gets out of bed for a few minutes.

4. M. B., *Spunk* 8 (1916): 62 and Anon., *Spunk* 20 (1928): 45. *Spunk* was a monthly magazine published by the patients of the Pennsylvania State Tuberculosis Sanatoria. In the poem and letter that follow, two young patients, one at the facility at Cresson and the other one at Mount Alto, describe their experiences.

> C is for the Cure that makes us better;
>
> R is for the Rules we must obey;
>
> E is for the Eats which fill our stomachs;
>
> SS are for the SongS learned in our play;
>
> O is for the Outlook from our windows;
>
> N is for the nurses sweet and gay—
>
> Putting them together they spell Cresson
>
> Where we children dearly love to stay.
>
> —M. B., age 13, one of the Kiddies.

Mt. Alto Sanatarium

March 20, 1928
Dear Pop:

I am as happy as can be. I had to change trains three times, it is a wale of a ride. I thought they had a nice big bus, but it is a small auto-truck ride, bounce you so much you think he is looking for bumps.

When I left philadelphia I did not see any snow, but gee whiz she snow out here drown you almost. The first thin I had to do was take a shower bath. I made friends so quick I couldn't remember all their names. They give me so much to eat, I have a stomach ache almost. We are up at six, wash up, breakfast one hour sleep, one hour rest, just lie down and talk to each other. Tell mother to be good and I am getting sweets after every meal, prunes sliced peaches and other nice things. My friend tell me Saturday we go to movies, Sunday we have ice cream. Radio in our ward gramephone. Plenty of fun, after lunch three hours sleep after supper one hour sleep. Give love to Uncle and Aunt Rosie. Tell Uncle plenty of work out here if he can clean all the snow out here. Not so cold as I thought it was. Send Uncle John address. I play so much after I got here I was glad when it was bedtime, it was seven when we go to bed. My temperature was high today nurse said stay in bed until doctor see me. That hard flame still choke me in the throat. Air can't be beat, hope you be straighten out; don't forget fishes. I may write Aunt May soon. Love and kisses to mother and you, write back write away a long letter too. Don't mean maybe. Love to all. Your loving son.

Children's Hospital
South Mountain, Pa.

P.S. Dempsey and Tunney fight movies tonight. I am sending another letter write behind this.

5. From 1936 to 1940 the Federal Writers' Project of the Works Progress (later Work Projects) Administration conducted interviews with individuals born in slavery. These first-person accounts were written out as narratives and typically involved some attempt by the interviewers to reproduce in writing the spoken language of the people they interviewed. These accounts are now available online at the American Memory collection: *Born in Slavery,* at memory.loc.gov/ammem/snhtml/snhome.html. In many of the interviews individuals spoke very briefly of the medical care they received as children and the remedies manufactured in their homes. These accounts are excerpted below.

Ann Rice, *South Carolina Narratives,* vol. 14, part 4, 11

When we got sick all the medicine we took was turpentine—dat would cure almost any ailment. Some of the niggers used Sampson snake weed or pooch leaves boiled and tea drunk.

Annie Young, *Oklahoma Narratives,* vol. 13, 358

When any of my family was sick I always sent for de doctor. We had a few of our own home remedies dat we used also. We boiled poke root and bathed in it for a cure for rheumatism. A tea made from may apples was used for a physic.

Robert Bryant, *Missouri,* vol. 10, 64

We never had no doctor. My mother would go out in de woods and get herbs and if I had de stomach ache we would put a little bit of turpentine one a piece of sugar. If I had de headache we would put a piece of brown paper and vinegar on horse radish leaves on de head. In two or three hours us kids would be out playin' and kickin' up our heels. We would go out and get some goose grass and make a little bit of tea and pour it down for de stomach ache. We would get dis black root for constipation. We used turnip and scraped it and would bind de foot when it was frost bit.

James Bolton, *Georgia Narratives,* vol. 4, part 1, 94

Garlic was mostly used to cure wums [worms]. They roasted the garlic in hot ashes and squez the juice outen it and made the chilluns take it. Sometimes they made poultices outen garlic for the pneumony. We saved a heap of bark from wild cherry and poplar and black haw and slippery ellum trees and we dried out mullein leaves. They was all mixed and brewed to make bitters. When someover a nigger got sick, them bitters was good for—well ma'am, they was goid for what ailed 'em! We took 'em for rheumatiz, for fever, and for the misery in the stummick and for most all sorts of sickness. Red oak bark tea was good for sore throat.

Georgia Baker, *Georgia Narratives,* vol. 9, part 1, 49

Mammy Mary usd all sorts of tees made up for us, 'cordin' to whatever ailment us had. Ecneset tee was for colds. De fust thing dey silus done for sore throat was give us tee made of red oak bark wid alum. Scurvey grass tea cleant us out in the springtime, and dey made us weer little secks of assfidy [asefetida] 'round our necks to keep off lots of sorts of miseries. Some folkses hung de left hind foot of a mole on a string 'round deir babies necks to make 'em teethe easier. I never done nothin' lak dat to my babies 'cause I never believed in no such foolishness. Some babies is jus' netchelly.

6. Another activity of WPA Federal Writers Project involved interviews with Americans about their lives and customs. Some were transcribed as narratives and others as dialogue. They can be accessed online as part of the American Memory Project at memory.loc.gov/ammem. The following excerpts discuss children's illnesses, their treatment, and home remedies.

Interview with Mr. C. A. Kirshtien [?] in 1938
    A native of New York, Mr. Kirshtien lived in the South during his childhood and spent his summers in Tennessee.

There were several primitive but apparently effective remedies for illness practiced in my mother's family. When we children had a cough, mother would give us boiled water that had been sweetened, with a piece of clean cherry bark floating in it.

    It was believed that to prevent fever for a whole year, a child should pick the first three violets he found in the spring, and eat them. Some of us used to eat violets all summer long, because we got to like the taste of them!

    A recipe for Insomnia: Bruise a handful of anise seeds and steep them in waters then place in small bags, and bind one bag over each nostril before going to bed.

    As a cure for mumps I have seen a negro rub the oil from a 3 can of sardines on his cheeks, and then eat the sardines. The swelling would usually go down, too. Probably the messaging helped.

A popular cure for warts, practiced by both blacks and whites, was to gather as many pebbles as you had warts, rub one pebble on each wart, take them to a crossroads and throw the pebbles over your left shoulder. The warts were supposed to go with them.

Of course, there was one always effective way to stop hiccoughs. Just swallow nine gulps of water while standing on one foot.

Interview with Maria Gonsales [?] in Florida in 1938

Mrs. Gonsales was a squatter, having left her husband when he became mentally ill. In the interview she reported on her limited experience with medical care.

Out here we don't have much sickness neither like I hear tell they have in town. [Seems?] like someone is alway sick there. Sometimes one of my younguns has the colic an I give him plenty of castor oil and he soon gits well. If he [has?] a [tooth?] hurtin' I let him pack [snuff?] round it [?] it [will?] stop [?] real soon. [Snuff's?] good for ear ache too. If you blow it [down?] in the ear, it don't feel so good at first but soon helps.

Mr. Alex Samuels, interviewed in Atlanta, Georgia, in 1939

He was born in Prairie du Chien, Wisconsin, in 1884 and recalled the childhood illnesses and deaths in his family.

I had one sister, no brothers. My sister and my father died with diphtheria when I was about a year and a half old. Diphtheria killed them quickly in those days. The first thing I can remember was having my throat swabbed with a carbolic solution. The memory was clear enough to cause me to recognize the smell and taste years afterwards. Diphtheria, when it took a virulent form, was a much more dangerous disease than it is now. It was not uncommon for the mortality to go as high as fifty percent or more. During such epidemics no public funerals were held for those who died of the disease. People were afraid of contacting the disease themselves.

I was almost eight years old when I started school. The diphtheria had injured me somewhat, and a case of measles when I was seven kept me from starting earlier.

Mrs. Garrett, interviewed in West Asheville, North Carolina, in 1939

The interview is about her situation during the Great Depression. It begins by describing how four Garrett children showed up at the door of the principal's office in the public school asking for free lunches after having been absent for five weeks. A visit to the Garrett home reveals the family's poverty and struggles, beginning with the wait for Mr. Garrett to find a WPA job after the one he worked on ended. Mrs. Garrett describes her situation and the health of the children, including their poor diet.

"He goes back to work tomorrow," she said. "After he gets his first paycheck, we can get along. But we haven't had anything in the house to eat for a week now but two messes of flour and a peck of meal. The children has nothin' for breakfast but a biscuit or a slice of corn bread. They come home after school begging for food. But I can't give them but two meals a day. That's why I want to get free lunches."

So the family was given commodities by the welfare department; beans, flour, and dried milk. The school agreed to give them lunches, and a member of the parent-teacher association offered to find clothes and shoes for them.

"That's my baby," she said, indicating the two-year-old. "He shore has had a hard time." She enumerated the illnesses of his two short years; diphtheria, pneumonia, measles, and now an abscess in his ear. He had a bad cold also, and a sore on his upper lip, which his mother wiped every now and then with a not-too-clean cotton cloth. Like the other children, he had too waxen a look.

"The doctor says as how he should have orange juice every day, and tomatoes and onions mashed with potatoes, but I don't have no money to buy them things for him. I ain't nothing to give him but cereal." However, she admitted someone was sending him milk every day. She didn't know who.

She was still feeding the older children on biscuits, corn bread, and now "white beans," but not bread and beans at the same meal.

Mrs. Mary Wright Hill, interviewed in Athens, Georgia, in 1939

She spent thirty-three years as principal of a grammar school. She was educated at Atlanta University and was the first African American woman to be elected a principal in Athens.

"I would like to tell you how I managed to get running water in that school. Not long after I took charge and began to drink that well water I began to feel bad and didn't feel like doing my work as it should be done. No matter how hard I talked to city officials they wouldn't do anything about it. I took my drinking water from home and began to work on the State Board of Health about the conditions of the water in the section. They sent a representative down to investigate the matter. They asked me a million questions, of which they had a perfect right to do. I sent a boy to the well to get a fresh bucket of water and saw to it that the bottle I put the sample in was thoroughly clean. They took it and went on back to Atlanta. In about a month I got a report on that water. Headquarters said they didn't understand why there wasn't typhoid fever and other contagious diseases over there. Water was put in. . . .

"The [?] I have seen over there would make you sick. Often I have had a [kid?] come to school sick. Their parents at work, I have put a pallet on the floor by the heater many days and lay a sick child on it, give them milk and food, and take that child home or to some friend's house until the mother came home late in the afternoon. When I first started teaching in the school, I wore my good clothes. I have looked down on my dress and seen lice crawling on it, or have a sick child to vomit, or have bowel action and get it on me. I decided to war white dresses in order to see the lice when they fell on my white dress. I have had had people ask me, 'why do you war white dresses to school the year round? Are you not a nurse?' I would give them some nice answer and go on.

"I found it was necessary to know something about nursing and the care of children, not only my own, but those I taught. So I took a [correspondence?] course by mail and received my diploma from the Chatauqua School of Nursing, at Jamestown, New York. That course has been my salvation in caring for those children. Now when things [like?] I have just mentioned occur, I immediately get the [mercurochrome?] and wet their head in it. It kills every nit and louse on a child's head."

Mr. Charles E. Banister, interviewed in Oregon in 1939 about home medical practices

My mother had all kinds of home remedies she used to use on the children. I don't remember what particular ailment it was for, but we took catnip tea, and sassafras tea. Turpentine and sugar was given for worms, and sometimes people were dosed with straight turpentine, as in the case of my brother who died of diphtheria. It was the doctor who doped him, and he gave him too much.

Turpentine and lard rubbed on the chest was wonderful for colds, and if we had no turpentine we could use coal oil or kerosene.

We also had several kinds of poultices, flax seed poultice, bread and milk poultice, and beefsteak poultice, which my mother put on me whenever I came home with a black eye. But the very best poultice for sores was the angle worm poultice. It would draw all the smart out of even a bad felon. The worms were taken alive, placed upon the sore, and wrapped around with a bandage.

For earache sometimes mother used laudanum dropped into the ear with a dropper. There were pain killer pills to be got at the store, but the usual remedy for headaches was hot or cold packs applied to the head.

Among the foremost of remedies "handed down" in the family is the tea made of dung. In the case of my grandmother the most efficaciously medicinal dung is that of the swine, the common sty-pig, which, when dried and baked in an oven and made into a tea is said to cure evils of all sorts, from the slightest indisposition to measles and smallpox. I recall several years ago when I was in Baker, Oregon, that a child took sick with the measles. The grandmother procured the dung of a sheep, gave it the same treatment in the oven and made it into tea. This the child drank, being too young to know what the decoction was.

Poultices too were common. Chewed tobacco poultice would remove the heat from a bee sting in remarkably short order. Also a mud of spittle and dust was used on occasions of this sort. Then there was the mustard poultice, the tea-leaf poultice, and a poultice of gunpowder and milk which was used to combat ringworm. In this latter case it was sometimes customary to paint the offending "ring" with ink.

7. William Carlos Williams, "The Use of Force," in *On Doctoring: Stories, Poems, Essays,* ed. Richard Reynolds, MD, and John Stone, MD (New York: Simon and Schuster, 1995). Williams was a prolific writer who published poems, stories, novels, and other literary works during a career as a practicing physician in Rutherford, New Jersey. This story reveals many aspects of the physician-patient encounter.

They were new patients to me, all I had was the name, Olson. Please come down as soon as you can, my daughter is very sick.

When I arrived I was met by the mother, a big startled looking woman, very clean and apologetic who merely said, Is this the doctor? And let me in. In the back, she added. You must excuse us, doctor, we have her in the kitchen where it is warm. It is very damp here sometimes.

The child was fully dressed and sitting on her father's lap near the kitchen table He tried to get up, but I motioned for him not to bother, took of my overcoat and started to look things over. I could see that they were all very nervous, eyeing me up and down distrustfully. As often, in such cases, they weren't telling me more than they had to, it was up to me to tell them; that's why they were spending three dollars on me.

The child was fairly eating me up with her cold, steady eyes, and no expression to her face whatever. She did not move and seemed, inwardly, quiet; an unusually attractive little thing, and as strong as a heifer in appearance. But her face was flushed, she was breathing rapidly, and I realized that she had a high fever. She had magnificent blond hair, in profusion. One of those picture children often reproduced in advertising leaflets and the photogravure sections of the Sunday papers.

She's had a fever for three days, began the father, and we don't know what it comes from. My wife has given her things, you know, like people do, but it don't do no good. And there's been a lot of sickness around. So we tho't you'd better look her over and tell us what is the matter.

As doctors often do I took a trial shot at it as a point of departure. Has she had a sore throat?

Both parents answered me together, No. . . . No, she says her throat don't hurt her.

Does your throat hurt you? added the mother to the child. But the little girl's expression didn't change nor did she move her eyes from my face.

Have you looked?

I tried to, said the mother, but I couldn't see.

As it happens we had been having a number of cases of diphtheria in the school to which this child went during that month and we were all, quite apparently, thinking of that, though no one had as yet spoken of the thing.

Well, I said, suppose we take a look at the throat first. I smiled in my best professional manner and asking for the child's first name I said, come on, Mathilda, open your mouth and let's take a look at your throat.

Nothing doing.

Aw, come on, I coaxed, just open your mouth wide and let me take a look. Look, I said opening both hands wide, I haven't anything in my hands. Just open up and let me see.

Such a nice man, put in the mother. Look how kind he is to you. Come on, do what he tells you to. He won't hurt you.

At that I ground my teeth in disgust. If only they wouldn't use the word "hurt" I might be able to get somewhere. But I did not allow myself to be hurried or disturbed but speaking quietly and slowly I approached the child again.

As I moved my chair a little nearer suddenly with one cat-like movement both her hands clawed instinctively for my eyes and she almost reached them too. In fact she knocked my glasses flying and they fell, though unbroken, several feet away from me on the kitchen floor.

Both the mother and father almost turned themselves inside out in embarrassment and apology. You bad girl, said the mother, taking her and shaking her by one arm. Look what you've done. The nice man. . . .

For heaven's sake, I broke in. Don't call me a nice man to her. I'm here to look at her throat on the chance that she might have diphtheria and possibly die of it. But that's nothing to her. Look here, I said to the child, we're going to look at your throat. You're old enough to understand what I'm saying. Will you open it now by yourself or shall we have to open it for you?

Not a move. Even her expression hadn't changed. Her breaths however were coming faster and faster. Then the battle began. I had to do it. I had to have a throat culture for her own protection. But first I told the parents that it was entirely up to them. I explained the danger but said that I would not insist on a throat examination so long as they would take the responsibility.

If you don't do what the doctor says you'll have to go to the hospital, the mother admonished severely.

Oh yeah? I had to smile to myself. After all, I had already fallen in love with the savage brat, the parents were contemptible to me. In the ensuing struggle they grew more and more abject, crushed, exhausted while she surely rose to magnificent heights of insane fury bred of her terror of me.

The father tried his best, and he was a big man but the fact that she was his daughter, his shame at her behavior and his dread of hurting her made him release her just at the critical moment several times when I had almost achieved success, till I wanted to kill him. But his dread also that she might have diphtheria made him tell me to go on, go on though he himself was almost fainting, while the mother moved back and forth behind us raising and lowering her hands in an agony of apprehension.

Put her in front of you on your lap, I ordered, and hold both her wrists.

But as soon as he did the child let out a scream. Don't, you're hurting me. Let go of my hands. Let them go I tell you. Then she shrieked terrifyingly, hysterically. Stop it! Stop it! You're killing me!

Do you think she can stand it, doctor! Said the mother.

You get out, said the husband to his wife. Do you want her to die of diphtheria?

Come on now, hold her, I said.

Then I grasped the child's head with my left hand and tried to get the wooden tongue depressor between her teeth. She fought, with clenched teeth, desperately! But now I also had grown furious—at a child. I tried to hold myself down but I couldn't. I know how to expose the throat for inspection. And I did my best. When I finally got the wooden spatula behind the last teeth and just the point of it into the mouth cavity, she opened up for an instant but before I could see anything she came down again and gripping the wooden blade between her molars she reduced it to splinters before I could get it out again.

Aren't you ashamed, the mother yelled at her. Aren't you ashamed to act like that in front of the doctor?

Get me a smooth-handled spoon of some sort, I told the mother. We're going through with this. The child's mouth was already bleeding. Her tongue was cut and she was screaming in wild hysterical shrieks. Perhaps I should have desisted and come back in an hour or more. Not doubt it would have been better. But I have seen at least two children lying in bed of neglect in such cases, and feeling that I must get a diagnosis now or never I went at it again. But the worst of it was that I too had got beyond reason. I could have torn the child apart in my own fury and enjoyed it. It was a pleasure to attack her. My face was burning with it.

The damned little brat must be protected against her own idiocy, one says to one's self at such times. Others must be protected against her. It is a social necessity. And all these things are true. But a blind fury, a feeling of adult shame, bred of a longing for muscular release are the operatives. One goes on to the end.

In a final unreasoning assault I overpowered the child's neck and jaws. I forced the heavy silver spoon back of her teeth and down her throat till she gagged. And there it was—both tonsils covered with membrane. She had fought valiantly to keep me from knowing her secret. She had been hiding that sore throat for three days at least and lying to her parents in order to escape just such an outcome as this.

Now truly she *was* furious. She had been on the defensive before but now she attacked. Tried to get off her father's lap and fly at me while tears of defeat blinded her eyes.

8 Advice on Child Health

Both laywomen and physicians wrote advice books on infant and child care, presenting information about medical problems and regimens for keeping babies and for children health.

1. An American Matron. *The Maternal Physician: A Treatise on the Nurture and Management of Infants, From the Birth Until Two Years Old. Being the Result of Sixteen Years' Experience in the Nursery,* 2nd ed. (Philadelphia: Lewis Adam, 1818). The anonymous author of America's first child health manual has recently been identified as Mary Palmer Tyler. In the book she identifies herself as the mother of eight children and a resident of New England. Many of her suggestions are taken from popular medical books on child rearing. The following excerpt discusses a common childhood ailment, measles, and its cure.

Measles

This disease is thus described by Dr. Wallis: "According to my conception, it is in general a febrile disease of the inflammatory kind, always infectious, electively affecting that membrane called scheiderian, which lines the inside of the nose, throat and lungs, and, in its progression, the skin; though I have seen the affection of the lungs so extremely slight, as not to call forth the least attention, where there was a diarrhoea attended through the whole course of the disease. Its progress is divided into three stages; the *first* precedes, the *second* attends, and the *last* succeeds the completion of the eruption. At the commencement, there are chillness and heat alternately succeeding each other; soon after, on the second day, the fever increases, attended with considerable sickness, great heat, thirst, languor, and loss of appetite; the tongue is white; there is a heaviness of the head and drowsiness, sneezing, brightness of the eyes, from whence flow a think humour; the eyelids swell, and most commonly there is a dry and very troublesome cough; sometimes vomiting and looseness are associates with these; the last of a dark green colour, when children are getting their teeth; and all these symptoms gradually increase, till the *eruptive* or *secondary* stage begins, which occurs generally on the fourth day, about which time small red spots, like flea bites, make their appearance on the face, which run into clusters, forming larger spots, rising above the skin, perceptible only to the touch, not to the sight; afterwards broad spots spread over the body downwards, not quite so prominent though of a higher colour than those of the face: when the eruption is finished the vomiting ceases, but the fever increases; and the cough, with the difficult of breathing, becomes more violent; a sweat and diarrhoea now and then supervene.

"On the sixth day, or thereabout, the *third stage* begins, on which the spots on the face grow dry, and give it a rough appearance; and in three days more they totally disappear from the whole body; for on the ninth day nothing is to be seen, except a dark coloured fine farina, or appearance like bran, all over the surface of the skin: at this period, the fever and cough are sometimes alleviated, sometimes increased, and terminate in a dangerous peripneumony, and not unfrequently a looseness succeeds the disease. . . .

"After this we are not to conclude the patient is out of danger, unless, during its course, some considerable evacuation has taken place, either by sweating, vomiting, urine, or looseness; for without something of this kind occurs, the cough will continue, the fever will return with additional violence, and the strength not be recovered except with great commotion in the system, and, consequently extreme danger.

"Through what we have here described is the most frequent mode of the measles appearance and progress, to their termination, yet sometimes they differ so much that authors have denominated them *anomalous,* or *irregular,* as deviating from the common course, or as in the eruption putting on the appearance of small-pox.

Characteristic signs. An infectious inflammatory fever for the most part, with which are associated a defluxion of a thin watery humour from the eyes, tickling in the nose, sneezing, dry cough, more or less violent; on the fourth day, sometimes sooner, sometimes later, though rarely, small spots running together, perceptible to the touch on the face, but broader on the body, not perceptibly elevated above the skin, break forth, which in three days after are converted into branny scales in part, and totally disappear upon the ninth day.

"*Cure.* In so mild a manner with the measles sometimes affect patients, that little is necessary to be done, except abstinence from all *animal food,* or heating applications; and drinking freely of thin watery acessent liquids, such as common fig drink, made agreeably acid with lemon-juice, apple water, or some such like fluids. But should the febrile symptoms run high, we must proceed as directed in the small-pox; but great attention must be paid to the affection of the lungs; oily emulsions and tinctures, may therefore be prescribed occasionally in conjunction with the other remedies, calculated to keep the febrile affections within proper limits.

"Should oily medicines disagree with the stomach, as is sometimes the case, we must have recourse to the class of demulcents, using the pectoral decoction, or that of linseed, as common drink.

"After the eruption is completed, slight opiates are serviceable; but as nature generally performs her crisis either by sweats, looseness, or urine, we must observe what way she directs her efforts, and proceed *as* we have before directed in cures of this kind, where they occur in fevers not eruptive.

"As soon as the redness of the skin goes off, and the spots begin to die away, gentle purgatives must be administered, at proper intervals, and the patient return to his usual mode of life gradually. Care also should be taken that patients expose not themselves too early to the cold air; for these are apt to bring on a very disagreeable cough, asthma, and consumption, from affections of the lungs, or of some other parts."

Much more is said by this learned author upon the variations in the measles, enumerating many distressing aspects sometimes assumed by this disease; but as I am not writing with an idea to make physicians, but merely to enable my readers to *nurse* their infants with the aid of the physician, or *prescribe* for them in slight and ordinary attacks, I shall not transcribe more on this subject, except one paragraph, which, I think, merits attention from the faculty in general.

"Few people have thought the measles to be a disease of sufficient consequence, to avail themselves of these assistances, which, as in the small-pox, might be derived from inoculation in this complaint. As for my own part, *practically*, I cannot say any thing on the subject; but if we may believe the authority of some who have made the experiment, or be allowed to depend on reasoning from analogy, our labours might be happily rewarded; for it is asserted, and appears probable, that from inoculation from infected blood, on the sixth day a slight fever manifests itself most commonly, though it is very moderate, unattended with loss of sleep and inflammatory symptoms; and it is neither succeeded by a hectic fever, cough, nor inflamed eyes; so that we find we should be freed from a train of the most dangerous symptoms, and consequently relieved, in many cases, from the most distressing apprehensions."

Surely the experiment is worth trying, provided it is attended with danger, which appears to be the case. All my children except the three youngest had this disease at the same time, and very favourably; they were not confined but a day or two, each one; indeed, some of them were able to go about the house during the whole course of the disease, although very feeble. The physician who attended them, treated the disease upon the same plan as he would have done the smallpox, in opposition to the ancient method of keeping the patients in bed from fear of their taking cold, and thereby increasing the defluxion, cough, &c. After two or three days, while the eruption was coming out, my children were able to run about, and disposed to play, in which they were indulged, and they recovered surprisingly fast; the cough left them with the other symptoms, and no ill consequences whatever occurred. Children in general, I believe, have the disease lighter than adults, partly from their youth, but chiefly from their simple manner of living, and regular habits.

It is a practice with me, whenever any of my family are seized with feverish symptoms for which I cannot readily account, to give them a draught of *saffron tea*, to defend the stomach in case the disease should prove eruptive; and I am confident it is often beneficial, although some physicians ridicule the practice as an *old woman's notion*, and say it intoxicates and inflames the blood. Every thing may be carried to excess; but it appears to me equally absurd to urge the intoxicating qualities of saffron, as an argument against the moderate and judicious use of it, as it would be to forbid the use of opium entirely, because it will occasion death when taken to excess. A few spoonsful of saffron tea, taken once or twice a-day, in all eruptive disorders, would greatly tend to prevent the retrocession of the eruption, from which such fatal effects so often arise, especially in very young children. I have always been in this practice, and never knew any eruption disappear till in its natural course it ought to do so, among all my children. Therefore, my fair readers, it is my sincere opinion, that you will do well, whenever your infants droop, and have highly feverish symptoms, to give them *a little saffron tea*, two or three times, and if the complaint is eruptive, it will assist nature in throwing it out; and no harm can result from it should it prove otherwise, as from long experience I am convinced, saffron, although a powerful stomachic, is perfectly harmless in its operation. A little snake root added to the saffron tea will often prove serviceable.

2. William Potts Dewees, *Treatise on the Physical and Medical Treatment of Children*, 3rd ed. (Philadelphia: Carey, Lea and Carey, 1829). Dewees wrote one of the first and most comprehensive American textbooks on the care of children. Excerpts on the disease of cholera infantum, a diarrhea disease that caused many infant deaths, are followed by excerpts on its treatment.

This is a disease almost peculiar to the climate of the United States. Children, in other countries, are liable, during dentition, or from other causes, to various affections of the alimentary canal, all of which differ from our endemic.

The exciting causes are, improprieties in diet and clothing; and it is likewise very often aggravated, by teething, worms, by premature weaning, and by a variety of adventitious circumstances.

Cholera infantum makes its approaches in different ways. In some instances, it comes on as a simple diarrhœa, though the stomach is also very apt to be affected; and in its more violent forms, there are vomitings and purgings, attended by no inconsiderable spasmodic uneasiness, constituting the cholera morbus of farther advanced life. In its ordinary forms, the fever, which soon supervenes, is of an irregular remittent character; the exacerbations being highest in the evening. The pulse is usually small, quick, and feeble, or irritated, and corded; but rarely full, strong, or voluminous. Determinations to the brain, or at least, this organ seems early to be affected sympathetically; as is manifested by a tendency to stupor or delirium, or sometimes even frenzy. The eyes, also denote this cerebral affection; they are either fierce, or languid, in expression; and when the patient sleeps, are half closed. Thirst is intense, and for a time really unquenchable—cold water is clamorously demanded; but if swallowed, is instantly rejected.

Treatment

The disease, as already stated, usually commences with a very disordered state of the alimentary canal; and, it seems to be admitted, that our earliest endeavours are to be directed to the evacuation of the stomach and bowels. As regards, however, the precise course to be pursued, to effect this purpose, there is not the same unanimity. Generally, purgatives are employed in preference to emetics; and especially the castor oil. Cases of a mild nature, may undoubtedly be treated in this way, and particularly if laudanum be occasionally added, when there is little or no fever. But, in the more violent forms of the disease, attended by vomiting, it will be impossible to get such medicines to be retained. It is, therefore, necessary that we attempt to allay the irritability of the stomach.

For this purpose, there is nothing so certain, or so prompt, as an injection of a gill of warm water, in which are dissolved three tea-spoonsful of common salt; this is for a child of a year old and upward, proportionally less for younger. And however frequent the discharges may be per anum, it must not be regarded; the injection must be given. If it operate immediately, and bring with it a fæcal or bilious discharge, the stomach becomes almost immediately quieted; and may then be repeated only pro re nata—that is, whenever the vomiting be again severe. Should it not bring any thing off, it must be repeated; and an attempt made to force it high into the bowels; or should the vomiting not cease, it must again be had recourse to.

This repetition of the injection will either procure the discharge required, or it will produce a most salutary irritation of the rectum, on which its chief efficacy depends. We would wish this fact to be remembered; for a common injection of molasses, oil, and water, will do little or no good, though it may procure a stool, as it lacks the stimulating ingredient, the salt, on which its virtue depends. So decided and effective is this simple plan, that we have a hundred times seen it relieve entirely, almost without the aid of any other remedy.

The great desideratum in cholera infantum, is to tranquilize the stomach; if the disease has been provoked by any irritating matter in the stomach itself, it should be our first endeavor to remove it, by encouraging the puking, by draughts of warm, or even cold water, where the warm will not be drunk, until no foreign substance appears in the matter thrown up—but do not let us administer an emetic; for, so long as nature continues her efforts to dislodge the offensive substance, it cannot be required, as she will certainly succeed if she be aided by warm water; and it can never be otherwise than injurious, after it has cast off the irritating material.

When this complaint attacks very young children, nearly the same plan should be pursued—that is, an injection of the same materials must be given, of nearly the same strength, but of less bulk, and this repeated when necessary—or should the first not succeed in allaying the irritation of the stomach, it should be repeated in half an hour. A tea-spoonful of strong coffee, without sugar or milk, every fifteen minutes, should be given to very young children especially; but we believe all ages would profit by it in larger doses. We have, in a number of instances since we first tried it, seen it act like a charm.

3. Catharine Beecher, *A Treatise on Domestic Economy* (Boston: Marsh, Capen, Lyon, and Webb, 1841). Beecher was a reformer whose *Treatise* offered advice to women about the management of domestic life. Her discussions of health and child care quote the experts of the day. In the excerpts below from her chapter on the care of infants she offers her own observations and opinion.

In regard to the importance of giving animal food to children, at all, there are many popular notions, which are very incorrect. Many seem to think that animal food is more nourishing than vegetable, and, when a child is weak and thin, will for this reason give it meat. This is an entire mistake. Experiments, repeatedly made by chemists, prove the contrary; and tables are made out, showing the relative amount of nourishment in each kind of food. From these tables it appears, that, while beef contains thirty-five per cent. Of nutritious matter, rice and wheat contain from eighty to ninety-five per cent. One pound of rice, then contains as much nourishment as two pounds and a half of beef. The reason why meat has been supposed to be more nourishing, is that, on account of its stimulating property, the stomach works faster, and digests it quicker; while the withdrawal of a meat diet produces a temporary loss of strength, just as the withdrawal of other stimulants are followed by consequent languor.

The result of the treatment of young children in the Orphan Asylum, at Albany, New York, is one upon which all who have the care of young children should deeply ponder. This institution was established in 1829–1830; and during the six succeeding years, its average number of children was eighty. For the first three years, their diet was meat once a day, fine bread, rice, Indian puddings, vegetables, fruits, and milk. Considerable attention was given to clothing, fresh air, and exercise; and they were bathed once in three weeks. During these three years, from four to six children were continually on the sick list, and sometimes more; one or two assistant nurses were necessary; a physician was called two or three times a week; and in this time there were between thirty and forty deaths. At the end of this time, the management was changed, in these respects. Daily ablutions of the whole body were practised; bread of unbolted flour was substituted for that of fine wheat; and all animal food was banished. More attention was also paid to clothing, bedding, fresh air and exercise. The result was, that the nursery was vacated, the nurse and physician no longer needed, and for two years not a single case of sickness or death occurred. The third year, also, there were no deaths, except of those two idiots, and one other child, all of whom were new inmates, who had not been subjected to this treatment. Their teachers also testified that there was a very manifest increase of intellectual vigor and activity, while there was much less irritability of temper.

The preceding general views of medical writers, furnish the ground for several more minute directions. An infant should be washed all over, every morning, with warm water, and, in cool weather, in a warm room. The head should be thoroughly washed, and brushed clean with a soft brush. If, by neglect, a covering of dirt forms at the roots of the hear, the yolk of an egg, rubbed in and combed out while damp, will remove it without trouble. After washing, fine starch should be sprinkled, from a muslin bag, in creases of fat, under the knees and in the groin.

Do not give any stimulating food or drinks, such as tea, coffee, spices, pepper, mustard, and the like; and the less animal food given, the better. The Writer knows a family of eleven children, all but one born with robust constitutions, and reared in the country, through early childhood, in fine health. But they were allowed to eat meat, twice a day, with butter and gravy; and every one, in afterlife, suffered severely, either from chronic cutaneous eruptions, or from dyspepsy, or from liver complaints or from excessive nervous excitability. Not one escaped.

4. Elizabeth Blackwell, *The Laws of Life, With Special Reference to the Physical Education of Girls* (New York: George P. Putnam, 1852). Blackwell was the first woman in the United States to obtain a regular medical degree. She was a reformer whose writings about health focused extensively on prevention. The following excerpt comes from the concluding section of her book.

What then must be done in order to save the rising generation from the physical weakness and disease, with their attendant evils, which prevails so widely in the present race, and which are rapidly increasing in extent?

I answer, 1st. The domestic habits of our households must be changed for children; their food, dress, sleeping apartments, and hours for rising and retiring, must be regulated with scrupulous regard for their physical welfare, and according to the principles so often laid down in the course of our re-marks.

2d. The system of school discipline must be essentially modified. The period of life from seven to sixteen being regarded as the special season of physical growth, the bodily development must be considered as the basis of all true education; we must cease to force the learning of a later period upon the youthful mind at that age. A system of scientific gymnastic training should be adopted—every kind of sport encouraged—the accomplishments of riding, dancing, singing, swimming, archery, &c., should be taught; the moral and religious nature should be educated by the intercourse and influences of every day. The *habits* of intellect should be carefully trained in conversation and in those studies which are suitable to the age; these studies should be such as require the aid of the senses—writing, drawing, the study of charts and maps, the living languages and a variety of other subjects, might be employed to advantage. There should be frequent expeditions into the country or to the sea-side, where in direct intercourse with nature, the child in conversation with its teacher, would learn with the utmost avidity and happiness—for such expeditions our city enjoys rare advantages; an hour's journey by steamboat or omnibus would bring the children into the midst of the magnificent country which borders the Hudson; or spread them along the shores of the Atlantic.

The idea of physical development should never be forgotten in any study; no pursuit should place the child under unfavorable conditions of position, atmosphere, &c., and direct physical exercise should constantly terminate the short periods of mental application. Lofty, well ventilated halls, and a large piece of ground partly shaded by trees, should be essential elements of every establishment for education.

Such changes could easily be brought about in our school system; it only needs that public opinion should be roused to the necessity of an ample provision for the physical education of the young—that mothers should realize the immense mischief that is done to their daughters by neglecting the body and overtasking the mind, and that they should resolve as a duty of primary importance to give them a strong physical organization. Public sentiment thus requiring the true method of education, would soon find its wants satisfied by the necessary institutions, and intelligent teachers would gladly welcome the change, for they clearly perceive the evils of the present system—though they are quite unable, alone, to remedy them.

5. L. Emmett Holt, MD, *The Care and Feeding of Children: A Catechism for the Use of Mothers and Children's Nurses* (New York: D. Appleton, 1894). Holt was one of the most prominent pediatricians of the late nineteenth and early

twentieth centuries. This book was originally written as a pamphlet for the nurses at the New York Babies Hospital, where Holt was physician in chief. It went through seventy-five printings and was the most-used professional guidebook of the twentieth century until the publication of Dr. Spock's *The Common Sense Book of Baby and Child Care.* Note that Holt addressed, in a question-and-answer format, topics ranging from the risks of playing with babies to the onset of contagious illnesses.

At what age may playing with babies be begun?
Never until four months, and better not until six months. The less of it at any time the better for the infant.

What harm is done by playing with very young babies?
They are made nervous and irritable, sleep badly, and suffer in other respects.

When should children be played with?
If at all, in the morning, or after the midday nap. Never just before bedtime.

How does measles begin?
Gradually, like an ordinary cold in the head, with cough, sneezing, running eyes and nose. The eruption usually appears on the fourth day, first on the face and neck.

How does scarlet fever begin?
Generally it comes suddenly, with vomiting, high fever, and sore throat. The eruption appears upon the second day, first upon the neck and chest.

How does diphtheria begin?
Sometimes suddenly, but usually very gradually, with sore throat and often swelling of the glands of the neck, with white patches upon the tonsils, or a very free discharge from the nostrils.

At what period are these diseases contagious?
From the very beginning of the symptoms. Measles and scarlet fever are quite likely to be communicated in the early stages as when the eruption is fully out.

How long should a child with any of these disease be kept away from other children?
In measles, two weeks after the rash is gone; in scarlet fever, at least four weeks after the rash has gone, and longer if the peeling is not over or if the ears are running; in diphtheria, at least three weeks after the throat is well, and four weeks if the case has been severe.

What should be done if a child shows the first symptoms of a serious illness?
The child should be put to bed. If it is an infant, the food should be diluted to one half of the usual strength. If an older child, only fluid food should be given. If the child seems feverish take the temperature. If the bowels are constipated give a teaspoonful of castor oil, but no other medi-

cations without the doctor's orders. Send for the doctor at once, and until he comes carefully exclude all the other children from the room.

6. J. Compton Burnett, *Delicate, Backward, Puny, and Stunted Children: Their Developmental Defects and Moral Peculiarities Considered as Ailments Amenable to Treatment by Medicines* (Philadelphia: Boericke and Tafel, 1896). Burnett discusses homeopathic treatments and offers examples of children he has treated successfully. Medical books journals commonly published case reports such as those excerpted below.

Blighted by Suppressed Ringworm

Young organisms are stunted by many acute diseases: this no one denies, "he has never got over the effects of measles." It is an often-told and ever-believed story—That vaccination very frequently blights the young organisms. I have often shown, and do now solemnly re-affirm, that the suppression of common ringworm frequently also blights the organisms of the sufferers; by *suppressed* I mean the ordinary external wash-and-scour method of ridding the outside of the body of the outside manifestations of the malady, the inward disease-essence remaining choked-up within.

A little stunted maid of 12 years was brought to me on June 27, 1892, because she was undersized and deaf. The glands under the right ear are indurated and enlarged; her tongue pippy; she is dusky in the neck. Patient had had ringworm for two years, and when that was cured (?), she went deaf.

She has been twice vaccinated.
Rx Bacill. 30.
July 25.—She has begun to grow!
Rx Rep
August 26.—Her teeth are clearing.
Ib. CC.
September 26.—Is growing; hearing much better; teeth getting cleaner and of a better colour.
Ib. C.

And thus the treatment was continued till the summer of 1893, at which date I find in my case-records the following note:—"Has grown enormously; her glands are better; still deaf;" since when I have not seen her, but quite lately I heard from her mother that patient is in good health and away at school at the seaside, but she is still hard of hearing.

Arrested development of eyes and teeth

A frail, undersized, almost toothless girl of 16 was brought to me on November 11, 1887, principally for her eyes. She had been at the ophthalmic hospitals, and also under the best ophthalmic surgeons for "inflammation of the nerve of the sight," and was informed that she would probably go blind. However, she had mended under their own care till the present time so far that spectacles were of some slight service. She suffers much from headaches, which are worse in bed at night. Her teeth are indented in dots, notched, and imbedded more or less in tartar. Much toothache.

Rx Luet. CC.
December 9.—Headache better; toothache gone.
Rx Tc. Geranium Robertianum 3x, 3iv, five drops in a tablespoonful of water night and morning
January 4, 1888.—Headache much worse, also toothache.
Rx Luet. CC.
February 1.—About the same; tuberculous teeth.
Rx Bacill. 30.
March 9.—Much pain in the right side of the face; worse on getting warm in bed.
Rx Trit. 3 Aurum met. four grains dry on the tongue at bedtime
May 9.—Very drowsy; pains now worse after food
Rx Thuja Occid. 30
June 17, 1891 Been going the round of oculists gain. Typically tuberculous teeth; much frontal headache.
Rx Bacill. CC.
July 15.—Headache worse; eyes ache very much; teeth beginning to clean a little
Rx Rep. (1000).

And thus the treatment went on till the summer of 1893, when patient's teeth and general physique were notably improved, inclusive of her eyes; but just as the teeth are still imperfect though very much improved, so are her eyes; and I have now ordered the mechanical dentist for her teeth and the mechanical oculist for her eyes, as further organic improvements is not to be expected.

Spectacles come in for the organically irremediable; but to start children in life with spectacles without first trying to mend their ocular defects vitally is hardly worth of really scientific physicians.

A truism?

Quite so, but bespectacled children are all over the place nevertheless, and practically no one ever tries to cure eyes.

7. Hancock County Teacher, *The Lament of the Decayed Tooth* (Hancock County Public Health Service, 1929). This document is an example of health education materials used to teach public school children the rules of proper personal hygiene

> I am a poor decayed tooth.
>
> Would I were strong and well!
>
> Where are the foods my owner should eat?
>
> I see nothing

But CANDY and FROSTED CAKE,

ICE-CREAM and CHEWING GUM!!

Yea, my soul crieth for LIME

And for IRON. . . . If my owner

Would drink MILK and eat

VEGETABLES

And lunch on FRESH FRUITS

How I would improve!!!

Instead I . . . But where are my friends?

Come, RHEUMATISM! Come, CARDIAC INFECTION!

And where are you, INFLAMED TONSILS?

But what do I hear? . . . To the Dentist's?

The right Foods? . . . Oh, oh, oh, what JOY!

I shall be a decayed tooth no longer!

My owner realizes my sterling worth at last!

I am SAVED, thanks to that BLESSED HANCOCK COUNTY NURSE!

8. Eleanor Glendower Griffith, *Cho-Cho and the Health Fairy* (New York: Child Health Organization of America, 1920). This is another example of health education materials from the 1920s. Authors typically would use poems and stories to make the health lessons fun and interesting for children.

The House the Children Built

Once upon a time there lived a good and beautiful Fairy named Health, and she was very happy, for all around were flowers and trees and birds and in the midst of these, her house.

Now, Health's house was built of bricks and shingles and lovely colored glass. One day when the sky was blue and the sun shining, down the road came an ugly old Witch. Her face was hard and her eyes were very cruel. She stopped in front of Health's lovely garden and from her pocket drew forth a yellow ball and threw it with all her strength toward the house.

It settled on the roof, and where it fell there sprang forth fire, which spread and spread over the house, until it was a mass of flames. Fairy Health ran to the well for water, but before her tiny hands could draw water up from the well, her house was burnt beyond all help.

When the Witch, whose name was Ignorance, saw the harm she had done, she laughed a cruel laugh and hobbled down the road.

Poor little Fairy Health sank upon the grass in her garden and cried. At last she was conscious of a voice and looking up, saw in a green bush quite near a lovely Bird, who said: "Keep up your courage, Fairy, for I will tell you how to build your house anew."

Health dried her eyes upon a sweet geranium leaf, and asked him how that could possibly be done.

The Bird replied: "It can be done by the hands of Children alone. Every time a Child learns to eat the right food, a brick shall be added to your house, every time a Child learns to sleep in the sweet fresh air, a shingle shall be put upon the roof. And every time a Child learns to play and be happy, a colored glass shall be added to the windows."

"But alas!" said Fairy Health, "How shall we teach the Children these things?"

"I will go to the Teachers who are wise and good," said the Bird, "and tell them what to do."

So the Bird, whose name was Education, started on his journey. He took his brother Rumor with him, to help tell the Teachers, because there were a great many Teachers to be told about the Children's health.

Far and near these wise birds traveled, to little towns and to big cities, and everywhere the Teachers listened to their story, until in all that great country, the Children were taught to eat wholesome food, to sleep in the sweet fresh air, and to play and be happy.

And as the Children grew healthy and happy, the bricks were added to the Fairy's house, and shingles were put upon the roof. Lovely glass filled up the broken windows, and once again there stood among the trees and flowers, a house so beautiful that strangers, passing by, paused to admire it. Health often invited them to rest in her garden, and as she refreshed them with sparkling water from the well, she told the story of her house, and how Children had rebuilt it for her.

9 Images of Child Health and Providers

The following images come from the National League for Nursing Archives, 1894–1952. They are undated but clearly of mid-twentieth-century vintage and show typical scenes of children receiving health care or health education.

THEME ONE: INFANT CARE

A nurse from the Los Angeles City Health Department demonstrating infant care to a new mother

A nurse bathing a baby as three other children watch

A nurse caring for an infant as a mother lies in bed and her five children observe

A member of the Visiting Nurse Association demonstrating infant care and bathing techniques to parents

THEME TWO: NURSING CARE OF CHILDREN

A nurse examining a small boy's throat

A nurse helping a young boy on crutches take his first steps (Image from the United States Public Health Service)

A nurse examining the ears of a preschool child

A nurse weighing an infant while other children watch

THEME THREE: MEDICAL AND DENTAL CARE OF CHILDREN

A dentist examining a young boy's teeth while others look on

A physician examining an infant while the mother and a nurse look on

A doctor examining a child in the school health room (Image from the Avon Avenue School, Newark, New Jersey)

THEME FOUR: HEALTH EDUCATION

Seventh-grade girls participating in demonstrations preparing children's food, clothing, and toys, and in bathing infants

Children at a makeshift hand-washing assembly line (From the Agricultural School, Atlantic County, New Jersey)

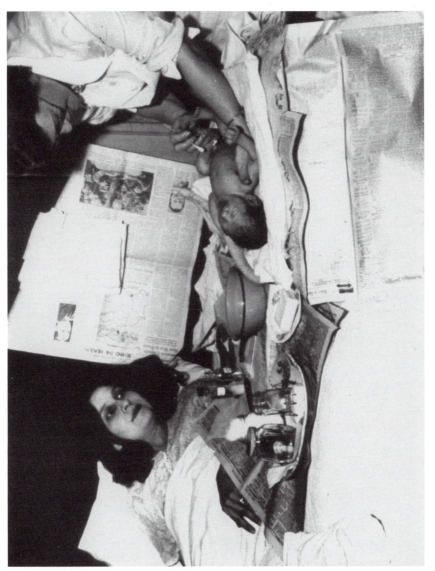

A nurse from the Los Angeles City Health Department demonstrating infant care to a new mother

A nurse bathing a baby as three other children watch

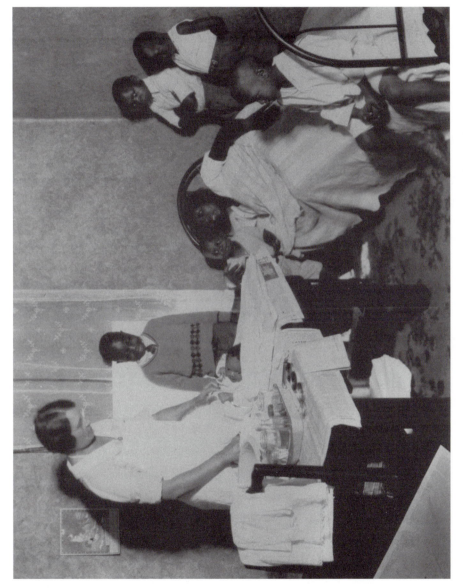

A nurse caring for an infant as a mother lies in bed and her five children observe

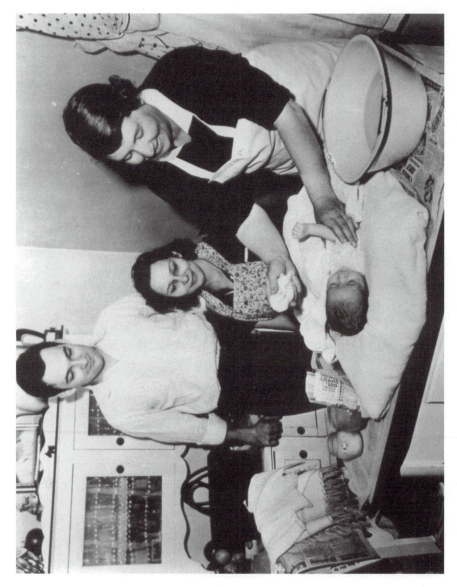

A member of the Visiting Nurse Association demonstrating infant care and bathing techniques to parents

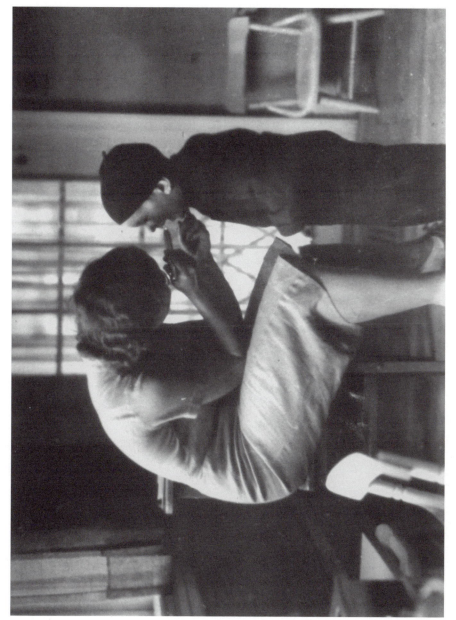

A nurse examining a small boy's throat

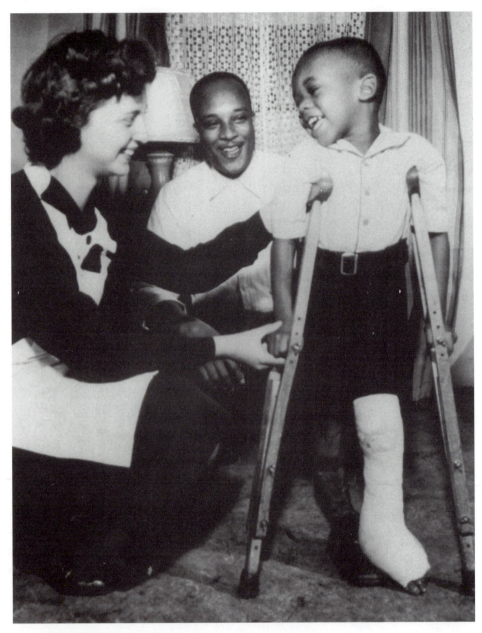

A nurse helping a young boy on crutches take his first steps (Image from the United States Public Health Service)

A nurse examining the ears of a preschool child

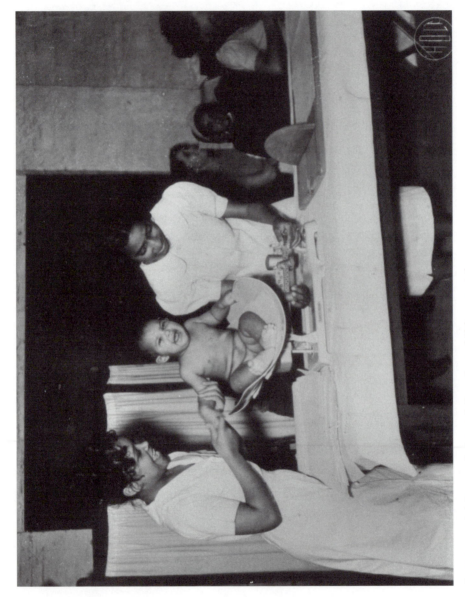

A nurse weighing an infant while other children watch

166

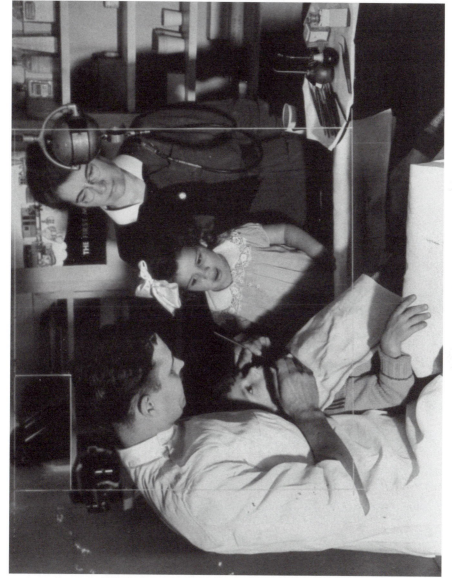

A dentist examining a young boy's teeth while others look on

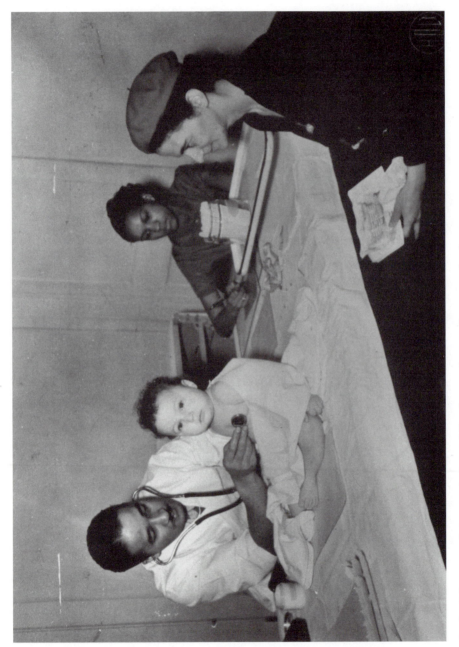

A physician examining an infant while the mother and a nurse look on

A doctor examining a child in the school health room (Image from the Avon Avenue School, Newark, New Jersey)

Seventh-grade girls participating in demonstrations preparing children's food, clothing, and toys, and in bathing infants

Children at a makeshift hand-washing assembly line (From the Agricultural School, Atlantic County, New Jersey)

10 Institutions for Children

Beginning in the mid-nineteenth century, institutions for the sick and dependent were erected by philanthropists and municipalities. Some had separate wings for children, but in other cases separate institutions were built for them, as children were seen as a class needing special protection and moral guidance.

1. *On the Causes of Idiocy; Being the Supplement to a Report by Dr. S. G. Howe and the Other Commissioners Appointed by the Governor of Massachusetts to Inquire into the Condition of the Idiots of the Commonwealth, Dated February 26, 1848* (Edinburgh: MacLachland and Stewart, 1858; reprint New York: Arno, 1972). In 1850 the Massachusetts legislature funded a School for Idiotic and Feeble-Minded Youth, which was directed by noted physician and reformer Samuel Gridley Howe. In this report he and others assess the causes of idiocy. A summary of the work of the school included in the report is also excerpted below.

It may be assumed as certain, that in all cases where children are born deformed, or blind, or deaf, or idiotic, or so imperfectly and feebly organized that they cannot come to maturity under ordinary circumstances, or have the seeds of early decay, or have original impetuosity of passions that amount to moral insanity,—in all such cases the fault lies with the progenitors. Whether they sinned in ignorance or in willfulness, matters not as to the effect of the sin upon the offspring. The laws of God are so clear that he who *will* read may do so. If a man violates them ignorantly, he suffers the simple penalty; if he violates them knowingly, he has remorse added to his suffering; but in no case can the penalty be remitted to him.

No. 35. Jonas ——, aged 8 years. His body is well-proportioned and strong, but very small. Face has the deformed look of idiocy. The sides of his head seem to be at a fever heat. He is almost all the time in violent motion. His appetite is not only voracious, but evidently morbid and insatiable; for, after eating heartily at table, he swallows anything he can lay his hands upon, raw potatoes, the bark of trees, chips of wood, and even small stones. He has been known to swallow pebbles as large as chestnuts. He hears and seems to understand the meaning of some sounds, but has no speech. He has no sense of propriety, no affection, no attachment; his brothers and sisters are no more to him than the dog and cat.

His father was intemperate to the last degree. His mother was of a very scrofulous habit of body.

Results of the Experimental School for Teaching and Training Idiotic Children in Massachusetts (extracted from the Third and Final Report on the School, by Dr. S. G. Howe, 1852).

Of the whole number of pupils of whom account is to be made, four, the youngest of whom was about six years of age, could not sit erect, and had no use of their limbs when they entered the school; they could not even put victuals to their mouths. Two of these only proved to be proper subjects, and remained. They have both greatly improved: they can sit up at a desk or table, and one can use his legs and toddle about by holding on to the wall.

Seven had very imperfect use of their limbs. They could walk about a room feebly, but could not help themselves. Of these seven, four only remained; and of these four, three have greatly improved; the other has not.

Seventeen were filthy in their habits. Of these, thirteen have greatly improved. Most of them are now habitually clean, and always desirous of being so. The other four have as yet made little improvement.

Twenty-two could not dress themselves. Of the twelve who remained over a year, eight now dress themselves without assistance.

2. *Fourteenth Annual Report (Year 1884) of the Board of Directors of the Children's Hospital of the District of Columbia* (Washington, D.C.: 1885). The Children's Hospital of the District of Columbia was incorporated in 1870 as a charitable organization for the medical and surgical treatment of the diseases of children. Admission was fixed at age twelve but without respect to color, creed, or sex. At the time of this report the hospital had seventy-two beds, with an average daily census of forty-four patients. Staffing included a resident physician, two assistants, a matron, five nurses, five servants, a cook, two laundresses, and a chambermaid. There were, in addition, four attending physicians and four assistants, as well as an outdoor physician.

Letter of the President to the Commissioners, in answer to their Communication Requesting a Detailed Statement of the Operations of the Children's Hospital for the Fiscal Year Ending June 30, 1884.

The Honorable Commissioners of the District of Columbia

Gentlemen: Agreeably to your request of the 1st inst., I furnish herewith a "detailed statement of the operations of the Children's Hospital of the District of Columbia, for the fiscal year ending June 30th, 1884."

During the year two thousand one hundred and fifty-two (2,152) indigent children have received medical and surgical treatment in this Institution. Of this number, one hundred and eighty-three (183) have occupied beds in the Hospital, with all their wants gratuitously supplied, and one thousand nine hundred and sixty-nine (1,969) have been treated in the Dispensary. On the first of July 1883, there were fifty-one (51) children in the wards of the Hospital; and during the year, one hundred and thirty-two (132) were admitted—fifty-six (56) white, and seventy-six (76) colored. Of this number, eighty-nine (89) were fully cured and discharged—white, forty-eight (48), black, forty-one (41); twenty (20) were discharged, upon the application of parents and friends, improved—ten (10) white, and ten (10) black; five were discharged, improved—two (2) white, and three (3) black; eight (8) were removed by their parents, and twenty-three (23) have died—three (3) white, and twenty (20) black—leaving thirty-nine (39) children under treatment in the wards, on the 1st of July, 1884. Of the large number of children under treatment in the Dispensary during the year, seven hundred and sixty-nine (769) were white, and twelve hundred (1,200) colored.

During the year, forty-two (42) surgical operations were performed—twenty-two in Hospital proper, and twenty (20) in Dispensary.

As illustrative of the time and attention bestowed upon the children under treatment, your attention is called to the fact that ten thousand six hundred and ninety-two (10,692) prescriptions were compounded for their relief.

The mortality during the year has principally been confined to the colored children, caused to a great extent by their indifferent hygienic surroundings before being brought to the Hospital, and their liability from that and other causes to contract consumption; a number of children are also brought to the Hospital, when the diseases from which they are suffering, have made such inroads that very little can be done for them save to temporarily relieve their suffering. . . .

Your obedient servant,
(Signed) Samuel V. Niles,
President of the Children's Hospital, District of Columbia

3. *Seventh Annual Report of the Children's Homeopathic Hospital of Philadelphia* (Philadelphia: C. R. Deacon, 1885). Excerpts from the hospital reports reveal the similarities between homeopathic and regular medical care of sick children.

Report

Besides the cases treated in the wards, a vast amount of suffering is relieved in the Out-Patient Department attached to the hospital.

A glance at the Report of the Medical Staff will show with what success various cases have been treated. Surely this proof of the power to relieve these afflicted children should incite us to greater efforts in bringing health and happiness to the little ones put under our care, who would otherwise spend lives of pain and suffering.

The demands for food, clothing, medicines, instruments, etc., are constant, and we appeal to the public, especially to those who have little ones of their own, and who thus know the utter helplessness of sick children, to aid us in our work both by prayers and contributions.

We tender our heartfelt thanks to the churches, Sunday-schools, societies, the press, and to all who have so kindly assisted us by their contributions. We would especially remember the children, whose gifts are always most acceptable, and who, by bringing them in person, brighten the faces and gladden the hearts of the little sufferers. We trust our many helpers will continue their interest and will ever try to enlist the sympathy of their friends in our good works.

The monthly average number in the Hospital for 1884 was thirty one, and the average expense per month of each child was five dollars and ninety-eight cents; average monthly expense for matron, nurses, help, groceries, etc., one hundred and eighty-five dollars and thirty-one cents.

Seeing the need of isolated wards in case an epidemic, such as diphtheria, scarlatina, whooping-cough, measles, or inflammation of the eyes, should break out from cases exposed to such diseases before admission and developing afterward, the Directors have fitted up three large rooms in the building on Carlisle street, away from the main building, for use in such emergencies, so that the inmates may be protected from such as risk as formerly existed.

We have received in the Hospital fifty-seven cases of eczema capitis, out of which number we have discharged (cured) forty-eight, and have in the Hospital at present nine afflicted with it, all of whom are in a fair way of recovery. Such has been our success in this particular disease that we have had two children's homes placed in our charge for hospital treatment and have convinced five Homes of the superior advantages of Homeopathy.

An interesting case or two we will draw attention to—one that of a little girl who was found six months ago in a deserted house. When discovered by the police, shut up alone, the child was so weak from loss of food and drink—having had nothing for nearly two days—that she could scarcely utter a sound. She had been placed to board with a family that had moved out, shutting up the house, leaving the helpless little thing to sob and cry and starve and die. Both lower limbs and the right arm were completely paralyzed. Now, under homeopathic care and treatment, she can walk and use her right arm and is well and healthy.

Still another case we will mention—that of a little boy from Mt. Ephraim, N.J. When he was admitted he resembled in his movements more an animal than a human being. His lower limbs had been so deformed by rachitis that he could not walk. He moved about the room by the aid of a stick, with a hop and a jump, much in the manner of a kangaroo. Our surgeon operated on him—straightened his limbs by sawing out pieces of the bones, then breaking them and setting the limbs in a straight direction. This made good legs for him when he healed. He was discharged at the end of six months, walking nicely, though still on crutches. We received a letter from him lately stating that he is now able to help his father. A brighter, finer looking boy than he is now you will not find.

In fact, many emaciated, pale, haggard, puny, and suffering children come to us that go away plump, healthy and bright.

Charles B. Kellogg
Secretary

Out-Patient Report
    From May 1st, 1883 to January 1st, 1885

Total Prescriptions	24006
New cases	4247
Hospital Cases	
Total Surgical	71
Total Medical	104

4. *Second Annual Report of the New York State Hospital for the Care of Crippled and Deformed Children for the Year Ending September 30, 1902* (Albany, N.Y.: 1903). The excerpts below come from the report of the surgeon in chief and superintendent. His report details the demand for care from the parents.

To the Board of Managers, New York State Hospital for the Care of Crippled and Deformed Children:

Gentlemen.—I have the honor to submit for your consideration a report of the operations of your hospital for the year ending September 30, 1902.

As mentioned in my report a year ago the hospital was opened for the reception of patients early in December 1900.

On the first of October, 1901 there were 19 patients under treatment. Since that time 16 new patients have been received; 10 have been discharged leaving 25 under treatment on October 1, 1902.

There were 81 formal, written, applications for admission, in most cases accompanied by the necessary affidavit. In addition, over 75 verbal applications were made to members of the Medical Staff, mostly from New York city, nearly all of which were eligible. As no vacancies existed, and as the waiting list was already large and as we seek to favor, so far as is right and proper, the "up State" applications, no formal record was made of these applications. It may be safely stated that 150 applications for admission have been made during the year. Of the 35 treated, 22 were boys and 13 were girls, and 17 were received from New York county and 18 were received from counties outside of New York.

There are, at present, under treatment, 15 patients with hip joint disease; 1 patient with congenital dislocation of the hip joint; 1 patient with Pott's disease of the spine; 2 patients with club food; 3 patients with deformities of infantile paralysis; 1 patient with lateral curvature of the spine and 2 with white swelling of the knee. Total, 25 patients.

It was not until last June that the operating room was equipped for work. On June 10th the first surgical operations were performed. Altogether, 7 operations were performed, on various occasions, and all successfully.

The one great burden which has fallen upon your executive officer has not been the daily routine connected with the conduct of the hospital, but the frequent necessity of declining a poor suffering child who sadly needs our care.

Respectfully yours,
Newton M. Shaffer, M.D. Surgeon-in-Chief and Superintendent

5. Miss Robin, "Memories of Bellevue and Bellevue Children," *Trained Nurse* 8 (1892): 567–77. In this article, a trained nurse at New York's Bellevue Hospital describes some of her patients.

Lina is the next memory picture which stands before me. She is lying back on pillows in a baby's perambulator. She has straight, black hair, which is kept back from her face by a round comb. Black eyes which twinkle like a canary's, a delicate, refined face, with a clear white skin, which is too often flushed with fever. She is dead—that is to say, completely paralyzed—below the waist, and otherwise deformed in a manner terrible to see. Although she is nine years old, she has to be dressed like a little baby every day, and is then laid in her perambulator, another charitable gift, and is wheeled about wherever her fancy takes her. But however deformed the poor body may be, her heart and brain are sound and true.

I firmly believe in the law of compensation, and, as an illustration, you will find nowhere in New York a happier child. Never can I remember her unhappy. There were no fretful or even irritable days for her.

We were great friends, but on one point we had a disagreement. Lina has a great liking for strong tea, as nearly all invalids have, and I have a strong prejudice against it, thinking the milk better for her. "Lina," I remonstrate as she begs for more "if you drink so much tea you will be an old maid."

Silence for a moment, to turn this new idea over in her head. Lina with her other misfortune stammers, and she finally breaks out with "wha', wha', what is an old maid? Miss Robin, are you an old maid?"

"Yes, Lina," sadly and solemnly.

Another minute for reflection, and then with some surprise in the tone— "We', we', well then, I'—I just as lief be an old maid as not."

Oh, the sweet flattery of childhood! Lina gets her tea. Dear little child. You are almost the only one whose end I have been able to follow. Not long were you kept in your sad prison and I am sure that by that same most just and merciful law of compensation you must have gained an additional degree of happiness in heaven, which far more than repays your few years of suffering here.

Over in that corner bed behind the screen is a tall, thin, awkward lad of about twelve years of age. He is in bed most of the time from weakness and pain, but occasionally comes out of his seclusion and joins the noisy crowd. Especially is he given to nocturnal rambles and chats with the night nurse, for Stephen likes solitude. He was born and brought up in the heart of the Adirondack woods. A screen is placed about the bed, partly to please him and partly to keep him from the eyes of visitors, for Stephen is a gruesome object to look upon. He has chronic meningitis, and the swollen, ulcerated glands about his ears and neck are not for the eyes of strangers to gaze upon. It is hard to believe that even in this naughty world of ours there can be beings so selfish and hard as Stephen's relatives appear to have been. He was brought to Bellevue by the police. This is his story: His uncle, weary of the care of a chronic invalid, thought the easiest way of disposing of an unwelcome burden was to abandon him in the streets of a great city. It was sad to see the lad's homesickness at first. He could not be reconciled to exchanging his beloved woods for a crowded city hospital ward. Who could blame him? Day and night he moaned and wept. All we could do to please and comfort him was to no avail. To go home, to go home! Was his one cry.

Gradually, however, this wore away, and we felt well paid for our trouble to hear him say shyly one day to one of his nurses, "I like to be here." After this all went well. He had roused the sympathies of all, and the space round his bed was filled with colored cards and other little gifts from the doctors and other friends.

Poor Stephen! He died before I left Bellevue. Happy Stephen! For he received the grace of baptism which he would not have had in his mountain home. . . .

6. *Second Report,* River Crest, Phoenixville, Pennsylvania, Preventorium of Kensington Dispensary for the Treatment of Tuberculosis, 1915. Preventoria were begun in the early twentieth century to remove "pretubercular" children from their homes to the countryside, where they could enjoy fresh air and good food in the hope that this would prevent tuberculosis.

Report of Physicians

To "River Crest" Committee.
Ladies:
"River Crest," the Preventorium of the Kensington Dispensary, opened for the reception of the children June 21st, and fifty-three (53) children were

received during the season. Needless to say, they enjoyed every minute of the time and gained from two to ten pounds during their stay. Under the watchful eye of the Superintendent, Mrs. Ischler, and the attendants, no serious accidents occurred, and no illness to speak of—necessitating very few calls for the Physician or his assistant.

The Play Ground, recently constructed, was the home of the children from early morning until late at night. The Giant Stride, a new addition, was enjoyed by all, being a healthy exercise for them as well as an enjoyment.

There is at least one addition with which the Play Ground should be equipped for the comfort and pleasure of the children, and that is a Pavilion, wherein they may gather during damp or wet days. This will keep them in the fresh air, and carry out our rules, which require the children to be outdoors continually.

We would earnestly urge that there be great efforts made for the erection of the same.

(Signed) C. F. Doran, M.D.
J. E. Gotwals, M.D.

7. New Jersey State Institution for Feeble-Minded, Vineland, N.J., [report] undated, circa 1915. This excerpt from the report documents the institution's work with feeble-minded children. The institution opened in 1888 to provide for feeble-minded women of child-bearing age and by 1912 had become a large facility, caring for 1,500 patients of both sexes and all ages.

It is important and interesting to note that the training of the feeble minded child is identical with the training of a feeble minded adult of the same mental age, therefore, biological and social training are applied alike to the young, adolescent, and adult of a given mental grade, one of the conclusive factors in favor of the abolition of all age restrictions as a basis of admission. The first steps of the training consist in games, such as playing bean bag, buttoning shoe and dress button frames, lacing and unlacing, tying bows, fitting geometrical insets, all conducive to special objective development. It is highly essential that this sensory training be given to all such types. In adults of low mental grade, this training may progress no farther than a simple response, grading to complex sensory and manual acts, however, affording that individual its maximum degree of development and self-expression, keeping in constant exercise those evidences of a higher Being which have been their meager allotment.

As described in the following pages, the children of higher mental grade pass on through this training to the successive steps of manual and educational training under proper environmental conditions we find it necessary to intensively apply the school test under normal institutional conditions, in an attempt to demonstrate that patient's respective learning ability, one of the most important steps in the diagnosis of an atypical type of defective.

The obvious necessity for individual training, both for the mental and moral uplift of the patient and institutional community, bespeaks the urge for adequate provision in this respect.

It is interesting to note the wide range of selectivity according to the various aptitudes with regard both to the individual and to the type. Intelligent understanding of relative aptitudes must be exercised in order to conserve the proper class or individual for a given line of training or work. Imbeciles make excellent laundresses, and almost wholly has this class been conserved for this and allied domestic departures. The washing, mangling, ironing, yard, and linen room work of the entire Institution is done by this type of patient under the supervision of one trained employee with two high grade assistants, contributing largely to the health, happiness, and economic responsibility of this industrial community.

It must not be construed that nay one line occupies an individual patient's entire daily program. They are, in fact, given only a certain number of hours' of work, for which they have a certain aptitude, that is consistent with heir physical and mental well being. Their schedule is interspersed with work in the departments of music, gymnastics, industrial art, and agriculture.

8. *Biennial Report,* Children's Orthopedic Hospital (Seattle) February 1, 1920–February 1, 1922. Founded in 1907 with one bed in a ward of the Seattle General Hospital, it grew to a fully equipped hospital with 128 beds. The following is excerpts from the report of the Hospital Committee.

Social Service Agencies Cooperate

We are very much indebted to the American Red Cross, to the Public Health Nursing Department of the University of Washington, and the County and City welfare organizations for this co-operation. Nurses from these organizations visit children in remote parts of the county and state and give "follow up" care to those who have been in the Hospital for operations or remedial treatment. Another great advantage to the Hospital is that in making their round of visits through the country, these nurses discover children who need our care and, when possible, get them to us before it is too late to remedy existing illness or deformity. A very interesting illustration of the sort of help these nurses are giving us is the story of a Red Cross Nurse who drove her car from Gray's Harbor to Seattle in January with seven children that she had collected in the country about there, one a baby eleven months old. She passed one night in a hotel on the way, occupying two rooms with her brood of seven and arriving at the Clinic one Tuesday morning. After examination, three were left in the Hospital and four carried back for home treatment. The same nurse brought in four patients to a recent clinic.

Benefits of Massage Treatment

You have heard each year in these reports of the wonderful work that our surgeons are doing, straightening crooked legs and feet, mending diseased backs with the famous Albee operation, transplanting tendons, etc., but I think very little has been said of another form of treatment given there which though very slow often is productive of just as gratifying results. This is the Massage Treatment. Last May a boy of eight years came to the Hospital who had Infantile Paralysis when he was two years old and never walked afterward. Massage was advised and patiently and conscientiously persisted in, until, early in January, having been in the Hospital eight months, he walked out of the door and down the steps holding his father's hand but with no other support.

School Work and Manual Training

The Educational Department has two division, regular school and manual training. The school has an average attendance of 40. . . . Many children who are not able to be out of bed, some on Bradford Frames and others with hop trouble, in various positions take part in this work, crocheting, knitting or sewing, not only as a playtime occupation but as a help in gaining better control of muscles in hands and arms and serving as part of the general hospital scheme to help these children to become useful men and women. . . .

Splendid Work of Hospital Staff

Doctors' visits to the Hospital in the year just past numbered 181, which were 397 more than in 1920. . . . The staff of nurses has been increased with the added number of patients. We now have, besides the Superintendent, Assistant Superintendent and Night Superintendent, 5 graduate nurses, 4 undergraduate nurses, 3 pupil nurses, 7 ward helpers; also 1 Interne, 1 Historian, 1 Technician and 1 Dietitian.

Respectfully submitted,
Harriet O. Stimson, Chairman Hospital Committee

Superintendent's Report for Two Years (excerpted)

1921		
Number of Patients Applied	517	894
Number of Patients Accepted	488	872
Number of Patients Discharged Cured	134	293
Number of Patients Discharged Improved	61	131
Number of Patients Died	14	23
Number of Operations	305	630
Out-Patient Department		
Number of Children Treated	446	735
Number of Visits to Outpatient Department	1,152	1,826

11 Mental Hygiene

Americans were always concerned about the mental, emotional, and behavioral development of children. Medical discussion and intervention in these matters increased dramatically in the nineteenth century and became a critical part of life in the twentieth century.

1. Benjamin Rush, *Medical Inquiries and Observations upon the Diseases of the Mind* [facsimile of the Philadelphia 1812 edition] (New York: Hafner, 1962). Rush was the best-known physician of his day and shortly before his death published the first American textbook on diseases of the mind (what might today be termed psychiatry). Rush believed few children suffered from mental derangements, which he discusses in the excerpt below.

In entering upon the subject of the following Inquiries and Observations, I feel as if I were about to tread upon consecrated ground. I am aware of the difficulty and importance, and I thus humbly implore the *being*, whose government extends to the thoughts of all his creatures, so to direct mine, in this arduous undertaking, that nothing hurtful to my fellow citizens may fall from my pen, and that this work may be the means of lessening a portion of some of the greatest evils of human life.

Before I proceed to consider the diseases of the mind, I shall briefly mention its different faculties and operations.

Its faculties are understanding, memory, imagination, passions, the principle of faith, will, the moral faculty, conscience, and the sense of Deity.

Its principal operations, after sensation, are perception, association, judgment, reasoning and volition. All its subordinate operations, which are known by the names of attention, reflection, contemplation, wit, consciousness, and the like, are nothing but modifications of the five principal operations that have been mentioned.

The faculties of the mind have been called, very happily, internal senses. They resemble the external senses in being innate, and depending wholly upon bodily impressions to produce their specific operations. These impressions are made through the medium of the external senses. As well might be attempt to excite thought in a piece of marble by striking it with our hand, as expect to produce a sing operation of the mind in a person deprived of the external senses of touch, seeing, hearing, taste, and smell.

All the operations in the mind are the effects of motions previously excited in the brain, and every idea and thought appears to depend upon a motion peculiar to itself. In a sound state of the mind these motions are regular, and succeed impressions upon the brain with the same certainty and uniformity that perceptions succeed impressions upon the senses in their sound state.

In inquiring into the causes of the diseases of the mind, and the remedies that are proper to relieve them, I shall employ the term derangement to signify the diseases of all the faculties of the mind.

Having rejected the abdominal viscera, the nerves, and the mind as the primary seats of madness, I shall now deliver an opinion, which I have long believed and taught in my lectures, and that is, that the cause of madness is seated primarily in the blood-vessels of the brain and that it depends upon the same kind of morbid and irregular actions that constitute other arterial diseases. There is nothing specific in these actions. They are a part of the unity of disease, particularly of fever; of which madness is a chronic form, affecting that part of the brain which is the seat of the mind.

My reasons for believing the cause of madness to be seated in the blood vessels of the brain are drawn,

I. From its remote and exciting causes, many of which are the same with those which induce fever and certain diseases of the brain, particularly phrenitis, apoplexy palsy, and epilepsy, all of which are admitted to have their seats in a greater or less degree in the blood-vessels. Of thirty-six dissections of the brains of persons who had died of madness. Mr. Pinel says he could perceive no difference between the morbid appearances in them and in the brains of persons who had died of apoplexy and epilepsy. The sameness of these appearances however do not prove that all those diseases occupy the same parts of the brain: I believe they do not, especially in their first stage: they become diffused over the whole brain, probably in their last stages, or in the paroxysm of death. Dr. Johnson, of Exeter, in speaking of the diseases of the abdominal viscera, mentions their sympathy with each other, by what he very happily calls "an intercommunion of sensations." It would seem as if a similar intercommunion took place between all the diseases of the brain. It is remarkable they all discover, in every part of the brain, marks of a morbid state of the blood-vessels.

II. From the ages and constitutions of persons who are most subject to madness. The former are in those years in which acute and inflammatory arterial diseases usually affect the body, and the latter, in persons who labour under the arterial predisposition.

Madness, it has been said, seldom occurs under puberty. To the small number of instances of it that are upon record I shall add four more. Two boys, the one of eleven, and the other of seven years of age, were admitted into our Hospital with this disease (the latter during the time of my attendance in 1799) and both discharged cured. I have since seen an instance of it in the year 1803, in a child of two years old, that had been affected with cholera infantum; and another in a child of the same age, in the year 1808, that was affected with internal dropsy of the brain. They both discovered the countenance of madness, and they both attempted to bite, first their mothers, and afterwards their own flesh. The reason why children and persons under puberty are so rarely affected with madness must be ascribed to mental impressions, which are its most frequent cause, being too transient in their effects, from the instability of their minds, to excite their brains into permanently diseased actions. It is true, children are often affected with delirium, but this is a symptom of general fever, which is always induced like the few cases of madness in children that I have mentioned, only by corporeal causes.

2. Elizabeth Blackwell, *The Laws of Life, With Special Reference to the Physical Education of Girls* (New York: George P. Putnam, 1852). Blackwell was the first woman in the United States to obtain a regular medical degree. She was a reformer whose writings about health focused extensively on prevention. The following excerpt comes from the concluding section of her book; she warns against "overtasking" the minds of girls and neglecting their physical development.

What then must be done in order to save the rising generation from the physical weakness and disease, with their attendant evils, which prevails so widely in the present race, and which are rapidly increasing in extent?

I answer, 1st. The domestic habits of our households must be changed for children; their food, dress, sleeping apartments, and hours for rising and retiring, must be regulated with scrupulous regard for their physical welfare, and according to the principles so often laid down in the course of our remarks.

2d. The system of school discipline must be essentially modified. The period of life from seven to sixteen being regarded as the special season of physical growth, the bodily development must be considered as the basis of all true education; we must cease to force the learning of a later period upon the youthful mind at that age. A system of scientific gymnastic training should be adopted—every kind of sport encouraged—the accomplishments of riding, dancing, singing, swimming, archery, &c., should be taught; the moral and religious nature should be educated by the intercourse and in-fluences of every day. The *habits* of intellect should be carefully trained in conversation and in those studies which are suitable to the age; these stud-ies should be such as require the aid of the senses—writing, drawing, the study of charts and maps, the living languages and a variety of other sub-jects, might be employed to advantage. There should be frequent expedi-tions into the country or to the sea-side, where in direct intercourse with nature, the child in conversation with its teacher, would learn with the ut-most avidity and happiness—for such expeditions our city enjoys rare ad-vantages; an hour's journey by steamboat or omnibus would bring the children into the midst of the magnificent country which borders the Hudson; or spread them along the shores of the Atlantic.

The idea of physical development should never be forgotten in any study; no pursuit should place the child under unfavorable conditions of position, atmosphere, &c., and direct physical exercise should constantly terminate the short periods of mental application. Lofty, well ventilated halls, and a large piece of ground partly shaded by trees, should be essential elements of every establishment for education.

Such changes could easily be brought about in our school system; it only needs that public opinion should be roused to the necessity of an ample pro-vision for the physical education of the young—that mothers should real-ize the immense mischief that is done to their daughters by neglecting the body and overtasking the mind, and that they should resolve as a duty of primary importance to give them a strong physical organization. Public sen-timent thus requiring the true method of education, would soon find its wants satisfied by the necessary institutions, and intelligent teachers would gladly welcome the change, for they clearly perceive the evils of the present system—though they are quite unable, alone, to remedy them.

3. John Madison Taylor, "The Insane Disorders of Childhood," *Archives of Pediatrics* 11 (1894): 100–15. Taylor was a professor of diseases of children and a consultant to the Vineland Training School for Backward and Feeble-Minded Children. The article excerpted below describes some of the fac-tors causing mental disease in children.

It comes in the way of those who see much of children's diseases to meet with many cases of what may be collectively called insane disorders. A con-sideration of these rather in the line of their nature and requirements than of elaborate speculation as to causation and phenomena, may prove of use to the practical physician.

Insanity is rare in childhood arising from the same sources whence it comes in the adult, but mental defects are only too common and grow worse with startling rapidity unless most wisely handled. Minor mental deflections, or shortcomings, which may escape attention, form fertile ground for in-eradicably evil mental attitudes to take ready root. Active disease frequently disturbs the cerebral functions, and these may not recover with the subsidence of the acute processes, even though the structural damage be small. When this occurs, it is important carefully to direct even the simplest educational and disciplinary measures in order to inhibit further lapses and regain healthy tone.

In a long experience in dispensary work among children, such cases have occupied much of my attention, and certain principles of guidance have become formulated in my mind, which may be trite enough, but nevertheless prove of service to others.

My purpose is to call attention to the causal factors which should be scrutinized by the physician so soon as the least ground for apprehension arises, and after general consideration of these point out how to deal with suspicious phenomena.

The sources of these states are many and of wide reach. Some are the outcome of depressed physical powers due to want and misery; many more, however, are the result of careless usages, complications, and vice.

In certain parental tendencies, there lies danger. Vitiated appetites, as for alcohol, opium, or even tobacco, interlace with other or are themselves a ground for diseases of body as well as of mind. Tuberculous families frequently present instances of acute nervous disease terminating in swift fatalities, and offer also little resisting power against exciting causes. Then there are families of notably unstable nervous equilibrium in whom acute disease or overwrought emotions work sad havoc. Cultivation of emotions in the way of mundane or heavenly things, or, per contra, an undue asceticism or self-repression, may exercise a hurtful effect upon the offspring. When these various causes thus sketched out, and of limitless scope and variety are, become superadded, one to the other, by the marriage of a tuberculous father to a hysterical mother, or an alcoholic father to an over-conscientious, highly spiritual mother, disaster may be predicted for the issue. Again, upon the impressionable nature of developing nervous tissues in a child hyper-sensitive by heredity, exciting causes act only too overwhelmingly. Influences capable themselves of disturbing even a healthy minded child are many. Acute febrile diseases produce commonly delirium, which is itself a transient insanity, and this may pass utterly and quickly away, or leave an indelible stain upon the cerebrum. That surprising condition which we regard as accidental, because as yet we do not know how to explain its origin, known as precocity, is a source of peril if not an evidence of mental unsoundness. It is almost never a ground for parental gratulation and only rarely fulfils youthful promise and not seldom destines its possessor to neurosis.

The childish brain is very vulnerable at all times, and demands for its best development slow and undisturbed opportunities and wholesome conditions. Very much mental stimulus is always hurtful, although pure intellectual pushing is said by Charcot to be in itself incapable of harm, provided other wholesome physical and moral conditions are maintained. The emotions evidence themselves first in mere animal delightedness, even then running along the lines of ancestral traits. Here the parental coloring of mind, habit, or exterior is shown in curious faithfulness of detail. Even at this stage bad habits may become sketched in upon the impressionable receptive centres, which, either encouraged or neglected, form the ground for future calamitous happenings. The exciting cause of mental disturbances differs in some respects from those of the adult. One of the most serious is rapid alternations in temperature. Children notably bear heat and cold less well than grown folk, and a baby laid with its head defencelessly toward a hot stove has in several instances been driven into an acute mania. Children, however, bear pain unusually well so far as mental distress goes. Much attention has wisely been drawn of late by rhinologists to adenoid growths of the nasopharynx as a cause for mental degeneration. Disorders of the digestive organs may form fundamental perversions which result in a series of reflex irritations, setting up usually but transient disturbances of mind.

The cause being removed, recover ensues. Intestinal parasites produce a variety of nervous troubles, but very rarely actual insanity.

Hurtfully directed moral agencies are very efficient factors in disturbing the mind, both temporarily and in greater permanence. The shock of fright or overwhelming dread is powerful for harm even in children perfectly healthy. Religious teachings of a lurid hyperbolic type act as a lever by which great harm may be wrought. As a potent accessory factor superstition has in all times been an agent to dethrone unstable minds. Acute disease is a fertile source of harm; a scarlet fever, or typhoid, especially, if accompanied by hyperpyrexia, very often reduces a perfectly healthy, vigorous child to an imbecile or a maniac. Masturbation was aforetime credited with overmuch power for mental harm, but is certainly responsible for not a little.

A brutal, drunken father, aside from exerting effects on prenatal conditions, produces terror and woe among children as well as perverting their morals. Example is almost as powerful for harm as ancestral proclivities.

Children subjected to long periods of want and exposure are certain to fail of right development and to cause some stain of the moral senses if not of mental clarity. Hence the waifs and strays gathered up by the municipality or by philanthropic societies are of questionable mentality, and demand unusual care in implanting and encouraging the seeds of morality and right conduct. These must receive a more primitive form of instruction than others who have enjoyed a better start in life. Their fundamental concepts being at fault too advanced instruction only confuses wholesomely budding traits.

4. Lewis M. Terman, *Hygiene of the School Child* (Boston: Houghton Mifflin, 1914). Beginning in the late nineteenth century the schoolhouse came to be seen as a place where children's health could be assessed and promoted.

In these excerpts, Lewis Terman, a psychologist best known for his studies of gifted children, describes how educational hygiene can aid society and discusses some of the mental hygiene problems of school children.

School Hygiene as a part of the problem of conservation

The rapid development of health work in the schools during the last two decades is not to be regarded merely as an educational reform, but rather as the corollary of a widespread realization of the importance of preventive measures in the conservation of natural and human resources. The prevention of waste has become, in fact, the dominant issue of our entire political, industrial, and educational situation.

Health work in the schools must be extended

The fact that the school doctor has been called in to examine and advise does not signify that the gravity of the situation has been apprehended. Teachers have simply found physical defects and impediment to the pupil's school progress and desire their removal. The school doctor spends some three to six minutes in the examination of each pupil, looking only for the gross and external symptoms of defectiveness. Having usually the point of view of the physician, his search is for disease. His training has not always fitted him to discover incipient deviations from the normal or even to see the necessity of doing so.

Our plea is for a broader conception of the functions and scope of educational hygiene. The usual attention given to heating, lighting, ventilation, and gross physical defectiveness is but the merest beginning. The school instead of causing sickness and deformity must be made to preserve the child from all kinds of morbidity, repair his existent deformities, combat his unfavorable heredity and the bad conditions of his environment; in a word, fortify his constitution and render him physically and mentally fit for the struggles of life.

No other agency compares with the school in the opportunities offered for contributing to the health of the succeeding generation. We cannot legislate desirable habits of living into men and women, but we may be able to mold after our ideals the hygienic habits of the child.

Hysteria

Children should never be punished or blamed for such hysterical symptoms, nor should their attention be needlessly directed toward their disorder. There may be no conscious pretension on the child's part. The special class has been used to advantage in such epidemics to prevent the spread of the contagion, and soon brings about a cure of those already afflicted. The Basel special class of 1904, organized for this purpose, went on with the regular school work, and by means of suggestive treatment applied in the form of simple gymnastic exercises, warm lunches, etc., all the cases were speedily cured.

Dementia praecox

Dementia praecox is a form of adolescent insanity which usually involves fantastic day-dreaming, sexual imagination, brooding over disappointments, and (the most central symptom) a discrepancy between thought and action. As described by Jelliffe (26), it is most likely to develop in those "who are abnormally brilliant, but whose lights are turned inward." The patient may be gentle in disposition; of dreamy, lofty, exclusive, disdainful demeanor; conceited, egotistic, given to deep ruminations and always unpractical.

In order to escape such dangers, children need to be taught to "avail themselves of the power of the concrete." School work should feed the instinct of workmanship instead of starving it. . . . Nothing is more subversive of sanity than a regime of inactivity and repression which creates a smouldering volcano of sentiment and frothy desire.

5. John B. Watson, *Psychological Care of Infant and Child* (New York: W. W. Norton, 1928). Watson was a prominent behavioral psychologist who believed that mothers were responsible for rearing healthy children through effective training and inculcation of habits. In the introduction to his book, excerpted below, he elaborates on his beliefs.

Parents—mothers especially—resent still more strenuously any advice or instructions on how to care psychologically for their children. What parents want advice on how much affection they should bestow on their children or any word about how their children should be handled and treated hourly in the home? "I can't take my child up in my lap! I can't let my children sleep together! I can't let my child play all around me all I want to! I can't slap him or scold him if I care to! I have to begin talking sex to him the moment he is born! Who ever heard of such a thing?" And do not think this is a backwoods attitude. On the main streets of every city, village, and town you find just such parents. You find the same resistance in the homes of college professors and in the homes even of pediatricians. Even in the homes of "advanced" mothers—mothers who are listening eagerly for words of wisdom about the care of their children you find the complaint—"The behaviorists are on the right track but they go too far."

It is a serious question in my mind whether there should be individual homes for children—or even whether children should know their own parents. There are undoubtedly more scientific ways of bringing up children which will probably mean finer and happier children.

Since the behaviorists find little that corresponds to instincts in children, since children are made not born, failure to bring up a happy child, a well adjusted child—assuming bodily health—falls upon the parents' shoulders. The acceptance of this view makes child-rearing the most important of all social obligations.

Since the most serious faults in the rearing of children are to be found on the emotional side I have put especial emphasis upon the growth of emotional habits. The other two phases taken up are day and night care and the kind and amount of sex instruction that should be given.

6. *Are You Training Your Child to Be Happy?* Children's Bureau Publication 202 (Washington: D.C.: U.S. Department of Labor, 1930). This booklet included twelve lessons prepared by a psychologist with experience as director of a "habit clinic" in Boston. The following excerpt offers advice on being a parent.

> DO YOU HAVE A HAPPY BABY?
>
> Does he laugh and coo while you work?
>
> Does he play quietly by himself while you work?
>
> Does your little child like the food you give him?
>
> Is he ready and willing to go to bed at bedtime?
>
> Does he love the new baby?
>
> Does he play happily with other children?
>
> Then he is happy and good.
>
> Does our baby cry all day?
>
> Does he get mad and kick and scream?
>
> Does your little child spit out the food he does not like?
>
> Does he beg you not to put him to bed?
>
> Does he tease the new baby?
>
> Of course, you do not want these things.
>
> We can help you to make your baby happy, but you must help, too. You must try very hard.
>
> You must never stop trying.
>
> You are tired and busy some days. Your baby is crying,
>
> You say, "This one time does not matter. I will pick him up. Then he will stop crying."
>
> Then your smart little baby says to himself, "Hurrah, I was the boss that time! I can be boss next time."
>
> Before you know it, he will cry again. Will you pick him up again?
>
> Do you always give him what he wants?
>
> Then he will not be happy long.

Read this little book. It will help you to keep your baby happy and good.

MARY AND HER MOTHER

Mary's mother took her to kindergarten when she was 4 years old. Mary could not take off her coat. Her mother did it for her. She could not hang it up. Her mother did that for her, too. She could not feed herself. She could not cut with scissors. She could not make pictures. Her mother had always done these things for her.

She came to school every day, but she did not learn. When she walked she fell down. She could not talk much. She acted like a stupid little girl.

The teacher said to her mother, "Was she a sick little baby?"

"Oh, no," said her mother, "she was always well. She was so strong she began to creep and walk too early. She got into my things and broke them. So I never let her walk. I do everything for her."

The teacher said, "Poor mother and poor little Mary ! You wanted to be good to your baby, but you were bad to her. Children must be doing things all the time. They must be active. That is the way they learn. When you do not let them move about you keep them from learning. You make them act like stupid children. Will you help me try to show how bright Mary really is?"

Of course, Mary's mother said "Yes." She let Mary dress herself. She let her feed herself. She let her run and climb.

In school Mary did these things, too. Soon she was a busy little girl. She did not act stupid any more. She learned how to do new things every day.

Her mother came to the teacher and said, "I used to be happy when I could do things for Mary. I did not know I was making her seem stupid. Now I am happy when I see her *do things for herself.*"

7. D. A. Thom, *Guiding the Adolescent* (Washington, D.C.: U.S. Department of Labor, Children's Bureau, 1933). This publication offered advice to parents on guiding the adolescent from childhood to "healthy, happy adulthood." The following excerpt discusses the problem of delinquency, applying the latest psychological theories.

In dealing with human behavior, whether good or bad, it is essential to appreciate and understand that conduct is always motivated by some inner force. Some environmental factor may be the precipitating cause, but it is the state of mind that determines whether or not trivial and inconsequential events will result in conduct of a disrupting character.

It has been pointed out by those interested in juvenile delinquency that chronic offenders usually started on their delinquent careers before reaching the age of adolescence. Probably one half of these offenders came from families that had histories of much asocial activity. Many of these chronic offenders came from homes which were badly disorganized, often to an extent which led the children to leave home at an early age. In considering the soil in which delinquency is likely to develop, it is often found, therefore, that it has been well fertilized with poverty and vice and also by mental and physical inadequacies. This does not mean, of course, that all delinquents spring from such unhappy and inadequate backgrounds. Delinquency may be a problem even in the best-regulated families. The background is but one of the factors that need consideration in the effort to understand conduct. It is obvious, however, that children reared in such an environment would not be likely to acquire the essential habits and personality traits to permit them to meet life in an adequate way during that adolescent period when things matter so much and when experience is so limited.

Besides the family background of the child, one must also consider certain inadequacies and handicaps of the child himself which would tend to make for difficulties in meeting the ordinary demands of life. Illness, mental inadequacy, physical handicaps—such as defects of hearing and vision, residuals of infantile paralysis, a chronic heart condition, and the like—are all particular obstacles which certain individuals have to overcome before they can fit into the social scheme of things successfully. These must be considered carefully in any effort to understand both the contributing and the precipitating factors leading to asocial activity.

A tendency that leads distinctly away from the wise handling of undesirable conduct but that is nevertheless common among many parents is an unwillingness to face fairly and squarely a situation as it actually exists. This leads to the use of artificially produced excuses. Mary's mother explains that her daughter would not have stayed out late at night and played about with undesirable company if she had not been led astray by her friend who was older and wiser. Tom's father complains in indignation that the school teacher who expelled his son for cheating had never given the boy a fair deal. Another father attempts to protect his son who has been apprehended for taking an automobile by explaining that it was a boyish prank and that the youngsters had just been out for a lark. A very solicitous mother finds an excuse for the truancy and mild indiscretions of her 18-year-old boy in the fact that he had always been ill and never had a good time.

It is quite natural for the youth in trouble to accept as a means of protecting himself from criticism these excuses which the self-deceived parent offers; and although he may not accept them as the true reasons for his misdeeds, he nevertheless appreciates that they serve the purpose of letting him off without punishment or reprimand. Notwithstanding that there is a constant and progressive innate tendency leading toward the socialization of the individual, and that asocial activity can be looked upon, in a general way, as self-eliminating, this is not likely to work out in the individual case unless the youth is permitted to learn from his own experiences that his asocial activity does not pay. If, on the contrary, he finds in his delinquencies ways and means of overcoming all the difficulties and hardships in life and of acquiring those things which, for the moment at least, bring pleasure and satisfaction without having to meet the responsibilities that actually attach themselves to such conduct, it is but to be expected that asocial trends will continue.

12 Child Health and the State

Over the course of the twentieth century, federal, state, and local governments as well as private philanthropic groups paid increasing attention to matters of child health, evaluating needs and suggesting solutions to problems identified by various studies.

1. Anna Steese Richardson, *Better Babies and Their Care* (New York: Frederick A. Stokes, 1914). Richardson reported for the magazine *Women's Home Companion* about a baby health contest held in conjunction with a livestock exposition. She then wrote this book, profiling the "better babies" campaigns across the nation. The following excerpt details women's responses to "better baby" contests.

One of the most interesting features of the Better Babies Contests which I have visited has been the amazement of some mothers when they discover that, with a little care and attention, they could work such wonders in their babies. As an example, in one city near New York, the physicians in charge of the examinations at a contest asked me if I would attend a meeting or "dress rehearsal" of the examination a few weeks before the contest. They wanted a demonstration of just how babies are examined by a scorecard. So all the arrangements were made, the physicians agreeing to have a real baby on hand for a "model," to undergo the full examination.

The baby was scored precisely as if a regular contest were under way, and was penalized 5 points for a rough skin and 15 points for an eruption. The mother protested vigorously. The doctors showed her a fine eruption over the abdomen and under the armpits. She declared that the child had always had the marks—they were a sort of birthmark. The doctors explained that such an eruption indicated overfeeding. Here was a bottle-fed baby getting too heavy fare. The mother admitted that she knew nothing about modifying the milk. The doctors told her how it should be done.

The roughness of the skin was due to mosquito bites, numbers of them. The mother said that she couldn't help that and neither could the baby. That was the fault of the mosquitoes! The doctors did not agree with her. They explained that a careful mother protected her child from the mosquitoes with a netting, that mosquitoes carried disease, that the itching sores made the baby nervous.

The mother listened resentfully, especially when she saw that by the card her baby scored only 89. Nevertheless, she must have thought a great deal about what those doctors said, because when the real contest was held in her city six weeks later, she entered her baby and carried it off first prize, scoring 98 per cent. The chairman of the committee in charge of the work wrote me that this mother had lightened the quality of the baby's food and the rash had disappeared. She had cleared the house of mosquitoes, and the baby's skin was smooth as a rose petal! Which shows that a Better Babies Contest makes mothers think—and act. Also, that a child can be made healthier and happier with just a little thought and attention.

2. S. Josephine Baker, *Fighting for Life* (New York: Macmillan, 1939). Baker, a pioneering physician and public health activist, was most noted for her work as director of the Bureau of Child Hygiene in the New York City Health Department. Among other efforts she developed programs for educating the mothers of newborns, baby health stations, and schemes for distributing clean milk. The following excerpt from her autobiography describes her work in 1908 to lower infant mortality rates.

I had served my time in [a] long hot summer in Hell's Kitchen when I walked up and down tenement stairs to find in every house a wailing skeleton of a baby, doomed by ignorance and neglect to die needlessly. It struck me suddenly that the way to keep people from dying of disease was to keep them from falling ill. After speaking with my superiors I came out of that office the bewildered Chief of the newly created Division of Child Hygiene. I had no staff; I had no money; all I had was an idea.

I tried an experiment. The closing of schools in June meant that the thirty-odd nurses on school inspection duty would be at liberty. It was also the beginning of the diarrhoeal season which, if this summer of 1908 was going to be anything like its predecessors, would kill its 1500 babies each week. I went to a district with a high baby death rate—a complicated, filthy, sunless and stifling nest of tenements on the lower east side. The Registrar of Records sent me the name and address on the birth certificate of every baby whose birth had been reported on the previous day. Within a few hours, a graduate nurse visited with the mother and her baby and [went] into detail of just how the baby should be cared for. That summer there were 1200 fewer deaths in that district than the previous summer.

It was never clear whether in pioneering in child hygiene being a woman was more of an asset than a liability. From the point of view of publicity, it was superb. I have a feeling that if a man had been given this position it would have been just another bureau; but for a woman to get this job, well, that was news.

Looking back, I remember how I felt when, after we had our baby health stations established and doing well in the Brownsville section of Brooklyn, a petition was forwarded to my desk signed by thirty-odd Brooklyn doctors, protesting bitterly against the Bureau of Child Hygiene because it was ruining medical practice by keeping babies well, and demanding that it be abolished in the interests of the medical profession. That petition cheered me up like a cocktail.

3. An Act for the Promotion of the Welfare and Hygiene of Maternity and Infancy, Sixty-Seventh Congress, Sess. 1, 1921. Better known as the Sheppard-Towner Act, this legislation involved the federal government in the promotion of child health at the local and state levels. An excerpt of the act, which was approved November 23, 1921, shows that the government took special care to forbid officials to enter homes if parents objected.

Be it enacted by the Senate and House of Representatives of the United States of America in Congress assembled, That there is hereby authorized to be appropriated annually, out of any money in the Treasury Act, to be paid to the several States for the purpose of cooperating with them in promoting the welfare and hygiene of maternity and infancy as hereinafter provided.

Sec. 2. For the purpose of carrying out the provisions of this Act, there is authorized to be appropriated out of any money in the Treasury not otherwise appropriated, for the current fiscal year $480,000, to be equally apportioned among the several States, and for each subsequent year, for the period of five years $240,000, to be equally apportioned among the several States in the manner hereinafter provided: *Provided further,* That the additional appropriations herein authorized shall be apportioned $5,000 to each State and the balance among the States in the proportion which their population bears to the total population of the States of the United States, according to the last preceding United States census: *And provided further,* That no payment out of the additional appropriation herein authorized shall be made in any year to any State until an equal sum has been appropriated for that year by the legislature of such State for the maintenance of the services and facilities provided for in this Act.

So much of the amount apportioned to any State for any fiscal year as remains unpaid to such State at the close thereof shall be available for expenditures in that State until the close of the succeeding fiscal year.

Sec. 3. There is hereby created a Board of Maternity and Infant Hygiene, which shall consist of the Chief of the Children's Bureau, the Surgeon General of the United States Public Health Service, and the United States

Commissioner of Education, which is hereafter designated in this Act as the Board. The Board shall elect its own chairman and perform the duties provided for in this Act.

The Children's Bureau of the Department of Labor shall be charged with the administration of this Act, except as herein otherwise provided, and the Chief of the Children's Bureau shall be the executive officer. It shall be the duty of the Children's Bureau to make or cause to be made such studies, investigations, and reports as will promote the efficient administration of this Act.

Sec. 4. In order to secure the benefits of the appropriations authorized in section 2 of this Act, any State shall, through the legislative authority thereof, accept the provisions of this Act and designate or authorize the creation of a State agency with which the Children's Bureau shall have all necessary powers to cooperate as herein provided in the administration of the provisions of this Act: *Provided,* That in any State having a child-welfare or child-hygiene division in its State agency of health, the said State agency of health shall administer the provisions of this Act through such divisions. If the legislature of any State has not made provision for accepting the provisions of this Act the govern or such State may in so far as he is authorized to do so by the laws of such State accept the provisions of this Act and designate or create a State agency to cooperate with the Children's Bureau until six months after the adjournment of the first regular session of the legislature in such State following the passage of this Act.

Sec. 5. So much, not to exceed 4 per centum, of the additional appropriations authorized for any fiscal year under section 2 of this Act, as the Children's Bureau may estimate to be necessary for administering the provisions of the Act, as herein provided, shall be deducted for that purpose, to be available until expended.

Sec. 6. Out of the amounts authorized under section 5 of this Act the Children's Bureau is authorized to employ such assistants, clerks, and other persons in the District of Columbia and elsewhere, to be taken from the eligible lists of the Civil Service Commission, and to purchase such supplies, material, equipment, office fixtures, and apparatus, and to incur such travel and other expenses as it may deem necessary for carrying out the purposes of this Act.

Sec. 7. Within sixty days after any appropriation authorized by this Act has been made, the Children's Bureau shall make the apportionment herein provided for and shall certify to the Secretary of the Treasury the amount estimated by the bureau to be necessary for administering the provisions of this Act, and shall certify to the Secretary of the Treasury and to the treasurers of the various States the amount which has been apportioned to each State for the fiscal year for which such appropriation has been made.

Sec. 8. Any State desiring to receive the benefits of this Act shall by its agency described in section 4, submit to the Children's Bureau detailed plans for carrying out the provisions of this Act, within such State, which plans shall be subject to the approval of the board *Provided*, That the plans of the States under this Act shall provide that no official, or agent, or representative in carrying out the provisions of this Act shall enter any home or take charge of any child over the objection of the parents, or either of them, or the person, standing in loco parentis or having custody of such child. If these plans shall be in conformity with the provisions of this Act and reasonably appropriate and adequate to carry out its purposes they shall be approved by the board and due notice of such approval shall be sent to the State agency by the chief of the Children's Bureau.

Sec. 9. No official, agent, or representative of the Children's Bureau shall by virtue of this Act have any right to enter any home over the objection of the owner thereof, or to take charge of any child over the objection of the parents, or either of them, or of the person standing in loco parentis or having custody of such child. Nothing in this Act shall be construed as limiting the power of a parent or guardian or person standing in loco parentis to determine what treatment or correction shall be provided for a child or the agency or agencies to be employed for such purpose.

4. Michael M. Davis, Jr., *Immigrant Health and the Community* (New York: Harper and Brothers, 1921). In these excerpts from chapter 12, "Immigrant Diets and American Food," Michael Davis, director of the Boston Dispensary, reported on immigrant health to individuals concerned with helping immigrants Americanize—what was then called "social betterment."

The Italian children are put on the adults' diet as soon as they are out of swaddling clothes. The larger the abdomen the stronger and healthier the mother considers the child. A diet of milk, strained cereal, and fruit juices is unknown to an Italian mother. The children learn to take tea or black coffee and bread without butter, for breakfast. Usually this means a meal of 200 to 250 calories, composed of carbohydrates, instead of one of 500 calories, combining protein, carbohydrates, mineral matter, and fats. At noon the meal often consists again, as with the adults, of bread with a piece of bologna and more tea or coffee. At supper time comes the big meal of the day. Too large an amount of macaroni or rice, and lard, is usually included in the diet, with few vegetables and little fruit, and often the children suffer from constipation because of this excess of starch.

Very often bringing a child back to normal health and development is only a matter of readjusting diet. With a slight knowledge of their predilections this can be done. They do not need to be encouraged to eat macaroni, vermicelli, or spaghetti. They are quite ready to eat oatmeal or rolled oats if these are cooked in milk and with raisins. Undernourished children should be given soups and milk, plain or in custards.

The Jewish children suffer from too many pickles, too few vegetables, and too little milk. Enuresis is quite common among these children, induced by the highly spiced foods in their diet and the pickles eaten at and between meals.

For undernourished children among the Jews, it is necessary not only to urge the use of milk, but to plan when it may be taken, as it cannot be taken at the same meal with meat. Therefore midmorning and midafternoon meals of milk must be introduced. This is impossible for the children who eat in school, unless there is a school lunch.

Among the Syrians, Armenians, Greeks, and Turks we usually find the children well nourished, with plenty of growth material and mineral matter in their diets. They do not have milk and fruit in as large quantities as they should, because of the expense.

The undernourished children need more milk added to their diets. Wheat is used extensively either whole or cracked; it is cooked in water until nearly done, then milk is added for the last few minutes' cooking. Even the candy and sweetmeats, called medley, is made with wheat. The green-leaved vegetables are not used in cream soups, but are cooked in stock. This must be remembered in diets for children.

The Polish children, and those of other Slavic people, come from sturdy stock. Upon arrival in this country they have round, well-shaped heads, rosy cheeks, and strong bodies. With their kerchiefs over their heads they make fascinating pictures of health. They have had an abundance of milk and fresh air in their own countries.

Here they live at first in crowded districts. Milk is counted as a drink, not something to eat; therefore, because the family income is small, it is left out of the diet almost entirely. If these children are fortunate enough to belong to Polish families that have saved or bought land in the country, for tobacco or onion farms, they have goats' milk, vegetables, and fruit. Otherwise they eat what the grown-ups have, and they pay the price. Sometimes they are constipated, with accompanying ill feelings; sometimes they are underweight.

5. The American Academy of Pediatrics, with the cooperation of the U.S. Public Health Service and the U.S. Children's Bureau, *Child Health Services and Pediatric Education*, Report of the Committee for the Study of Child Health Services (New York: Commonwealth Fund, 1949). Shortly after World War II the American Academy of Pediatrics undertook a study of child health services to investigate the reasons why large numbers of children did not receive preventive and curative care compatible with good pediatric practice. The following excerpts from the report analyze trends in child health and future needs.

The United States may feel justly proud of the gains which have been made in protecting the health of its children. Mortality in infancy and childhood has decreased; certain diseases which accounted for a high proportion of deaths twenty-five or even ten years ago have become less frequent or have largely disappeared. The death rate among preschool children (ages one to five) has shown a decline from 20 deaths per 1000 population in 1900, to 10 in 1920, to 2 in 1945. Among school-age children (ages five to fifteen) the rate has declined from 4 in 1900, to 3 in 1920, to 1 in 1945.

The phenomenal record of improvement for the preschool ages is due mainly to the control of communicable diseases. It is a striking fact that among preschool children the death rate from all causes in 1945 was less than the combined death rate from pneumonia, influenza and the other communicable diseases in 1935. The reduction in mortality from diarrheal diseases, scarlet fever, whooping cough, and measles has been particularly noteworthy. During the last fifteen years the death rate in this age group from diarrheal diseases, although still important, has been cut to one tenth of its former level.

The rapidly changing mortality picture has brought about major shifts in the relative importance of the various cases of death and consequently, new concepts regarding the chief problems and objectives in child health today. Accidents are now responsible for about 1 in every 4 deaths among children beyond the age of one year, outranking every other cause of death in this age group. Among children of school age chronic illnesses are increasing in importance as morbidity and mortality from acute diseases diminish. Today rheumatic heart disease is at the top of the list of causes of death from disease. A rather surprising finding is the entrance of cancer, including leukemia, into the picture as one of the leading causes of death among children.

Where children receive the best that modern medical science offers, health records are outstanding. But if we look within the averages, there is little room for complacency.

Infant mortality serves as one useful index of general health conditions. The national average in 1946 was 34 deaths under one year for every 1000 live births, the lowest ever attained up to that date. Utah, Oregon, and Connecticut succeeded in bringing their death rates below 28. On the other hand, in New Mexico the rate was 78, three times the rate in the best states and the same as the national average of twenty-five years ago.

The rate in isolated counties was about a third higher than in the greater metropolitan counties. A striking contrast often exists between the infant mortality rate of greater metropolitan counties and that of the isolated rural counties in the same state. For example, in Arlington County, Virginia, which is a greater metropolitan county, the infant mortality rate was 25, but in the isolated rural counties of Virginia the rate was 59, almost two and a half times as high.

There are many factors other than geographic location which influence the level of child health. Where there are poor sanitary conditions, families crowded together, ignorance of proper hygiene, babies born at home with no help at all, or at best the help of a midwife, infant mortality is high. This situation is illustrated forcefully in the nonwhite population, as for example,

Negro and Indian families. The national infant mortality rate in 1946 for nonwhite infants was 50 as compared with 32 for white infants. In New Mexico the rate for nonwhite was still at the startling height of 152, a condition due essentially to the notoriously poor health conditions among Indians.

In respect to death from premature birth, progress has also been made, but the fact remains that a large number of premature babies die needlessly. There has been a gradual decline from 15.4 per 1000 live births in 1935 to 12.1 in 1946. However, premature birth still ranks as the leading cause of infant death in the United States. If all ages are considered together, it is one of the ten leading causes of death. In 1946 premature birth was recorded as the cause of death of nearly 40,000 infants, more than one third of all deaths during the first year of life.

The cost to the nation from infant deaths is demonstrated vividly by a comparison with the experience of World War II. From Pearl Harbor to V-J Day 281,000 Americans were killed in action. During the same period 430,000 babies died in the United States before they were a year old—3 babies dead for every 2 soldiers.

Throughout the study we have recognized the inferior position of children in minority groups with respect to medical care. Children of migrant workers and children of certain racial groups have special problems. They belong to the low income group, thus often being excluded from private practice. Moreover, hospitals and clinics to which they would be eligible on the basis of their economic status are frequently closed to them because of admission policies based on residence or race.

6. *Report to Congress on Fiscal Year 1991 Maternal and Child Health, Title V: Maternal and Child Health Service Block Grant* (Rockville, Md.: U.S. Department of Health and Human Services, Public Health Service, 1995). In 1995 Congress received a report from the Secretary of Health and Human Services describing the activities supported by Title V of the Social Security Act. The following excerpts come from the executive summary of the findings.

Citizens of the United States should be able to enjoy universal access to good health care. Mothers and children should receive particular attention, because children are every nation's most important resource, and investing in their future is sound public policy. The United States spends more per capita on personal health care than any other country in the world, thus raising the expectation that mothers and children will enjoy significantly improving health status. However, while there has been slow, steady progress in many areas of maternal and child health (MCH), progress has not been uniform, and in some important variables health status has not improved at all or has even declined.

The infant mortality rate is the health variable most widely recognized as a measure of the Nation's MCH status. With its definition generally accepted as a standard worldwide, it serves as a simple point of comparison among counties. Many feel it provides a rough assessment of a country's resolve to address the multifaceted interconnected antecedents of infant death—poverty, lack of equal educational opportunities, and inability to provide universal access to health care. In 1990, the U.S. infant mortality rate was 9.2 infant deaths per thousand live births, a fall of 6 percent from 9.8 infant deaths per 1,000 in 1989. . . . Lowering the infant death rate to 7 will probably require universal access to prenatal care and a sincere effort to address the other antecedent social and economic risks.

Not only is the Nation's progress in reducing infant mortality somewhat erratic, but this country also has one of the world's worst infant mortality rates among industrialized nations. In 1990, 20 other industrialized nations, all with fewer technological resources than the United States, had lower infant mortality rates. These low rates in other countries are most likely the result of their comprehensive medical care systems that provide virtually all pregnant women and infants with regular health care visits.

The proportion of low-birth-weight babies, those weighing less than 5.5 pounds at birth, has not changed significantly since the 1970's. It is generally accepted that low birthweight is the single most important contributor to infant death, with risks of death in the first year 20 times greater than for babies with normal birthweight. Not only has the rate remained constant since the 1970's and early 1980's, but it actually increased slightly between 1987 and 1991, from 6.9 percent to 7.1 percent. It is extremely unlikely that the Year 2000 goal of 5 percent will be reached, given the recent rise in the incidence of low birthweight.

Although there has been slow improvement in general MCH status, disparity between he rates for certain racial and ethnic minorities and those for whites is unacceptable and seems to be increasing. Traditionally, the infant mortality rate for African Americans has been about twice that for whites; however, the difference in 1990 was 2.4 times (18 per thousand to 7.7 per thousand). Not only is the infant death rate for African Americans significantly higher, but so is the rate for American Indian/Alaskan Natives and Puerto Ricans, who have much higher rates than poor whites. Similarly, for low birthweight the rate for African Americans is more than twice that for whites. For Puerto Ricans, it is also significantly higher. There are similar disparities in neonatal and postneonatal mortality rates. These important indicators show a persistent and increasing disparity between rates for racial and ethnic minorities and those of whites.

There is a clear correlation between health status and poverty in the United States. There are almost 13 million children living in poverty, accounting for 37 percent of the Nation's 33 million people in poverty. In 1990, 15.1 percent of white children under 18 years of age, 44.2 percent of African Americans, and 39.7 percent of Hispanics lived in poverty. In 1990, nearly 2 of every 5 poor people were children under 18, and nearly 1 out of every 5 children in the United States lived in poverty.

Having health insurance is one important prerequisite for gaining access to health care, and most mothers and children have some form of health insurance. Yet, in 1991 more than 35 million Americans had no insurance, and 17.1 million of those were either women of childbearing age or children under 18 years of age. More than 8 million children, or 12.6 percent, had no health insurance throughout 1991. The problem is worse for African American children and Hispanic children, for whom the rates without insurance are 15.1 percent and 26.7 percent respectively.

While many nations have universal comprehensive medical care systems, the lack of a coordinated infrastructure in the United States contributes significantly to the slow improvement of some, and lack of improvement in many other MCH indicators. Improving incrementally the many components of the health care system seems to be the approach of choice for the last decade. While this has led to better health care for some, it has not led to improving health status for many others, and those from ethnic and racial minorities have been particularly left behind.

III Bibliography

13 Demographic and Epidemiologic Surveys

OVERVIEWS

Alter, George. 1997. "Infant Mortality in the United States and Canada." In *Infant and Child Mortality in the Past*. Edited by Alain Bideau, Bertrand Desjardins, and Hector Perez Brignoli, 91–108. Oxford: Clarendon.

Anderton, Douglas L., Richard E. Barrett, and Donald J. Bogue. 1997. *The Population of the United States*, 3rd ed. New York: Free Press.

Kunitz, Stephen J. 1984. "Mortality Change in America, 1620–1920." *Human Biology* 56: 569–82.

Meckel, Richard A. 2001. "Disease and Death." In *Boyhood in* America. Edited by Priscilla Ferguson Clement and Jacqueline S. Reinier, 205–209. Santa Barbara, Calif.: ABC-CLIO.

———. 2003. "Infant Mortality." In *History of Childhood*. Edited by Paula Fass et al. New York: Macmillan.

Steckel, Richard. 2000. "The African American Population of the United States, 1790–1920." In *A Population History of North America*. Edited by Michael R. Haines and Richard H. Steckel, 483–528. New York: Cambridge University Press.

Warren, Christian. 1997. "Northern Chills, Southern Fevers: Race-Specific Mortality in American Cities, 1730–1900." *Journal of Southern History* 63: 23–56.

EARLY SETTLEMENT THROUGH THE CIVIL WAR

Archer, Richard. 1990. "New England Mosaic: A Demographic Analysis of the Seventeenth Century." *William and Mary Quarterly* 47: 447–501.

Coelho, Philip R. P., and Robert A. McGuire; Steckel, Richard H. (reply). 2000. "Diets Versus Diseases: The Anthropometrics of Slave Children." *Journal of Economic History* 60: 232–46.

Davis, Eric Leiff. 1993. "The Era of the Common Child: Egalitarian Death in Antebellum America." *Mid-America* 75: 135–63.

Duffy, John. 1953. *Epidemics in Colonial America.* Baton Rouge: Louisiana State University Press.

Norton, Susan. 1971. "Population Growth in Colonial America: A Study of Ipswich, Massachusetts." *Population Studies* 25: 318–440.

Smith, Daniel B. 1978. "Mortality and Family in the Colonial Chesapeake." *Journal of Interdisciplinary History* 8: 403–27.

Steckel, Richard H. 1986. "A Dreadful Childhood: The Excess Mortality of American Slaves." *Social Science History* 10: 427–65.

———. 1986. "A Peculiar Population: The Nutrition, Health, and Mortality of American Slaves from Childhood to Maturity." *Journal of Economic History* 46: 721–41.

———. 1988. "The Health and Welfare of Women and Children 1850–1860." *Journal of Economic History* 48: 333–45.

Vinovskis, Maris. 1972. "Mortality Rates and Trends in Massachusetts before 1860." *Journal of Economic History* 32: 182–213.

———. 1976. "Angels Heads and Weeping Willows: Death in Early America." *Proceedings of the American Antiquarian Society* 86: 273–302.

CIVIL WAR THROUGH THE PRESENT

Bean, Lee L., et al. 1992. "High Risk Childbearing and Infant Mortality on the American Frontier." *Social Science History* 16: 337–63.

Boone, Margaret S. 1989. *Capital Crime: Black Infant Mortality in America.* Newbury Park, Calif.: Sage.

Centers for Disease Control. 1999. "CDC on Infectious Diseases in the United States: 1900–99." *Population and Development Review* 25: 635–40.

———. 1999. "CDC on Vaccines and Children's Health: United States 1900–1998." *Population and Development Review* 25: 391–95.

Chay, Kenneth Y., and Michael Greenstone. 2000. "The Convergence in Black and White Infant Mortality Rates during the 1960's." *American Economic Review* 90: 326–32.

Cheney, Rose A. 1984. "Seasonal Aspects of Infant and Child Mortality: Philadelphia 1865–1920." *Journal of Interdisciplinary History* 14: 561–85.

Condran, Gretchen A., and Rose A. Cheney. 1982. "Mortality Trends in Philadelphia: Age- and Cause- Specific Death Rates, 1870–1930." *Demography* 19: 97–123.

Condran, Gretchen A., and Eileen Crimmins. 1980. "Mortality Differentials between Rural and Urban Areas of States in the Northeastern United States, 1890–1900." *Journal of Historical Demography* 6: 179–202.

Condran, Gretchen A., and Ellen Kramerow. 1991. "Child Mortality among Jewish Immigrants to the United States." *Journal of Interdisciplinary History* 22: 223–54.

Dwork, Deborah. 1981. "Health Conditions of Immigrant Jews on the Lower East Side of New York, 1880–1914." *Medical History* 25: 1–40.

Ewbank, D. 1987. "History of Black Mortality and Health before 1940." *Milbank Memorial Quarterly* 65, suppl. 1: 100–28.

Federal Interagency Forum on Child and Family Statistics (FIFCFS). 2001. *America's Children: Key National Indicators of Wellbeing, 2001.* Washington, D.C.: U.S. Government Printing Office.

Fingerhut, Lois, and Joel Kleinman.1989. *Trends and Current Status in Childhood Mortality.* Washington, D.C.: National Center for Health Statistics.

Fishback, Price V., Michael R. Haines, and Shawn Kantor. 2001. "The Impact of the New Deal on Black and White Infant Mortality in the South." *Explorations in Economic History* 38: 93–122.

Ginsberg, Caren A. 1989. *Sex-Specific Mortality and the Economic Value of Children in Nineteenth-Century Massachusetts.* New York: Garland.

Gould, Tony. 1995. *A Summer Plague: Polio and Its Survivors.* New Haven, Conn.: Yale University Press.

Gutman, Myron P., and Kenneth H. Fleis. 1996. "The Social Context of Child Mortality in the American Southwest." *Journal of Interdisciplinary History* 26: 589–618.

Haines, Michael R. 1985. "Inequality and Childhood Mortality: A Comparison of England and Wales, 1911, and the United States, 1900." *Journal of Economic History* 45: 885–912.

Hardy, Anne. 1992. "Rickets and the Rest: Child-Care, Diet and Infectious Children's Diseases, 1850–1914." *Social History of Medicine* 5: 382–412.

Hummer, Robert A., et al. 1999. "Race, Ethnicity, and Infant Mortality in the United States." *Social Forces* 77: 1083–118.

Johnson, Nan E., and Khalida P. Zaki. 1988. "Racial and Residential Differences in U.S. Infant Death Rates: A Temporal Analysis." *Rural Sociology* 53: 207–19.

King, Charles R. 1991. "Childhood Death: The Health Care of Children on the Kansas Frontier." *Kansas History* 14: 26–36.

Legare, Jacques. 1989. "Infant Mortality among the Inuit (Eskimos) after World War II." *Genus* 45: 55–64.

Louden, Irvine. 1991. "On Maternal and Infant Mortality, 1900–1960." *Social History of Medicine* 4: 29–73.

Meckel, Richard. A. 1985. "Immigration, Mortality, and Population Growth, 1840–1880." *Journal of Interdisciplinary History* 15: 393–421.

———. 1996. "Health and Disease." In *Encyclopedia of the United States in the Twentieth Century,* vol. 2. Edited by Stanley I. Kutler et al., 757–86. New York: Charles Scribner's Sons.

Mortality of Children under Age 5: World Estimates and Projections, 1950–2025. 1988. New York: United Nations.

Preston, Samuel H., and Michael R. Haines. 1991. *Fatal Years: Child Mortality in Late Nineteenth-Century America.* Princeton, N.J.: Princeton University Press.

Rice, Jon F. 1977. "Health Conditions and Native Americans in the Twentieth Century." *Indian History* 10: 14–18.

Swedlund, Alan C. 1990. "Infant Mortality in Massachusetts and the United States in the Nineteenth Century." In *Disease in Populations in Transition.* Edited by Alan Swedlun and George J. Armelagos. New York: Bergin & Garvey.

Trafzer, Clifford E. 1999. "Infant Mortality on the Yakima Indian Reservation, 1914–1964." *American Indian Culture and Research Journal* 23: 77–96.

INTERNET SOURCES

America's Children, available at www.childstats.gov/americaschildren/.
National Center for Health Statistics, available at www.cdc.gov/nchs/hus.htm.

14 Framing Child Death, Disease, and Health

Aries, Phillipe. 1975. *Western Attitudes toward Death from the Middle Ages to the Present.* Translated by Patricia M. Ranum. Baltimore: Johns Hopkins University Press.

Avery, Gillian, and Kimberley Reynolds, eds. 2000. *Representations of Childhood Death.* New York: St. Martin's.

Baker, Bernadette. 2000. "The Hunt for Disability: The New Eugenics and the Normalization of School Children." *Teachers College Record* 104: 663–703.

Brown, Eleanor. 1999. "Victorian Visual Memory and the 'Departed' Child." *Archivist* 115: 22–31.

Brumberg, Joan Jacobs. 1988. *Fasting Girls: The Emergence of Anorexia Nervosa as a Modern Disease.* Cambridge, Mass.: Harvard University Press.

Burnham, John C. 1996. "Why Did Infants and Toddlers Die? Shifts in Americans' Ideas of Responsibility for Accidents: From Blaming Mom to Engineering." *Journal of Social History* 29: 817–37.

Conrad, Peter, and Deborah Potter. 2000. "From Hyperactive Children to ADHD Adults: Observations on the Expansion of Medical Categories." *Social Problems* 47: 559–82.

Daly, Ann. 1997. "Status Lymphaticus: Sudden Death in Children from 'Visitation of God' to Cot Death." *Medical History* 41: 70–85.

Dorey, Annette K. Vance. 1999. *Better Baby Contests: The Scientific Quest for Perfect Childhood Health in the Early Twentieth Century.* Jefferson, N.C.: McFarland.

Dye, Nancy Schrom, and Daniel Blake Smith. 1986. "Mother Love and Infant Death." *Journal of American History* 73: 329–53.

Engelhardt, H. Tristram, Jr. 1974. "The Disease of Masturbation: Values and the Concept of Disease." *Bulletin of the History of Medicine* 48: 234–48.

English, Peter C. 1999. *Rheumatic Fever in America and Britain: A Biological, Epidemiological, and Medical History.* New Brunswick, N.J.: Rutgers University Press.

Fairchild, Amy. 2001. "The Polio Narratives: Dialogues with FDR." *Bulletin of the History of Medicine* 75: 488–534.

Feldberg, Georgina D. 1995. *Disease and Class: Tuberculosis and the Shaping of North American Society.* New Brunswick, N.J.: Rutgers University Press.

Feudtner, Chris. 2002. "Juvenile Diabetes and the Origins of Managerial Medicine." In *Formative Years: Children's Health in America, 1880–2000.* Edited by Alexandra Minna Stern and Howard Markel, 208–32. Ann Arbor: University of Michigan Press.

Gardner, John W., and Robert C. Dinsmore. 1995. "Evolution of the Concept of Febrile Seizure as It Developed in American Medical Literature, 1800–1980." *Journal of the History of Medicine and Allied Sciences* 50: 240–363.

Golden, Janet. 1999. "'An Argument That Goes Back to the Womb': The De-medicalization of Fetal Alcohol Syndrome, 1973–1992." *Journal of Social History* 33: 269–98.

Greenberg, Michael, and Daniel Wartenberg. 1990. "Network Television Evening News Coverage of Infectious Disease Events." *Journalism Quarterly* 67: 142–46.

Herndl, Diane Price. 1998. "Critical Condition: Writing about Illness, Bodies, Culture." *American Literary History* 10: 771–85.

Hughes, Evans. 2002. "The Discovery of Child Sexual Abuse in America." In *Formative Years: Children's Health in America, 1880–2000.* Edited by Alexandra Minna Stern and Howard Markel, 233–59. Ann Arbor: University of Michigan Press.

Kett, Joseph. 1978. "Curing the Disease of Precocity." In *Turning Points: Historical and Sociological Essays on the Family.* Edited by John Demos and Sarane Spence Boocock, 183–211. Chicago: University of Chicago Press.

Koestler, Francis A. 1976. *The Unseen Minority: A Social History of Blindness in America.* New York: D. McKay.

Lakoff, Andrew. 2000. "Adaptive Will: The Evolution of Attention Deficit Disorder." *Journal of the History of Behavioral Sciences* 36: 149–69.

Lane, Harlen. 1984. *When the Mind Hears: A History of the Deaf.* New York: Random House.

Lerner, Laurence. 1997. *Angels and Absences: Child Deaths in the Nineteenth Century.* Nashville, Tenn.: Vanderbilt University Press.

Lockwood, Rose. 1978. "Birth, Illness, and Death in 18th Century New England." *Journal of Social History* 12: 111–28.

Lomax, Elizabeth. 1977. "Heredity of Acquired Disease? Early Nineteenth-Century Debates on the Cause of Infantile Scrofula and Tuberculosis." *Journal of the History of Medicine and Applied Sciences* 32: 356–57.

McClary, Andrew. 1980. "Germs Are Everywhere: The Germ Threat as Seen in Magazine Articles, 1890–1920." *Journal of American Culture* 3: 22–46.

Meckel, Richard. 1997. "Racialism and Infant Death: Late 19th and Early 20th Century Sociomedical Discourses on African American Infant Mortality." In *Migrants, Minorities and Health: Historical and Contemporary Studies.* Edited by Lara Marks and Michael Worboys, 70–92. London: Routledge.

———. 2002. "Going to School, Getting Sick: The Social and Medical Construction of 'School Diseases' in the Late 19th Century." In *Formative Years: Children's Health in America, 1880–2000.* Edited by Alexandra Minna Stern and Howard Markel, 185–207. Ann Arbor: University of Michigan Press.

Morey, Ann-Janine. 1996. "In Memory of Cassie: Child Death and Religious Vision in American Women's Novels." *Religion and American Culture* 6: 87–104.

Neuman, R. P. 1976. "Masturbation, Madness, and the Modern Concepts of Child-hood and Adolescence." *Journal of Social History* 8: 1–27.

Pollock, Philip H., III, Stuart A. Lilie, and Elliot M. Vittes. 1993. "On the Nature and Dynamics of Social Construction: The Case of AIDS." *Social Science Quarterly* 74: 123–35.

Prescott, Heather Munro. 2002. "'I Was a Teenage Dwarf': The Social Construction of 'Normal' Adolescent Growth and Development in the United States." In *Formative Years: Children's Health in America, 1880–2000.* Edited by Alexandra Minna Stern and Howard Markel, 153–82. Ann Arbor: University of Michigan Press.

Rogers, Naomi. 1989. "Dirt, Flies and Immigrants: Explaining the Epidemiology of Poliomyelitis, 1900–1916." *Journal of the History of Medicine and Allied Sciences* 44: 486–505.

Rosenberg, Charles. 1992. "Framing Disease: Illness, Society, and History." In *Framing Disease: Studies in Cultural History.* Edited by Charles Rosenberg and Janet Golden. New Brunswick, N.J.: Rutgers University Press.

———. 1995. "Catechisms of Health: The Body in the Prebellum Classroom." *Bulletin of the History of Medicine* 69: 175–97.

Safford, Philip L., and Elizabeth J. Safford. 1996. *A History of Childhood Disability.* New York: Teacher's College.

Simonds, Wendy, and Barbara Katz Rothman. 1992. *Centuries of Solace: Expressions of Maternal Grief in Popular Literature.* Philadelphia: Temple University Press.

Slater, Peter. 1977. *Children in the New England Mind.* Hamden, Conn.: Archon Books.

Stannard, David E. 1974. "Death and the Puritan Child." *American Quarterly* 26: 456–76.

Stearns, Peter N., Perrin Rowland, and Lori Giarnella. 1993. "Girls, Boys, and Emotions: Redefinitions and Historical Change." *Journal of American History* 80: 36–74.

———. 1996. "Children's Sleep: Sketching Historical Change." *Journal of Social History* 30: 345–66.

Taylor, Karen J. 1985. "Venereal Disease in Nineteenth-Century Children." *Journal of Psychohistory* 12: 431–63.

Tomes, Nancy. 1998. *The Gospel of Germs: Men, Women, and the Microbe in American Life.* Cambridge, Mass.: Harvard University Press.

Trent, James W. 1994. *Inventing the Feeble Mind: A History of Mental Retardation in the United States.* Berkeley: University of California Press.

Wells, Robert V. 1999. *Facing the "King of Terrors": Death and Society in an American Community, 1750–1990.* New York: Cambridge University Press.

Wilson, Daniel. 1994. "Covenants of Work and Grace: Themes of Recovery and Redemption in Polio Narratives." *Literature and Medicine* 13: 22–41.

Yosifon, David, and Peter N. Stearns. 1998. "The Rise and Fall of American Posture." *American Historical Review* 103: 1056–95.

Zaborney, John J. 1996. "'What Meaneth the Heat of this Great Anger?' The Religious Response to Colonial New England's Diphtheria Epidemic, 1735–1740." *New England Journal of History* 53: 30–37.

Ziporyn, Terra. 1988. *Disease in the Popular Press: The Case of Diphtheria, Typhoid Fever, and Syphilis, 1880–1920.* Westport, Conn.: Greenwood.

15 Health Care and Health Care Providers

PARENTS AND COMMUNITY

Abel, Emily K. 2000. *Hearts of Wisdom: American Women Caring for Kin, 1850–1940.* Cambridge, Mass.: Harvard University Press.

Apple, Rima. 1987. *Mothers and Medicine: A Social History of Infant Feeding, 1850–1950.* Madison: University of Wisconsin Press.

Curry, Lynn. 1999. *Modern Mothers in the Heartland: Gender, Health, and Progress in Illinois, 1900–1930.* Columbus: Ohio State University Press.

Fett, Sharla M. 2002. *Working Cures: Healing, Health and Power on Southern Slave Plantations.* Chapel Hill: University of North Carolina Press.

Goldstein, Alice. 1994. "Childhood Health-Care Practices among Italians and Jews in the United States, 1910–1940." *Health Transition Review* 4: 45–62.

Grant, Julia. 1998. *Raising Baby by the Book: The Education of American Mothers.* New Haven, Conn.: Yale University Press.

McMillian, Sally. 1994. "Antebellum Southern Fathers and the Health Care of Children." *Journal of Southern History* 605: 13–32.

———. 1990. *Motherhood in the Old South: Pregnancy, Childbirth, and Infant Rearing.* Baton Rouge: Louisiana State University Press.

Tannenbaum, Rebecca J. 2002. *The Healer's Calling; Women and Medicine in Early New England.* Ithaca, N.Y.: Cornell University Press.

Ulrich, Laurel Thatcher. 1990. *A Midwife's Tale: The Life of Martha Ballard Based on Her Diary.* New York: Alfred A. Knopf.

PEDIATRICS AND PRIMARY HEALTH CARE

Abt, Arthur F. 1965. *Abt-Garrison History of Pediatrics.* Philadelphia: Saunders.

Apple, Rima. 1987. *Mothers and Medicine: A Social History of Infant Feeding, 1850–1950.* Madison: University of Wisconsin Press.

Baker, Jeffrey P. 1994. "Women and the Invention of Well Child Care." *Pediatrics* 94: 527–31.

———. 1996. *The Machine in the Nursery: Incubator Technology and the Origins of Newborn Intensive Care.* Baltimore: Johns Hopkins University Press.

Brosco, Jeffrey P. 2002. "Weight Charts and Well Child Care: When the Pediatrician Became the Expert in Child Health." In *Formative Years: Children's Health in America, 1880–2000.* Edited by Alexandra Minna Stern and Howard Markel, 91–129. Ann Arbor: University of Michigan Press.

Buhler-Wilkerson, Karen. 1989. *False Dawn: The Rise and Decline of Public Health Nursing, 1900–1930.* New York: Garland.

———. 2003. *No Place Like Home: A History of Nursing and Home Care in the United States.* Baltimore: Johns Hopkins University Press.

Colon, A. R. 1999. *Nurturing Children: A History of Pediatrics.* Westport, Conn.: Greenwood.

Cone, Thomas E. 1979. *History of American Pediatrics.* Boston: Little, Brown.

———. 1985. *History of the Care and Feeding of the Premature Infant.* Boston: Little, Brown.

Desmond, Murdina MacFarquar. 1998. *Newborn Medicine and Society: European Background and American Practice (1750–1975).* Austin, Tex.: Eaken.

English, Peter. 1989. "Pediatrics and the Unwanted Child in History: Foundling Homes, Disease, and the Origins of Foster Care in New York City, 1860–1920." *Pediatrics* 73: 699–711.

Faber, Harold K., and Rustin McIntosh. 1966. *History of American Pediatric Society, 1887–1965.* New York: McGraw-Hill.

Fadiman, Ann. 1997. *The Spirit Catches You and You Fall Down: A Hmong Child, Her American Doctors, and the Collision of Two Cultures.* New York: Farrar, Straus and Giroux.

Golden, Janet L. 1996. *A Social History of Wet Nursing in America: From Breast to Bottle.* New York: Cambridge University Press.

Graebner, William. 1980. "The Unstable World of Benjamin Spock: Social; Engineering in a Democratic Culture, 1917–1950." *Journal of American History* 67: 612–29.

Halpern, Sydney A. 1988. *American Pediatrics: The Social Dynamics of Professionalism, 1880–1980.* Berkeley: University of California Press.

Hutchins, Vince L. 1997. "A History of Child Health and Pediatrics in the United States." In *Health Care for Children: What's Right, What's Wrong, What's Next.* Edited by Ruth E. K. Stein, 79–106. New York: United Hospital Fund of New York.

Jones, Kathleen. 1983. "Sentiment and Science: The Late Nineteenth-Century Pediatrician as Mother's Advisor." *Journal of Social History* 17: 79–96.

King, Charles R. 1993. *Children's Health in America: A History.* New York: Twayne.

Kunitz, Stephen J. 1983. "The Historical Roots and Ideological Functions of Disease Concepts in Three Primary Care Specialties." *Bulletin of the History of Medicine* 57: 412–32.

Levenstein, Harvey. 1983. "'Best for Babies' or 'Preventable Infanticide'? The Controversy over Artificial Feeding of Infants in America, 1880–1920." *Journal of American History* 70: 75–94.

Maier, Thomas. 1998. *Dr. Spock: An American Life.* New York: Harcourt Brace.

May, Charles D. 1960. "The Future of Pediatricians as Medical Specialists in the U.S." *American Journal of the Diseases of Children* 100: 661–68.

Markel, Howard. 1988. "Caring for the Foreign Born: The Health of Immigrant Children in the United States, 1890–1925." *Archives of Pediatric and Adolescent Medicine* 152: 1020–27.

———. 1996. "Academic Pediatrics: The View of New York City a Century Ago." *Academic Medicine* 71: 146–51.

Meckel, Richard A. 1990. *Save the Babies: American Public Health Reform and the Prevention of Infant Mortality 1850–1929.* Baltimore: Johns Hopkins University Press.

———. 2001. "Pediatrics." In *The Family in America.* Edited by Joseph Hawes and Elizabeth Shores, 764–73. Santa Barbara: ABC-CLIO.

Murphy, Lamar Riley. 1991. *Enter the Physician: The Transformation of Domestic Medicine, 1760–1860.* Tuscaloosa: University of Alabama Press.

Pawluch, Dorothy. 1995. *The New Pediatrics: A Profession in Transition.* New York: Aldine de Gruyter.

Pearson, Howard A. 1988. *The Centennial History of the American Pediatric Society, 1888–1988.* New Haven, Conn.: American Pediatric Society.

Peitzman, Steven J. 1996. "When Did Medicine Become Beneficial? The Perspective from Internal Medicine." *Caduceus* 12: 39–44.

Prescott, Heather Munro. 1998. *A Doctor of Their Own: The History of Adolescent Medicine.* Cambridge, Mass.: Harvard University Press.

Quiroga, Virginia. 1986. "Female Lay Managers and Scientific Pediatrics at Nursery and Child's Hospital, 1854–1910." *Bulletin of the History of Medicine* 60: 194–208.

Stern, Alexandra Minna, and Howard Markel, eds. 2002. *Formative Years: Children's Health in America, 1880–2000.* Ann Arbor: University of Michigan Press.

Viner, Russell. 1998. "Abraham Jacobi and German Medical Radicalism in Antebellum New York." *Bulletin of the History of Medicine* 72: 434–63.

———. 2002. "Abraham Jacobi and the Origins of Scientific Pediatrics in America." In *Formative Years: Children's Health in America, 1880–2000.* Edited by Alexandra Minna Stern and Howard Markel, 23–46. Ann Arbor: University of Michigan Press.

Wasserman, Manfred. 1972. "Henry L. Coit and the Certified Milk Movement in the Development of Modern Pediatrics." *Bulletin of the History of Medicine* 46: 359–90.

Weiss, Nancy Potisham. 1977. "Mother, the Invention of Necessity: Dr Benjamin Spock's *Baby and Child Care.*" *American Quarterly* 29: 519–46.

CHILD AND ADOLESCENT PSYCHOLOGY

Bach, William G. 1974. "The Influence of Psychoanalytic Thought on Benjamin Spock's *Baby and Child Care.*" *Journal of the History of Behavioral Sciences* 10: 91–94.

Dale, Nance R. 1970. "G. Stanley Hall and John B. Watson as Child Psychologists." *Journal of the History of Behavioral Sciences* 6: 303–16.

Herman, Ellen. 2001. "Families Made by Science: Arnold Gessell and the Technologies of Modern Adoption." *Isis* 92: 684–715.

Horn, Margo. 1989. *Before It's Too Late: The Child Guidance Movement in the United States, 1922–45.* Philadelphia: Temple University Press.

Jones, Kathleen W. 1999. *Taming the Troublesome Child: Taming the Troublesome Child: American Families, Child Guidance, and the Limits of Psychiatric Authority.* Cambridge, Mass.: Harvard University Press.

Lomax, Elizabeth, Jerome Kagen, and Barbara Rosenkrantz. 1978. *Science and Patterns of Child Care.* San Francisco: W. H. Freeman.

O'Donnell, John M. 1979. "The Clinical Psychology of Lightner Witmer: A Case Study of Institutional Innovations and Intellectual Change." *Journal of the History of Behavioral Sciences* 15: 2–17.

Richards, Barry. 1988. "Lightner Witmer and the Project of Psychotechnology." *History of the Human Sciences* 1: 201–19.

Richardson, Theresa R. 1989. *The Century of the Child: The Mental Hygiene Movement and Social Policy in the United States and Canada.* Albany: State University of New York Press.

Riley, Denise. 1983. *War in the Nursery: Theories of Child and Mother.* London: Virago.

Ross, Dorothy. 1972. *G. Stanley Hall: The Psychologist as Prophet.* Chicago: University of Chicago Press.

Rubenstein, Eli A. 1948. "Childhood Mental Disease in American: A Review of the Literature before 1900." *American Journal of Orthopsychiatry* 18: 314–21.

Schlossman, Steven. 1978. "The Parent Education Game: The Politics of Child Psychology in the 1970s." *Teachers College Record* 79: 788–808.

Slaff, Bertram. 1989. "History of Child and Adolescent Psychiatry Ideas and Organizations in the United States: A Twentieth-Century View." *Adolescent Psychiatry* 16: 31–52.

Snodgrass, Jon. 1984. "William Healy (1869–1963): Pioneer Child Psychiatrist and Criminologist." *Journal of the History of the Behavioral Sciences* 20: 332–39.

CHILD AND ADOLESCENT DEVELOPMENT

Anderson, John E. 1956. "Child Development in Historical Perspective." *Child Development* 27: 181–96.

Bryson, Dennis Raymond. 1993. "Lawrence K. Frank: Architect of Child Development, Prophet of Bio-Technocracy." Ph.D. dissertation, University of California, Irvine.

Cairns, Robert B. 1983. "The Emergence of Developmental Psychology." In *History, Theory, and Methods.* Edited by William Kessen. Vol. 1: *Handbook of Child Psychology.* Edited by Paul H. Mussen. New York: John Wiley and Sons.

Cravens, Hamilton. 1993. *Before Head Start: The Iowa Station and the Nation's Children.* Chapel Hill: University of North Carolina Press.

Grant, Julia. 1994. "Caught between Common Sense and Science: The Cornell Child Study Clubs, 1925–45." *History of Education Quarterly* 34: 433–52.

———. 1999. "Constructing the Normal Child: The Rockefeller Philanthropies and the Science of Child Development, 1918–1940." In *Philanthropic Foundations: New Scholarship, New Possibilities.* Edited by Ellen Condliffe Langemann, 131–50. Bloomington: Indiana University Press.

Kett, Joseph. 1977. *Rites of Passage: Adolescence in America, 1790 to the Present.* New York: Basic Books.

———. 1978. "Curing the Disease of Precocity." In *Turning Points: Historical and Sociological Essays on the Family.* Edited by John Demos and Sarane Spence Boocock, 181–211. Chicago: University of Chicago Press.

Lomax, Elizabeth. 1997. "The Laura Spellman Rockefeller Memorial: Some of Its Contributions to Early Research in Child Development." *Journal of the History of the Behavioral Sciences* 13: 283–93.

Markowitz, Gerald, and David Rosner. 2000. *Children, Race, and Power: Kenneth and Mamie Clark's Northside Center.* New York: Routledge.

Prescott, Heather Munro. 2002. "'I Was a Teenage Dwarf': The Social Construction of 'Normal' Adolescent Growth and Development in the United States." In *Formative Years: Children's Health in America, 1880–2000.* Edited by Alexandra Minna Stern and Howard Markel, 153–76. Ann Arbor: University of Michigan Press.

Rhodes, Sonya L. 1979. "Trends in Child Development Research Important to Day Care Policy." *Social Service Review* 53: 285–94.

Schlossman, Steven. 1981. "Philanthropy and the Gospel of Child Development." *History of Education Quarterly* 21: 275–99.

Sears, Robert R. 1975. *Your Ancients Revisited: A History of Child Development.* Chicago: University of Chicago Press.

Senn, Milton J. E. 1975. "Insights on the Child Development Movement." *Monographs of the Society for Research in Child Development* 40: 1–99.

Smuts, Alice B. 1996. "Science Discovers the Child, 1893–1935: A History of the Early Scientific Study of Children." Ph.D. dissertation, University of Michigan.

Tanner, James M. 1981. *History of the Study of Human Growth.* New York: Cambridge University Press.

White, Sheldon H. 1990. "Child Study at Clark University, 1894–1904." *Journal of the History of the Behavioral Sciences* 26: 131–50.

Young, James Harvey. 1979. "Height, Weight, and Health: Anthropometric Study of Human Growth in Nineteenth-Century American Medicine." *Bulletin of the History of Medicine* 53: 214–43.

Zenderland, Leila. 1988. "Education, Evangelism and the Origins of Clinical Psychology: The Child-Study Legacy." *Journal of the History of Behavioral Sciences* 24: 152–65.

INSTITUTIONAL CARE

Buck, Peter. 1985. "Why Not the Best? Some Reasons and Examples of Child Health and Rural Hospitals." *Journal of Social History* 18: 413–31.

Drachman, Virginia G. 1984. *Hospital with a Heart: Women Doctors and the Paradox of Separatism at the New England Hospital, 1862–1969.* Ithaca, N.Y.: Cornell University Press.

Evans, Helen Hughes. 1995. "Hospital Waifs: The Hospital Care of Children in Boston, 1860–1920." Ph.D. thesis dissertation, Harvard University.

Golden, Janet, ed. 1989. *Infant Asylums and Children's Hospitals: Medical Dilemmas and Developments.* New York: Garland.

Hendricks, Rickey. 1982. "Feminism and Materialism in Early Hospitals for Children: San Francisco and Denver, 1875–1915." *Journal of the West* 32: 61–69.

Hendricks, Rickey, and Mark S. Foster. 1994. *For a Child's Sake: History of Children's Hospital, Denver, Colorado, 1910–1990.* Niwot: University Press of Colorado.

Hunt, Marion. 1980. "Women and Childsaving in St. Louis: Children's Hospital, 1879–1979." *Missouri Historical Society Bulletin* 36: 65–79.

Lomax, Elizabeth. 1996. *Small and Special: The Development of Hospitals for Children in Victorian Britain.* London: Wellcome Institute for the History of Medicine.

Quiroga, Virginia. 1989. *Poor Mothers and Babies: A Social History of Childbirth and Child Care Hospitals in Nineteenth-Century New York City.* New York: Garland.

Radbill, Samuel X. 1979. "Hospitals and Pediatrics, 1776–1976." *Bulletin of the History of Medicine* 53: 286–91.

Rosenberg, Charles. 1987. *The Care of Strangers: The Rise of America's Hospital System.* New York: Basic Books.

Rothman, David J., and Sheila M. Rothman, eds. 1987. *Children's Hospitals in the Progressive Era: Two Investigations of Substandard Conditions.* New York: Garland.

Schmeling, Kathleen. 1990. "Every Child Is Worthy of Kindness and Care: The Founding and Early Development of Children's Hospital of Michigan, 1886–1922." *Michigan History* 74: 24–31.

Smith, Clement. 1983. *The Children's Hospital of Boston: "Better Built than They Knew."* Boston: Little, Brown.

16 Child Health, Philanthropy, and the State

GENERAL

Abel, Emily K. 1996. "Appealing for Children's Health Care: Conflicts between Mothers and Health Officials in the 1930s." *Social Service Review* 70: 282–304.

Altensteter, C., and J. W. Bjorkman. 1978. "Policy, Politics, and Child Health: Four Decades of Federal Initiative and State Response." *Journal of Health Politics, Policy, and Law* 3: 196–234.

Anderson, Paul Gerard. 1999. "The Origin, Emergence and Professional Recognition of Child Protection." *Social Service Review* 63: 222–44.

Baca, Oswald G. 2000. "Infectious Disease and Smallpox Politics in New Mexico's Rio Abajo, 1847–1920." *New Mexican Historical Review* 75: 105–27.

Berger, L. R, and S. R. Johansson. 1980. "Child Health in the Workplace: The Supreme Court in *Hammer v. Dagenhart* (1918)." *Journal of Health Politics, Policy and Law* 5: 81–97.

Brosco, Jeffrey P. 1999. "Policy and Poverty: Child and Community Health in Philadelphia, 1900–1930." *Archives of Pediatric and Adolescent Medicine* 149: 1381–87.

Butler, John A., Barbara Starfield, and Suzanne Stenmark. 1984. "Child Health Policy." In *Child Development Research and Social Policy*, vol 1. Edited by Harold Stevenson and Alberta Siegerl, 110–88. Chicago: University of Chicago Press.

Currie, Janet M. 1995. *Welfare and the Well-being of Children*. Chur, Switzerland: Harwood Academic.

Derickson, Alan. 1992. "Making Human Junk: Child Labor as a Health Issue in the Progressive Era." *American Journal of Public Health* 82: 1280–90.

Fee, Elizabeth. 1990. "Public Health in Practice: An Early Confrontation with the 'Silent Epidemic' of Lead Paint Poisoning." *Journal of the History of Medicine and Allied Sciences* 45: 570–606.

Foltz, A. M. 1980. "Care and Carelessness in Federal Child Health Policy." *Journal of Public Health Policy* 1: 141–49.

Galishoff, Stuart. 1998. "Newark and the Great Polio Epidemic of 1916." *New Jersey History* 94: 101–11.

Giglio, James N. 1983. "Voluntarism and Public Policy between the World War I and the New Deal: Herbert Hoover and the American Child Health Association." *Presidential Studies Quarterly* 13: 430–52.

Golden, Janet. 1996. "The Iconography of Child Public Health: Between Medicine and Reform." *Caduceus: A Humanities Journal of Medicine and the Health Sciences* 12: 55–72.

Grob, Gerald. 1991. *From Asylum to Community: Mental Health Policy in America.* Princeton, N.J.: Princeton University Press.

Hufbauer, Karl. 1986. "Federal Funding and Sudden Infant Death Research, 1945–80." *Social Studies of Science* 16: 61–78.

Mahowold, Mary Briody. 1993. *Women and Children in Health Care: An Unequal Majority.* New York: Oxford University Press.

Markowitz, Gerald, and David Rosner. 2003. *Deceit and Denial: The Deadly Politics of Industrial Pollution.* Berkeley: University of California Press.

Medley, Sara Sullivan. 1882. "Childhood Lead Toxicity: A Paradox of Modern Technology." *Annals of the American Academy of Political and Social Science* 461: 63–73.

Patel, Kant, and Mark E. Rushefsky. 1999. *Health Care Politics and Policy in America.* 2nd ed. New York: M. E. Sharpe.

Postol, T. 1993. "Public Health and Working Children in Twentieth-Century America: A Historical Overview." *Journal of Public Health Policy* 14: 348–54.

Romanovsky, Peter. 1978. "To One Common End: The United States Public Health Service and the Missouri Child Hygiene Movement, 1919–1921." *Bulletin of the History of Medicine* 52: 251–65.

Smith, Jane S. 1990. *Patenting the Sun: Polio and the Salk Vaccine.* New York: William Morrow.

Zelizer, Viviana. 1985. *Pricing the Priceless Child: The Changing Social Value of Children.* New York: Basic Books.

MATERNAL AND INFANT WELFARE

Adams, Sean Patrick. 2000. "'Who Guards Our Mothers, Who Champions Our Kids?' Amy Louise Hunter and Maternal and Child Health in Wisconsin, 1935–1960." *Wisconsin Magazine of History* 83: 180–201.

Almgren, Gunnar, Susan P. Kemp, and Alison Eisinger. 2000. "The Legacy of Hull House and The Children's Bureau in the American Mortality Transition." *Social Service Review* 74: 1–27.

Barney, Sandra Lee. 2000. *Authorized to Heal: Gender, Class, and the Transformation of Medicine in Appalachia, 1880–1930.* Chapel Hill: University of North Carolina Press.

Chepatis, Joseph B. 1972. "Federal Social Welfare Progressivism in the 1920's." *Social Service Review* 46: 213–29.

Klaus, Alisa. 1993. *Every Child a Lion: The Origins of Maternal and Infant Health Policy in the United States and France, 1890–1920.* Ithaca, N.Y.: Cornell.

Koven, Seth, and Sonya Michel, eds. 1993. *Mothers of a New World: Maternalist Politics and the Origins of Welfare States.* New York: Routledge.

Ladd-Taylor, Molly. 1994. *Mother-Work: Women, Child Welfare, and the State, 1890–1930.* Urbana: University of Illinois Press.

Lindenmeyer, Kriste. 1994. *The Right to Childhood: The U.S. Children's Bureau and Child Welfare, 1912–46.* Urbana: University of Illinois Press.

Meckel, Richard A. 1990. *Save the Babies: American Public Health Reform and the Prevention of Infant Mortality 1850–1929.* Baltimore: Johns Hopkins University Press.

Michel, Sonya. 1992. "The Paradox of Maternalism: Elizabeth Lowell Putnam and the American Welfare State." *Gender and History* 4: 364–86.

Moss, Nancy Ellen, and Karen Carver. 1988. "The Effect of WIC and Medicaid on Infant Mortality in the United States." *American Journal of Public Health* 88: 1354–61.

Schoen, Johanna. 1997. "Fighting for Child Health: Race, Birth Control, and the State in the Jim Crow South." *Social Politics* 4: 90–113.

Skocpol, Theda. 1992. "Statebuilding for Mothers and Babies: The Children's Bureau and the Sheppard-Towner Act. " In *Protecting Soldiers and Mothers: The Political Origins of Social Policy in the United States,* 480–524. Cambridge, Mass.: Harvard University Press.

SCHOOL HEALTH PROGRAMS AND HEALTH EDUCATION

Abbott, Devon Irene. 1988. "Medicine for the Rosebuds: Health Care at the Cherokee Female Seminary, 1876–1909." *American Indian Culture and Research Journal* 12: 59–71.

Baker, Bernadette. 2000. "The Hunt for Disability: The New Eugenics and the Normalization of School Children." *Teachers College Record* 104: 663–703.

Blackwell, Marilyn S. 2000. "The Politics of Public Health: Medical Inspection and School Nursing in Vermont." *Vermont History* 68: 58–84.

Child, Brenda. 1993. "Homesickness, Illness, and Death: Native-American Girls in Government Boarding Schools." In *Wings of Gauze; Women of Color and the Experience of Health and Illness.* Edited by Barbara Bair and Susan E. Cayliff, 169–79. Detroit: Wayne State University Press.

Cohen, Sol. 1983. "The Mental Hygiene Movement, the Development of Personality and the School: The Medicalization of American Education." *History of Education Quarterly* 23: 123–50.

Duffy, John. 1978. "School Vaccination: the Precursor to School Medical Inspection." *Journal of the History of Medicine and Allied Sciences* 3: 344–55.

———. 1979. "School Buildings and the Health of American School Children in the Nineteenth Century." In *Healing and History: Essays for George Rosen.* Edited by Charles Rosenberg, 161–78. New York: Science History.

Hackensmith, C. W. 1996. *History of Physical Education.* New York: Harper & Row.

Hammonds, Evelynn M. 1999. *Childhood's Deadly Scourge: The Campaign to Control Diphtheria in New York City, 1880–1930.* Baltimore: Johns Hopkins University Press.

Hutchinson, John F. 1997. "The Junior Red Cross Goes to Healthland." *American Journal of Public Health* 87: 1816–23.

Keene, Charles H. 1953. "The Development of School Health Services." *Journal of School Health* 23: 23–33, 51–59, 88–96.

Kraut, Alan. 1994. "East Side Parents Storm the Schools: Public Schools and Public Health." In *Silent Travelers: Germs, Genes, and the "Immigrant Menace,"* 226–56. New York: Basic Books.

Link, William A. 1988. "Privies, Progressivism, and Public Schools: Health Reform and Education in the Rural South, 1909–1920." *Journal of Southern History* 54: 623–42.

Makari, George. 1993 "Educated Insane: A Nineteenth-Century Psychiatric Paradigm." *Journal of the History of Behavioral Sciences* 29: 8–21.

Means, Richard K. 1960. "Contributions of the White House Conferences on Children and Youth to School Health Education." *Journal of School Health* 30: 323–33.

———. 1962. *A History of Health Education in the United States.* Philadelphia: Lea and Febiger.

Meckel, Richard A. 1996. "Open-Air Schools and the Tuberculous Child in Early 20th Century America." *Archives of Pediatric and Adolescent Medicine* 150: 91–96.

———. 2002. "Delivering Oral Health Services to Children in the Past: The Rise and Fall of Children's Dental Clinics." *Ambulatory Pediatrics* 2: 255–60.

Moran, Jeffrey P. 2000. *Teaching Sex: The Shaping of Adolescence in the 20th Century.* Cambridge, Mass.: Harvard University Press.

Park, Roberta J. 1989. "Healthy, Moral, and Strong: Educational Views of Exercise and Athletics in Nineteenth-Century America." In *Fitness in American Culture: Images of Health, Sport, and the Body, 1830–1940.* Edited by Kathryn Grover, 123–68. Amherst: University of Massachusetts Press; Rochester, N.Y.: Margaret Woodbury Strong Museum.

Prescott, Heather Munro. 2000. "The White Plague Goes to College: Tuberculosis Prevention Programs in Colleges and Universities, 1920–1960." *Bulletin of the History of Medicine* 74: 735–72.

Raymond, Diane. 1990. "Let's Say We've Got It: AIDS and Schoolchildren in the United States." *Harvard Educational Review* 60: 125–38.

Reise, William J. 1980. "After Bread, Education: Nutrition and Urban School Children, 1890–1920." *Teachers College Record* 81: 496–525.

Rosenberg, Charles E. 1995. "Catechisms of Health: The Body in the Prebellum Classroom." *Bulletin of the History of Medicine* 69: 175–97.

Smith, Ken. 1999. *Mental Hygiene: Classroom Films, 1945–1970.* New York: Blast Books.

Strong, Bryan. 1972. "Ideas of the Early Sex Education Movement in America, 1890–1920." *History of Education Quarterly* 12: 129–61.

Toon, Elizabeth. 1998. "Managing the Conduct of the Individual Life: Public Health Education and American Public Health, 1910–1940." Ph.D. dissertation, University of Pennsylvania.

Zimmerman, Jonathan. 1999. *Distilling Democracy: Alcohol Education in America's Public Schools, 1880–1925.* Lawrence: University of Kansas Press.

NATIVE AMERICAN CHILDREN AND GOVERNMENT HEALTH CARE AND POLICY

Abel, Emily K., and Nancy Reifel. 1996. "Interactions between Public Health Nurses and Clients on American Indian Reservations during the 1930s." *Social History of Medicine* 9: 89–108.

Benson, Todd. 1999. "Blinded with Science: American Indians, the Office of Indian Affairs, and the Federal Campaign against Trachoma, 1924–1927." *American Indian Culture and Research Journal* 23: 119–42.

Bergman, A. B., et al. 1999. "A Political History of the Indian Health Service." *Milbank Quarterly* 77: 571–604.

Kunitz, Stephen J. 1996. "The History and Politics of U.S. Health Care Policy for American Indians and Alaskan Natives." *American Journal of Public Health* 86: 1464–73.

Massing, Christine. 1994. "The Development of United States Government Policy toward Indian Health Care." *Past Imperfect* 3 (1994): 129–58.

Riggs, Christopher K. 1999. "The Irony of American Indian Health Care: The Pueblos, the Five Tribes, and Self-Determination, 1954–1968." *American Indian Culture and Research Journal* 23: 1–22.

Trennert, Robert. 1990. "Indian Sore Eyes: The Federal Campaign to Control Trachoma in the Southwest, 1910–1940." *Journal of the Southwest* 32: 121–49.

———. 1998. *White Man's Medicine: Government Doctors and the Navajo, 1863–1955.* Albuquerque: University of New Mexico Press.

U.S. Department of Health Education and Welfare. 1959. *Public Health Service, Indian Health Division: The Indian Health Program from 1800–1955.* Washington, D.C.: Public Health Service.

Index

Numbers in italics refer to illustrations.

Contributors

JANET GOLDEN is associate professor of history at Rutgers University. She is the author of *A Social History of Wet Nursing in America: From Breast to Bottle* (2001), the forthcoming *Message in a Bottle: The Making of Fetal Alcohol Syndrome,* and numerous articles and books.

KATHLEEN JONES is associate professor of history and adjunct faculty in the Science and Technology Studies program, Virginia Polytechnic Institute and State University. She is author of *Taming the Troublesome Child; American Families, Child Guidance, and the Limits of Psychiatric Authority* (1999). At present she is working on a book about the history of youth suicide.

KRISTE LINDENMEYER is associate professor and coordinator of the Public History Track at the University of Maryland Baltimore County. Her publications include *A Right to Childhood: The U.S. Children's Bureau and Child Welfare, 1912–1946; Ordinary Women, Extraordinary Lives: Women in American History;* and *Politics and Progress: American Society and the State since 1865* (with Andrew Kersten), as well as articles on the history of children and public policy.

RICHARD A. MECKEL is associate professor of American civilization and history at Brown University. He is author of *Save the Babies: American Public Health Reform and the Prevention of Infant Mortality, 1850–1929* (1998) as well as several articles and book chapters on the history of child health and welfare. He is currently at work on two books: *Classrooms and Clinics: The American School Hygiene Movement,* and *Children of the Nation: Child Health Policy in 20th Century America.*

HEATHER MUNRO PRESCOTT is professor of history at Central Connecticut State University. She is the author of *A Doctor of Their Own: The History of Adolescent Medicine* (1998) and several articles and book chapters on child and adolescent health issues. She is currently working on a book entitled *Student Bodies: The History of College Health.*

ELIZABETH TOON received her Ph.D. from the University of Pennsylvania's History and Sociology of Science Department in 1998. She is currently writing a history of interwar efforts by experts to educate Americans about health. She has taught at Cornell University and the University of Pennsylvania; in 2003–2005 she is a research associate at the Center for the History of Science, Technology, and Medicine/Wellcome Unit for the History of Medicine at the University of Manchester.